Gun Present

Gun Present

*Inside a Southern District Attorney's
Battle against Gun Violence*

SUSAN DEWEY, BRITTANY VANDEBERG,
AND HAYS WEBB

University of California Press

University of California Press
Oakland, California

Library of Congress Cataloging-in-Publication Data

Names: Dewey, Susan, author. | Vandeberg, Brittany, author. |
    Webb, Hays, author.
Title: Gun present : inside a Southern District Attorney's battle against
    gun violence / Susan Dewey, Brittany VandeBerg, Hays Webb.
Description: First edition. | Oakland : University of California Press,
    2024. | Includes bibliographical references and index. | Summary: "A
    book summary is provided under Additional Info below"— Provided
    by publisher.
Identifiers: LCCN 2023043891 (print) | LCCN 2023043892 (ebook) |
    ISBN 9780520393677 (cloth) | ISBN 9780520393684 (paperback) |
    ISBN 9780520393691 (ebook)
Subjects: LCSH: Firearms—Law and legislation—Alabama. | Firearms and
    crimes—Alabama. | Webb, Hays. | Public prosecutors—Alabama. | Gun
    control—United States. | Violent crimes—Law and legislation—
    United States.
Classification: LCC KFA379 .D49 2024 (print) | LCC KFA379 (ebook) |
    DDC 345.761/02—dc23/eng/20231005
LC record available at https://lccn.loc.gov/2023043891
LC ebook record available at https://lccn.loc.gov/2023043892

33 32 31 30 29 28 27 26 25 24
10 9 8 7 6 5 4 3 2 1

For all those engaged in the pursuit of justice

Contents

Acknowledgments

We are grateful for the support of staff and lawyers at the Tuscaloosa County District Attorney's Office. Support from the National Collaborative on Gun Violence Research and The University of Alabama helped make the work presented here possible. We are extremely grateful to Maura Roessner for taking on this project and to Linda Gorman for her meticulous copy-editing and to graduate students Harper Cook and Tori Stuecklen for their work compiling the index.

Introduction

Just feet from District Attorney Hays Webb's desk on the fourth floor of the Tuscaloosa County Courthouse, the office is abuzz with conversations among prosecutors. A police investigator, head slightly bowed, lopes through an open office door, his forehead already beaded with summer sweat from the short walk across the alley from the Sheriff's Office, to discuss the details of a gun case. "Another shooting? At 7:45 a.m. on a Tuesday?" asks a passing paralegal, her dismay softened by Alabama's characteristically languid vowels. An Assistant District Attorney gives her a quick hug as she passes on her way downstairs to court, trailed by a police investigator carrying a box of evidence, including a 9mm handgun a defendant was accused of using to commit murder.

Glancing down at the felony report in her hands, the first page emblazoned with a "Gun Present" stamp, its crimson ink bleeding out onto the page at a forty-five-degree angle, the Assistant District Attorney braces herself to review yet another several hundred pages of evidence photos, witness statements, phone records, and other information pertinent to the prosecution of criminal cases involving firearms. She puts down her coffee cup and sighs as she opens Filemaker, the office's internal case management system. She has 596 felony cases to prosecute, many of which involve a gun. Her files marked "Gun Present" span the gamut of human frailty, bad decisions, and just plain terrible luck. Drug deals gone wrong enough to involve a shooting that, despite the shooter's intentions, left the victim alive due to bad aim. Love triangle murders with the victim shot in the head at such close range the ballistics expert states that the defendant must have pressed the gun barrel directly against the victim's sweat-beaded forehead before pulling the trigger in the bed they used to share. Bystander shootings at apartment complexes that have become battlegrounds between rivals. Drive-by shootings committed by defendants with lengthy criminal histories.

Seeing "Gun Present" evokes vivid images of scenes from myriad cases. "Bang!" explodes the muffled reverberation of close-range gunfire in her mind as she looks at evidence photos taken at the crime scene, developing her theory of the case as she imagines a home invasion victim's absolute terror in their last living moments. "Bang!" goes the gun fired by another young shooter who, with more bravado than skill, fails to kill his teenage rival. "Bang!" ends the drug deal gone wrong.

She and her fellow felony prosecutors spend much of their time sorting through the detritus of such human suffering chronicled in police reports, victim and witness statements, crime scene photos, videos, and physical evidence related to near-daily violence as they search for truth while trying to make sense of the senseless. Murdering another human being for a half-pint mason jar of marijuana. For making too much noise next door at a Fourth of July party. For wanting to see other people. The list goes on.

The red "Gun Present" stamp on a felony report does not relate only to the actual misuse of a gun, as it also recognizes the increased danger any time a gun is present during the commission of any crime. These are the "what if" cases with guns—those scenarios that do not involve a shooting but nonetheless have significant potential for violence due to the presence of a firearm. "Bang!" could have screamed the sawed-off shotgun propped against decaying particleboard cabinets when police executed a search warrant in a mobile home following a confidential informant's controlled buy of a large amount of methamphetamine earlier that day.

"Bang!" could have resounded from the 9mm handgun and its multiple magazines the patrol officer found lodged under the front seat of a car driven by a man with multiple felony armed robbery and assault convictions. "It's my wife's gun," the driver tries to reason with officers as he puts his hands behind his back, his mind now in countdown mode until his parole officer inevitably revokes his freedom and sends him back to prison. "I didn't even know it was in there." "Bang!" could have sent a bullet racing into the body of the woman whose ex-boyfriend's family beat and pepper sprayed her while he waved his handgun in her direction, vowing to return and kill her. Indeed, "bang" could result from the presence of a gun during even a simple misdemeanor theft; the presence of a gun during any intentional criminal act changes the significance of the crime.

The Assistant District Attorney knows she must stay focused on the facts beyond change, and if they point to a crime, how to build her case with what she has—to be on the offensive instead of worrying constantly about what the defense is going to do. Her job is to see where the facts and law intersect when analyzing the evidence and assembling the state's case. Proper preparation demands that she challenge all from every source, and when confident that she has arrived at Truth, craft an unassailable story that resonates with those who will determine guilt or innocence. She understands that her witnesses and her victims may not want to talk. She believes it when they say they're scared, that they don't like police. She's less credulous when they say they are "too busy" to come talk to her at the courthouse about a criminal case. She understands it's an impossible position to be in, so she doesn't dwell on it. She can't. There are too many people, indeed an entire community, counting on her and her fellow prosecutors.

This is a book about prosecutors. It is also a book about guns. Yet there are a number of things that this book is not, and it is important to get those out of the way first to avoid disappointing readers who may have expected something else. This book is not a damning exposé of southern criminal justice practices, a collection of grand claims about the nature or state of justice in America, or a hand-wringing diatribe about ostensibly broken approaches to the administration of justice. You won't find any shocking accounts of corruption or analysis droning on about theories of little relevance to the gritty realities that make up the law in practice. Too many people who have never made an arrest, prosecuted a case, or worked in a correctional facility have already busied themselves with those approaches because it is easy to make sweeping generalizations and claims to truth from outside the everyday operations of criminal justice. When viewed from the interior depths of the law in practice, however, the picture becomes far less clear and the correctness of the popular notions now in vogue much less certain. In fact, although it was not the authors' intent, this book may well be seen as a defense of the system.

THE JUSTICE ASSEMBLAGE: THEORETICAL FRAMES

Coauthored by a district attorney, an anthropologist, and a geographer, all of whom have extensive experience as researchers and criminal justice practitioners, this book takes the reader inside the everyday operations of the law in practice at a courthouse in the Deep South. Scholarly and popular accounts typically depict prosecutors as the most powerful criminal justice actors because of their abilities to file criminal charges, choose the cases they pursue, make recommendations for bail amounts and sentencing, and make plea offers to defendants. Yet prosecutorial powers are simultaneously defined and limited by legislators who create criminal law and policy, by police who conduct criminal investigations and make arrests, by juries and judges who determine a defendant's guilt or innocence, by parole boards that make determinations about an incarcerated person's eligibility for freedom, and by voters who elect the district attorney (Bellin 2019). *Gun Present* illuminates the cultural and relational assemblages of actors, knowledges, and practices that comprise the everyday contexts in which prosecutors carry out their duties around one of the most pressing and politically charged challenges: the disposition of criminal cases involving guns.

Uniting and building on four transdisciplinary bodies of literature—assemblage theory, law and society, studies of discretionary decision-making in context, and violent and carceral geographies—this book argues that the everyday realities shaping the law in practice comprise a justice assemblage of individual people and the interactions they have with one another as they navigate the institutional structures and practices central to the administration of justice. This argument makes three significant contributions to both academic literature and popular discourse surrounding violent crimes committed with a gun. First, focusing on the work of prosecution in a midsize southern city provides powerful insights into what many scholars (e.g., Sklansky 2016; Arora 2018; Chambliss 2018) believe to be the tense position of elected district attorneys, who must aggressively prosecute violent crimes committed with a gun while simultaneously upholding their constituents' Second Amendment rights. Second, the book emphasizes that the violent crimes committed with a gun are hardly confined to major metropolitan areas; in fact, the number of crimes committed with a gun in the greater Birmingham, Alabama, area, which includes Tuscaloosa County, is disproportionately high and, when adjusted for population size, amounts to the second-highest homicide rate in the nation (Archibald 2021). Third, to our knowledge, no researchers have ever received total ethnographic access to a state prosecutor's office. This access allowed our research team to arrive at a nuanced understanding, from the vantage point of prosecutors, regarding the governing social and institutional cultures that together comprise the moral universe of a southern District Attorney's Office and, in turn, how criminal justice and community actors come together in the administration of justice, from arrest through investigation to prosecution.

Assemblage Theory

Philosopher Gilles Deleuze and psychoanalyst Félix Guattari (1980) originally conceptualized assemblage theory to understand systems and institutions as comprised of interlocking parts, rather than a unified whole.

Assemblages, translated from the French *agencement,* meaning "layout" or "arrangement," are dynamic and entail "a constructive process that lays out a specific kind of arrangement" (Nail 2017, 24). Assemblages are dialectic in that they are both abstract concepts and actually existing phenomena that structure society (Legg 2011). Scholars use the term *assemblage* as a descriptor, an ethos, and a concept to understand human relations within specific sociospatial formations (Anderson and McFarlane 2011). Assemblage theory allows us to theorize the social relations that structure the world as existing in constant reorientation and recomposition to one another while nonetheless constituting an order with tremendous collective expressive capacity (Anderson et al. 2012).

Assemblage theorists strongly caution against describing assemblages as analogous to networks, as doing so vastly dilutes the assemblage's social complexity. Assemblages are tetravalent—derived from *valency* in the sense of how chemists and biologists conceive of the combining powers of elements or molecules—with four types (*tetra*) of combining powers (*valency*) that operate along two distinct axes:

> first, between the intermingling *machinic assemblage* of bodies, actions, and passions (content) and that of a *collective assemblage* of bodies, acts, and statements (expression); and second, between territorial stabilizing *lines of articulation* and that of deterritorializing *lines of flight.* . . . A machinic assemblage (A) of two bodies encountering by chance (a line of flight (D)) also produces the encounter as a territory (C) and a space of articulation, thus articulating *together,* in expressive enunciation (B), something quite precise that could not be said if such compositions were not taking place (Dewsbury 2011, 150).

Conceiving of a particular social order as an assemblage, then, allows us to understand that social structure, and therefore social change, emerges through the everyday practices of human interaction (Dewsbury 2011).

As an ontology of relational practices, assemblage theory conceives of the social world as essentially relational, heterogenous, and fluid in ways that enable particular patterns and types of power to circulate, replicate, and, in turn, exert influence on the dynamic connections that structure social life (Cloatre 2018). Relationships and relational dynamics within the assemblage are processual and together form a precarious whole (Müller 2015). Affect plays a significant productive role in the process of bringing this precarious whole into being and stabilizing social relations within it through the creation of mutual wishes and desires among individuals and the social worlds of which they are a part (Müller and Schurr 2016).

Geographers, drawing on the work of philosopher Manuel DeLanda, have noted the utility of assemblage theory for analyzing democratic network governance, the coordination between actors and communities that, when taken together, constructs the social world and political action within it (Van Wezemael 2008). DeLanda builds on Deleuze and Guattari's original conceptualization of the assemblage to propose moving beyond the "reified generality . . . [of] 'society as a whole'" to envision "a multiscaled social reality" through which "a whole emerges from the interactions among its parts . . . [and] once it comes into existence it can affect those parts" (DeLanda 2006, 34). These parts include both the human and nonhuman world; for example, geographers note that disaster risk management assemblages attempt to manage disasters-in-the-making, yet in so doing, also create socio-environmental problems of their own (McGowran and Donovan 2021). Political geographers emphasize how ethnography, a method central to our project, has both the potential "to bring forward multiple voices to investigate the becoming of political events" and "even more promise for analyzing and intervening in the emergent politics of socio-material-affective assemblages" (Ghoddousi and Page 2020).

Geographers also note the importance of considering the role of objects within assemblages, which is particularly salient for our study of guns and their meaning within the justice assemblage. Describing objects as "smoldering furnaces of affects that are capable of creating, policing, and destroying the very contours of existence," geographer Ian Shaw explains,

> A world is a constellation of objects. These objects are constellated together because they affect each other . . . objects are constantly *affecting*. In their very existence, they force themselves upon each other, reducing, reshaping, channeling, annihilating, eroding, fusing, scouring, electrifying, and so on. An object, in this sense, is not defined by its brute materiality or an underlying "life." Either maneuver would be a form of reductionism. Instead, an object is precisely what it does . . . no object exists apart from its world: to exist is to affect and be affected by the world (Shaw 2012, 620–21).

Despite the tremendous utility of assemblage theory for the study of crime and justice, criminologists have been surprisingly slow and reluctant to adopt it. Our study, accordingly, represents a critical criminological intervention by conceiving of justice itself as an assemblage. In so doing, we unite and build on preliminary criminological theorizing about the potential for assemblage theory to provide new insights into, for example, the social processes by which communities and institutions define and respond to crime (Crewe 2010). Crime is itself an assemblage because it "is both a designation for an event and a category of acts and practices which are diverse and historically and geographically contingent" (Crockett Thomas 2020, 72) and those who commit crimes "are produced from their material and its affective relations with the rest of the world" (Crockett Thomas 2020, 75).

The limited body of criminological work that utilizes assemblage theory remains largely confined to analyses of affective assemblages, security assemblages, and surveillant assemblages. For example, feminist criminologists have examined rape trials to understand the courtroom as an affective assemblage with its own established practices and customs that interact with the top-down imposition of law and policy reforms to produce courtroom truths (Carline, Gunby, and Murray 2020). Domestic violence researchers likewise advocate for further development of an intersectional assemblage theory to understand the material and sociostructural processes that enable violence against women (Farr 2021). Studies of surveillant assemblages note therapeutic surveillance in drug courts' combination of personal relationships, intimate knowledge, and pastoral care (Moore 2011); the function creep of video surveillance images transferred from private sources to police as part of criminal investigations (Wilkinson and Lippert 2012); and the assemblage of penal governance at work in juvenile justice contexts (Gray 2013). Yet assemblages are inevitably products of their sociocultural contexts, and to understand how the justice assemblage takes shape, we turn to law and society scholarship.

Law and Society

Law and society scholarship focuses on how legal rules and decisions are both products of and negotiated within the social context that produced them. Law and society research regards the legal system as an abstract entity that realizes its concrete powers through the law in practice. For example, law and society research has examined how language is integral to all aspects of the law in practice due to the extraordinary weight words hold in legal settings, with linguistic analysis of the everyday practice and application of the law revealing the microdynamics of the legal process (Conley, O'Barr, and Conley Riner 2019). Likewise, anthropologist Robin Conley Riner (2016) has explored how communication strategies, such as linguistic and physical distancing between jurors and defendants, are critical aspects of capital trials because they function as a form of discursive violence that enables death sentencing (Conley Riner 2016).

Law and society researchers are attuned to the nuanced intersections between institutions and the social worlds that surround them and accordingly recognize ethnography's power to convey the nature of the law in practice. Early anthropological work in this area emphasizes that because institutions are the sum of individual ideas distilled in a common shape, different kinds of institutions collectively allow individuals to think different kinds of thoughts and respond to different kinds of emotions (Douglas 1986). More recent research recognizes the cross-cultural interrelations between law, custom, and justice, as law makes aspirational claims to truth, justice, and morality in all societies (Pirie 2013).

Cultural politics influence legal and governmental practices, and the law in practice is accordingly a tense site for the negotiation of tradition, justice, and morality, as is evident in tensions, revealed by ethnographic research in Hopi Tribal Court, between the language of Anglo-American law and Hopi culture (Richland 2008). Ethnographic research on the daily practices of French supreme courts demonstrates the foundational role of legal reasoning in constructing and altering the social realities that shape associations between people, things, and concepts (Latour 2010). According to Kohler-Hausmann (2018), the systemic nature of the intersections between law and society are likewise apparent in how jurisdiction-wide and politically driven policing priorities influence the types of cases seen at District Attorney's Offices, as occurred with the rise of stop-and-frisk policing that brought large numbers of misdemeanants into court. Prosecutors' everyday work is accordingly an ideal site to examine how legal decision-making occurs among individuals within institutions because prosecutors are fiduciaries accountable to and aligned with the interests of the public (Green and Roiphe 2020a).

Law and society research has also analyzed the court as a performance and a public spectacle. Some legal scholars have observed that contemporary courts are overburdened because they have historically been so successful in resolving cases and now face an overload of cases that in earlier eras would have been handled informally in the family or community (Flango and Clarke 2015). Levels of public confidence in politico-legal institutions are evident in public hearings, where individuals enact their social positions as part of a sensorial performance that impacts audiences both within and without the courtroom (Barrera 2013). Court's performative aspects are particularly evident in capital trials, where some researchers have argued that political machinations ultimately outweigh the additional due process requirements that such cases demand in the form of jurors and psychological experts (Kaufman 2020). Ethnographies of criminal courts, as mediators between policing and correctional facilities, have argued that important disconnects exist between dominant cultural understandings of the court as an impartial institution and institutional realities that can allow entrenched racism to flourish (Gonzalez Van Cleve 2016). Likewise, courtroom ethnography of sexual assault trials indicates the potential for forensic science, expert narratives, and witness accounts to publicly reinforce gender and race stereotypes (Hlavka and Mulla 2021).

Finally, law and society researchers have additionally explored the social role that evidence plays from investigation through trial as criminal justice professionals utilize evidence to create their narrative of a particular case. In homicide cases in the United Kingdom, for example, a reciprocal relationship exists between narrative and evidence, with detectives, scientists, and other experts embedding forensic science into narrative as they make their case for prosecution (Brookman et al. 2020a). Forensic evidence is a form of knowledge, with each piece possessed of its own social life and biography, and Swedish prosecutors engage in legal storytelling as they utilize forensic evidence to produce knowledge and this evidence, in turn, creates social relationships as cases move from crime scene to courtroom (Kruse 2016). Yet evidence is just one aspect of how prosecutors build a successful case. In sexual assault cases, for instance, forensic evidence is auxiliary, occasional, and nondeterminative in most rape cases, with victim willingness to testify and victim injuries the strongest predictors of case outcomes (Sommers and Baskin 2011). Understanding the social role each aspect of the legal process plays in the administration of justice also requires attending to legal actors' everyday use of discretionary decision-making in context.

Studies of Discretionary Decision-Making in Context

Studies of discretionary decision-making in context emphasize prosecutors' professional lives and identities as dynamic and in dialogue with political and judicial will, individual conscience, and office organizational cultures that may variously prioritize individual autonomy versus consistency across cases (Levine and Wright 2013). Some scholars contend that sovereignty, rather than discretion, best captures the scope of prosecutorial powers due to prosecutors' abilities to bring, or decline to bring, criminal charges against an individual even when legal reason exists to do so (Sarat and Clarke 2008).

Prosecutors, like all practicing lawyers, routinely need to reconcile legal objectivity and their duty to uphold the law with dilemmas in their community of practice (Levin and Mather 2012). According to Wright and Levine (2014), decision-making and approaches to professional role often shift throughout a prosecutor's career, with less-established prosecutors more likely to aggressively pursue cases and, without appropriate supervision, potentially cause harm in the forms of overcrowded trial dockets; procedural delays for victims, witnesses, and defendants; and pushing the limits of disclosure obligations.

Historically, prosecutors' discretionary latitude has prompted scrutiny, and during both the Progressive Era and now, progressive prosecutors were elected following popular support for criminal justice reform and believe(d) that crime is a social phenomenon better addressed by community services than prison; however, unlike today, Progressive Era prosecutors publicly announced their intentions to implement professional norms and practices to promote the values of fairness and proportionality (Green and Roiphe 2020b). Prosecutors' discretionary latitude, combined with their accountability to the public, prompts them to mitigate (or minimize) discretion's potential to result in harm. For example, Swedish prosecutors engage in "objectivity work" by appealing to regulations, duty, and professional standards while simultaneously responding to problems that arise in the exercise of discretion by restating their objectivity, correcting the issue, contrasting the problem with those of others, and recognizing human fallibility (Jacobsson 2008). In some cases, prosecutors may issue a public statement regarding their reasons for not pursuing a case to signal their stance on a given criminal justice issue, demonstrate accountability, and create a historical record of their decision (Roth 2020). Prosecutors' accountability to the public occurs in tandem with the dynamics of their interactions with other law enforcement actors. Prosecutors and law enforcement agents mutually monitor one another as part of a working group that brings charges in a criminal case, as prosecutors need a thorough investigation and evidence from police to prosecute the case and, in turn, law enforcement agents need prosecutors to build a compelling case by mobilizing a narrative around law enforcement agents' investigations and evidence (Richman 2003).

Just as prosecutors' discretionary powers are beholden to the public and to law enforcement agents, jurors' exercise of discretion figures prominently in prosecutors' minds as they craft their arguments in a criminal case. Jurors exercise discretion and engage in the interpretation of the law through the lens of their own lived experiences, acting as democratic interpreters between the law and those tasked with its practice (Carroll 2014). Prosecutors' discretion is both contingent and reflexive, with their case narratives developed through a creative and collaborative process with continual reference to jurors' potential interpretations of those narratives (Offit 2021). While prosecutors still exercise discretion during the voir dire jury selection process, individuals with implicit bias toward a case may nevertheless be selected as jurors (Bennett 2010), just as prosecutors and defense lawyers may exercise their own racial and other biases because there are so many ostensibly race-neutral reasons to strike jurors during voir dire (Bellin and Semitsu 2011).

The formulation of plea offers is one of the most explicit examples of prosecutorial power, giving rise to a robust literature critiquing the pervasive use of plea offers relative to trials and the concomitant diminished role of the trial in democratic governance (Burns 2009). A national survey of attorneys and judges on reasons for the dramatic decline of the jury trial found that while jury trials are the fairest and most preferred case resolution procedure, their decline is the result of perceived risks, costs, and delays; sentencing guidelines, mandatory minimums, and the bail system; and pressure on defendants to accept a plea offer rather than go to trial (Diamond and Salerno 2020). Others have argued that postplea sentencing arose as the paramount proceeding in most criminal justice cases due to mandatory minimums accompanying Federal Sentencing Guidelines in the 1980s and pressure on prosecutors to increase case disposition rates, along with changes in Department of Justice policies (Conrad and Clements 2017).

Critics of plea offers as the default case resolution method contend that many defendants who accept a plea might not have been charged to begin with absent this expedient option or would have received lenient sanctions from a jury trial (Bar-Gill and Ben-Shahar 2009). Similarly, researchers found that pleas offered in misdemeanor marijuana cases in New York City were more likely to include custodial sentence offers for black and Latino defendants and that black defendants were less likely to receive reduced charge offers (Andiloro, Johnson, and Kutateladze 2016). Scholars who remain hopeful about the future of jury trials contend that juries are fundamentally democratic institutions and jurors need better civic education to facilitate their collective action and knowledge about the true scope of the powers they wield in the courtroom (Chakravarti 2020).

Scholars have published extensive critiques regarding prosecutors' potentially harmful use of discretion. Angela Davis, for instance, argues that the increased politicization of prosecutors' offices, particularly the role of District Attorney, has resulted in racial and socioeconomic criminal justice inequalities for both victims and defendants from marginalized communities (Davis 2007). A former federal prosecutor contends that victims, especially victims from disadvantaged backgrounds, have lost power because of prosecutors' vast discretionary powers in comparison with the English Common Law tradition of private prosecutions, wherein victims brought charges against those who had wronged them to the courts rather than the contemporary reality in which the state brings charges irrespective of the victim's wishes or whether a victim exists (Capers 2020).

Critics have also suggested greater transparency with respect to prosecutorial misconduct, particularly the failure to disclose evidence and subsequent denial of a defendant's right to a fair trial, by sending letters to all impacted by the misconduct to reinforce the criminal justice system's legitimacy (Kreag 2019). Prosecutorial reform is not unsupported by District Attorney's Offices, but barriers to existing reform include prosecutorial norms, case-focused decision-making, policy ambiguities, and communication challenges. Likewise, prosecutors generally support the use of data to inform operational and case decisions, but barriers to utilizing such data include concerns about data accuracy and lack of resources to collect and analyze it (Olsen et al. 2018). To understand the cultural and spatial contexts in which the justice assemblage, and the discretionary decision-making that occurs within it, takes shape, we now turn to a discussion of violent and carceral geographies.

Violent and Carceral Geographies

Violent geographies comprise a body of research concerned with the dynamic ways in which violence manifests across time and space (Gregory and Pred 2007), while carceral geographies examine spaces of containment such as jails, prisons, and diffuse forms of monitoring (Moran, Turner, and Schliehe 2017). These approaches map the spatial aspects of how violence manifests psychologically, through fear and terror, and materializes in sites of harm or death where protections and laws are withdrawn, suspended, or utilized in exceptional manners (Hyndman and Mountz 2007; Oslender 2008). Violent geographies focus on how individuals and communities perceive violent phenomena at multiple scales, from the body to the neighborhood to the state (Watts 2008). This attention to space stems from the reality that violence is itself contingent on the contexts and actors involved, and, in turn, these contingencies manifest differently depending on these actors and contexts.

Criminology's interest in space stems from the Chicago School of Sociology, and in the past decade criminologists have encouraged expanding studies of five spaces: affective spaces (that cause particular feelings), parafunctional spaces (used for other than their intended purpose), container spaces (corralling people), virtual/networked spaces, and soundscapes/acoustic spaces (Hayward 2012). Violent and carceral geography's spatial focus engages with this criminological tradition by using a relational and material lens to explore the spatiality of violence and violent systems and is closely attuned to how criminal justice processes invoke space and place as well as the spatial forms taken by the law (O'Donnell, Robinson, and Gillespie 2020). Geographers who study violence are spatial detectives who investigate the imaginative and physical spaces created by the law and the co-constitutive relationship between people, places, and the law (Bennett and Layard 2015).

Violent and carceral geographies are also concerned with spatial injustice, which emphasizes how relations of power shape physical space and thereby render places meaningful to the law (Delaney 2016). For example, critical cartography is concerned with how maps' communicative power can foster or impede social justice, depending on how authorities use them, as in the example of how crime mapping research may be used to justify increased policing in already marginalized neighborhoods (Kindynis 2014). Geographer Ruth Wilson Gilmore (2007) famously connected spatial, political, and economic forces to argue that California's prison expansion emerged from politico-economic forces surrounding surpluses of finance capital, labor, land, and state capacity, resulting in mass incarceration.

Political-ideological stances on the nature of prison result in different visions of the physical forms justice should take. For instance, an ethnography of debates in Bloomington, Indiana, between conservative proponents of tough-on-crime approaches who supported constructing larger prisons and progressive reformers who supported building a "justice campus" found that, in practice, both political-ideological approaches supported expanding the carceral footprint (Schept 2015). These connections between the social worlds within and outside prison walls are also of interest to carceral geography, which acknowledges how a nuanced set of individuals, legal and institutional processes, and physical spaces comprise the boundaries between prison and the world outside it, with each accompanied by their own ideological and cultural norms (Turner 2016).

PARTICIPATORY METHODS AND ETHICS IN THE JUSTICE ASSEMBLAGE

On the red dirt road deep in the Alabama woods where Susan and her husband coaxed a self-sufficient farm from twenty acres of loblolly pine forest, every single resident belongs to one of two extended families. Road signs, the only indicators of human habitation throughout miles of dense subtropical foliage, bear their last names. Every few weeks a pickup truck driven by one of a few distant neighbor farmers pulls up, a thick sunburnt arm crooked outside the open window as the driver asks about mutual interests: "Y'all fixin' to sell any of them goats?", "Y'all interested in buyin' some hay I'm fixin' to cut?" One neighbor, who lives completely off the grid and has not seen the inside of a grocery store in decades, proposed bartering a few acres of Susan's forest in exchange for digging her a two-acre catfish pond, providing him with a place to put a family member's mobile home and providing Susan with a valuable source of protein. This is a rare part of the United States where people could live mostly without money—provided they can sell enough eggs or fresh produce to pay a hundred dollars or so of annual property taxes—by relying on each other. Hastily hand-painted wooden signs outside most farms read, "Eggs $2.50."

The Baptist preacher, whose chapel a few miles down the road posts new signs every week with the wit of country music—this week's sign curtly informs passersby "sin: a short word with a long sentence"—periodically drives up and walks around the farm until he finds Susan or her husband to tell them about a coming event he calls "the Rapture," a moment when everyone who belongs to his Evangelical Christian congregation will instantly vanish from Earth only to immediately reappear together in heaven. He wants Susan and her husband to join them there. Back in the Alabama woods, the state feels like a distant entity relative to the everyday concerns of food production, family, and religiosity. In this respect and in its people's reliance on each other for survival, it is a land that exists outside of time.

Life in the town, where most of this book is set, is a more expansive and socially complex variation on this tightly knit web of rural southern relationships. Most Alabama people fondly regard rural life and readily tell stories about family members' peach trees, honeybees, chickens, and woodland forays to hunt for deer, squirrels, and feral hogs. In June, when temperatures can reach eighty degrees before midmorning, the air outside the Tuscaloosa County Courthouse is redolent with the seductive honey-lemon smell of ripe peaches heaped in baskets on worn wooden shelves stacked against the metal frame of an open-sided truck. The truck's driver, who planted those peach trees and picked the fruit himself, jokes with everyone who passes on their way into the courthouse, as if he already knows them. Down here, *country* is a synonym for an endearing kind of wholesomeness and warmth highly regarded by most people. "I was raised in the country," Assistant District Attorney Shadrian Gayles explained to Susan when she praised him for his unfailing kindness and positivity despite his everyday work with people experiencing the absolute worst moments of their lives, "and so I know to be nice to everyone."

As coauthors, we are all part of the web of relationships that shape the cultural context in which we all live and work. The world we depict in this book is our everyday reality, rather than a distant "field site"—as the traditional research parlance would have it—where researchers might drop in for a few months or a year to observe as part of an extractive research enterprise. We are accountable to one another and to everyone whose words and actions form the substance of this book because we care deeply about the administration of justice and the people who carry out the indisputably difficult work of prosecuting criminal cases involving guns. Everyone featured in this book expressed great enthusiasm for our project and provided insights into its argument and structure, and, because we are southerners, we always remembered to hug, feed, and encourage each other every step of the way.

We believe our collaborative, community-based project presents a model for criminologists. Ideological brick walls all too often surround academic and professional practices in criminal justice, with many practitioners dismissing academics as lazy ivory tower elites who lack real-world experience and, in turn, many researchers dismissing practitioners as cynical pragmatists who lack evidence in support of their practices. The result, as any cursory examination of contemporary media will show, is a toxic political bifurcation of views on issues related to crime, law, and justice. Criminology currently lacks insights into the everyday operations of justice due to these toxic political bifurcations, which breed mistrust between academics and criminal justice practitioners. Studies of crime and justice also lack insights into the nuances of the everyday administration of justice due to primary reliance on secondary data from law enforcement agencies that fails to capture the dynamic human interactions that create and sustain institutional culture.

Researchers have already successfully bridged some of the gaps between criminal justice research and practice through ethnography, a well-established method that helps illuminate the dynamic interactions informing the administration of justice. Ethnography is a powerful method because it focuses on the elements of everyday life through focused observations of how members of a specific cultural community navigate, cocreate, and contest sociocultural norms. Ethnographic field notes transform these observations into vivid written descriptions of the nuances of how human interaction reinforces, mitigates, or contests dominant cultural understandings of a given topic under study (Emerson, Fretz, and Shaw 2011). Ethnography is likewise especially well suited to studying the legal and sociocultural meanings prosecutors ascribe to guns used in crimes, and accordingly helped us understand how these meanings engage with individual, organizational, and national debates through firsthand observations of how prosecutors carry out the law in practice.

Criminologists have successfully used ethnography in studies of police, courts, and prisons (Bucerius, Haggerty, and Berardi 2021), including in studies of police investigative units in the United Kingdom (Bacon 2016; Brookman et al. 2020a; Dabney and Brookman 2018), policing in France (Fassin 2013), US crime labs (Bechky 2021), and sexual assault trials in US courtrooms (Hlavka and Mulla 2021; Walenta 2019). Yet despite the rich ethnographic tradition of legal ethnography (Nader 1997), there are, to our knowledge, no ethnographies to date of state prosecutors. Legal scholar Anna Offit's (2022) *The Imagined Juror: How Hypothetical Juries Influence Federal Prosecutors* utilized ethnography to analyze how federal prosecutors draw upon somewhat simplistic preconceived notions about how an imagined jury would react to a given case, yet the author faced limitations due to confidentiality restrictions on her ability to write about specific cases and about her interactions with federal prosecutors.

Yet despite its many strengths as an immersive research method, ethnography follows traditional research methods in ultimately situating the project firmly within the researcher's control. Our collaboration accordingly combined ethnographic and participatory research methods with the goal of sharing control of research design, implementation, and analysis. Participatory research "represents a convergence of principles and values ... in which the community determines the research agenda and jointly shares in the planning, implementation of data collection and analysis, and dissemination of the research" (Wallerstein and Duran 2003, 28). Sometimes also called participatory action research (PAR) or mutual inquiry, its research design and methodology strongly emphasize community strengths in the development of research designed to help solve social problems. The philosophy undergirding participatory research positions researchers and community members as equal partners in praxis, the process by which theory becomes realized in the form of concrete action.

Informed by the noble intention of democratizing knowledge production, the participatory research process begins with researchers listening as community members articulate their concerns around a key set of themes, which creates an opportunity for structured dialogue to pave the way for social change on the community's terms (Wallerstein and Duran 2003). Participatory research originated in the 1960s, when social scientists began to align with activist causes designed to provoke social change, yet the emancipatory theory informing the method is much older. As early as the 1940s, social psychologist Kurt Lewin anticipated much later critiques of siloed knowledge production by strongly questioning the positivist politics of empirical objectivity in social science research (Adelman 1993).

All participatory research begins with the need to define the community serving as the focal point of analysis in a project. Participatory research defines community as

> a unit of identity . . . a sense of identification and emotional connection to other members, common symbol systems, shared values and norms, mutual (although not necessarily equal) influence, common interests, and commitment to meeting shared needs . . . [and participatory research] builds on strengths and resources within the community (Israel et al. 2003, 55).

For participatory researchers, a community can have physical parameters, such as a neighborhood or an office, or behavioral components, such as people who perform certain types of work, but the community must be clearly defined and bounded for researchers to design an effective project. Our project envisioned the Tuscaloosa County Courthouse as a community, with a particular focus on the prosecutors housed at the District Attorney's Office. In this unique setting, participatory research required Hays and his colleagues to place tremendous trust in Susan and Brittany as researchers and in Susan's and Brittany's willingness to become their students while listening, observing, and learning over the course of a year. It also meant Susan and Brittany always respected rules of confidentiality regarding data collected while providing their no-cost expertise as part of a mutually beneficial exchange (Goodman 2001).

Participatory research has six core values we embraced to ensure multiple standpoints and high ethical standards were cornerstones of our work: (1) commitment to relationships grounded in transparency and trust; (2) building on each party's strengths, resources, and interests; (3) working toward an equitable distribution of power; (4) equitable decision-making and mutual accountability; (5) flexibility in responding to all stakeholders' ongoing and evolving needs and priorities; and (6) regarding all products of the work as jointly belonging to all partners (Goodman et al. 2018). These six values informed every aspect of our collaboration.

Transparency and Trust

Participatory research's first core value is a commitment to relationships grounded in transparency and trust, which we achieved through very open initial conversations about Hays's priorities as district attorney and our goals as community-based researchers, followed by our jointly authoring the Institutional Review Board proposal to carry out the research and weekly discussions of our progress. This project began on the University of Alabama campus in fall 2020, when Hays's son Samuel was taking a class on domestic violence that Susan taught. One day after class, toward the end of the semester, Sam walked to the front of the amphitheater where our socially distanced class met and announced, in his unassuming way, "My father would like your phone number." Hays and Susan met not long after that and almost immediately decided to work together, and Susan invited Brittany to join us to create a truly innovative team: a prosecutor, an anthropologist, and a geographer.

When we first met, Hays had already been the Tuscaloosa County District Attorney for five years, during which he oversaw the prosecution of over one thousand criminal cases involving guns. Hays, a University of Alabama law school graduate, began his law career at the Tuscaloosa County Public Defender's Office before spending sixteen years in private practice as a criminal defense attorney. He ran unopposed for a second term as Tuscaloosa County District Attorney in 2022. Susan and Brittany, who work together at The University of Alabama, have worked as researchers and practitioners in a wide range of criminal justice contexts in the United States and internationally. Susan has worked in jails, prisons, parole, and transitional housing, and Brittany previously worked for the United Nations Office on Drugs and Crime.

In our view, building transparency and trust requires spending extensive amounts of time together. In Susan's and Brittany's experience, institutional ethnographers are most successful when they have a clear role within the organization and associated collegial relationships of trust with all organizational staff. This is particularly true for researchers who, as we did throughout this project, work in highly confidential settings where disclosure—whether intentional or not—of information could potentially compromise the outcome of a criminal investigation, cause further harm to victims, and even generate public mistrust of the justice process.

Our team was highly conscious of the many risks associated with our work and constantly reassessed our approaches as the project evolved to guard against the potential for our project to cause harm. Hays took the first step in introducing Susan, the project's ethnographer, to everyone in the office and explaining her role as a researcher. It was then up to Susan to build the collegial relationships necessary to build trust with the prosecutors, victim service officers, paralegals, and other staff she worked alongside throughout this project. By providing insights and observations throughout the project, Hays was a para-ethnographer and keenly reflexive epistemic partner (Holmes and Marcus 2008) who offered running commentary on the project throughout our time together.

Combining ethnography with participatory research as part of our collaboration required extraordinary transparency and trust because this method involved Susan's becoming embedded in the everyday workings of the office. Prosecutors, victim service officers, and paralegals did not alter their behavior around her because doing so would have meant completely changing their manner of interactions over an extended period of time. While some criminologists have insisted on the value of so-called "covert ethnography," where the researcher becomes part of a community without obtaining informed consent from participants (Calvey 2018), we found instead that becoming part of the office as a researcher enriched the research by allowing multiple opportunities for prosecutors to provide insights. It was common for prosecutors dealing with a particular case to note some version of "you should put this in your book" to Susan when they were engaged in casual conversation in the office. These mundane office interactions dramatically enriched the findings presented here and also allowed our team to maintain high ethical standards in our work together because our respective roles were always clear to one another.

Adhering to the core value of transparency and trust proved particularly valuable in the current divisive political climate, which has only served to amplify academia's generally poor reputation for many practitioners. This reality impacted our team's work together at times in the project's initial stages. "You're not a plant, are you?" Hays asked Susan early in our working relationship when he found her sitting at a colleague's computer. Before Susan could respond to explain her legitimate reason for being there, Hays immediately added, "Oh, well, we've got nothin' to hide here" and strode back to his office. Susan, who held a Central Office administration badge with the Wyoming Department of Corrections before moving to Alabama, deeply empathized with Hays's concerns. After all, what if Susan held misguided political beliefs about prosecutors and she had misrepresented her true purpose to defame them by selectively mobilizing evidence in support of a flawed argument? Such actions would always constitute a betrayal of both science and trust between researchers and participants because it involves searching for proof of an answer rather than searching for answers from truth, but this would be a particularly destructive choice in the current political climate. Only extensive amounts of shared time and goodwill, and the trust that comes with both, could help our team overcome these initial questions. Ultimately, we chose to trust one another to conduct ourselves with integrity.

Building on Each Party's Strengths, Resources, and Interests

Participatory research's second core value involves building on each party's strengths, resources, and interests (Goodman et al. 2018), which for our team meant a division of labor that regarded Hays and colleagues as experts throughout the study due to their extensive experience prosecuting criminal cases involving guns. Our team utilized Brittany's brilliance as a theorist alongside her extensive experience designing and implementing projects with international organizations, and Susan's expertise as an institutional ethnographer and vivid writer. Our innovative team chose to focus its energies on crimes involving guns, a priority area for Hays given the serious nature of these crimes and their tragic impact on our community. Thanks to the tremendous relationship of trust we built together as a team, Hays generously provided us with total access to all files, meetings, and proceedings. We accordingly divided our labor to maximize impact, with Hays using his professional expertise to guide the project's direction, Brittany theoretically conceptualizing the project and contextualizing our work within existing scholarship, and Susan conducting the ethnography and review of felony reports. Simply put, this project never would have been possible without each of our unique contributions to the project, and especially without Hays's enormous trust in Susan and Brittany. Uniting our diverse backgrounds led us to the momentous task of understanding how the law in practice coalesces around violent crimes committed with a gun in our community.

We each brought our own unique lifetimes of experiences with us to our collaboration and the writing of this book. Susan has spent most of her career working with women victimized by violence. In addition to her research, she has spent real and meaningful time in shelters for women abused by men who said they loved them, on the street with women who sold sex while trapped in addiction's peaty bog, in halfway houses for women trying to start over after their release from jail, and in prison with women whose lives had been derailed by their poor choices and circumstances. Yet Susan has also learned about the long half-life of violence while growing up in a military family proud of its soldiers who fought in every war in American history, starting with the first member of Susan's family to emigrate from Germany after enlisting to fight in the American Revolution because victory promised the otherwise impossible dream of owning land. One of Susan's earliest memories is of her father, a police officer with war-related PTSD, drinking too much beer and whistling as he attempted to mimic the sharp hiss of a bullet almost piercing his skull when he was a teenage soldier in the jungles of Vietnam. "I should have been dead," he wept, and then, a few hours later, woke up to work the night shift on the frontlines of the war on drugs in New York. "Wear your vest, Daddy!" elementary school–age Susan would yell when her father left his Kevlar vest slung over a second-hand kitchen chair.

"What if today's the day you get shot and you don't have it on?" "Well," he would say, "just make sure they play bagpipes at my funeral. I'd like that." Violence was never abstract, nor very far away.

Brittany spent most of her career working at the intersection of development and violence in the international context. In the small farming community in central Wisconsin where she grew up, guns and violence weren't one and the same. Rather, guns were at the very core of individual and community identity that defined rural culture and practices. The opening week of rifle season each fall was a much anticipated and sacred time. Students were excused from school, weddings and other social events were forbidden unless you wanted to lose friends, and while the men were putting the final touches on their deer stands, the women were confirming reservations and appointments for their "hunting widows" weekend of fun. Brittany fondly remembers the beautiful, stocked gun cabinet with whitetail deer etched into the glass that used to sit outside her bedroom. It wasn't until she began volunteering, working, and researching in sub-Saharan Africa that she became acutely aware of how context, actions, and individuals can produce very different understandings and operations of gun culture. As a Peace Corps volunteer in the North West province of South Africa, she recalls being surprised by the wooden box with the word *guns* painted on the side sitting at the entrance of a rural grocery store. Patrons would drop their rifles in it, grab their produce, and pick up their guns on their way out. The privileges of race and power wrapped up into being able to own a gun, put it in that box, and confidently retrieve it after shopping in postapartheid South Africa were not lost on her. Later, as she spent time living and working in East Africa, it seemed she couldn't go anywhere without the presence of a rusty, paint-chipped AK-47 nearby. Whether she was enjoying a dinner at a restaurant in Nairobi or being questioned at gunpoint by a fourteen-year-old boy manning a checkpoint in Somalia, guns acquired a new meaning of safety, security, and power. He who has the gun has all three.

Hays Webb is the District Attorney of the Sixth Judicial Circuit of Alabama, which encompasses Tuscaloosa County. He was appointed by Governor Robert Bentley in September 2016 to serve out the term of his predecessor. He was subsequently elected to a full term by the citizens of Tuscaloosa County on November 8, 2016. He ran unopposed for District Attorney in 2022. Hays enlisted in the United States Marine Corps at the age of seventeen and served from 1985 to 1989. He received his BS in Horticulture from Auburn University in 1993 and his J.D. from the University of Alabama School of Law in 1997. Hays worked as Assistant Public Defender for Tuscaloosa County from 1997 to 2001, when he left to pursue a career in private practice as a founding partner of the law firm Turner and Webb, PC. Hays describes himself as a great lover of freedom and a great believer in representative government. For him, firearm ownership is not only consistent with, but central to, freedom in fact. Hays believes very strongly that laws seeking to control guns do nothing to reduce crime, as most violent crime committed with a gun in our jurisdiction involves defendants who are either prohibited from possessing a firearm because of their previous felony convictions or by defendants using a stolen gun.

Working Toward an Equitable Distribution of Power

Participatory research's third core value involves working toward an equitable distribution of power (Goodman et al. 2018), which for us meant uniting resources from the courthouse and campus to coauthor grants and enrich students' education through the ability to discuss real-world examples of criminal cases in our campus classes, two of which were taught by Assistant District Attorneys, and involving students in data collection and analysis.

In addition to building familiarity and the trust that goes along with it, institutional ethnographers who have a clear organizational role can reciprocate their research access in meaningful ways. Our team regarded this reciprocity in research as a central aspect of our collaboration, and Susan accordingly spent April 2021 through November 2022 immersed in the internal case management system housing electronic records of all criminal cases prosecuted at the felony level. Hays initially advised us to focus our preliminary data collection on investigative reports of murder cases for three reasons: these cases typically involve violent crimes committed with a gun, the investigative reports' extensive length and detail, and the smaller number of murder cases relative to other types of felony cases involving guns. These investigative reports—also known as felony reports—often number over one hundred pages in length for a single homicide case and include police reports, witness statements, evidence photos, phone records, and all other information pertinent to the investigation, including video and audio recordings. Following completion of our analysis of patterns evident in murder cases, we expanded the scope of our inquiry to all investigative reports of criminal cases involving guns, which were easily identifiable in the database by the bright red stamp reading "Gun Present."

Susan's routine presence at an office computer throughout our project enriched our work tremendously by providing her with the opportunity to build meaningful professional relationships with everyone who worked at the office. As a professional listener and observer, Susan was always delighted to serve as a sounding board, or even just provide a sympathetic ear, for prosecutors who wanted to talk about the challenges and successes they experienced that day. She also routinely overheard prosecutors and victim advocates talking with victims and witnesses, some of whom were understandably emotional about their situation. These exchanges, while not included in the book to protect the confidentiality of people who did not consent to participate in research, provided invaluable context for the material that is featured here.

Susan also attended Hays's weekly meetings every Friday at 8 a.m. with all Assistant District Attorneys. Subjects discussed at these meetings, which commonly lasted between one and two hours, spanned an extraordinary gamut from philosophical discussions about prosecutors' responsibilities to pragmatic instructions on professional practices offered by visiting speakers as part of continuing legal education. These meetings provided tremendous insights into prosecutors' collective struggles and practices, while also furthering Susan's rapport with office colleagues. While Susan's role at these weekly meetings did not extend beyond observing, at Hays's recommendation she spent time at the end of each meeting speaking with prosecutors about victims and witnesses who did not want to participate in the prosecution of criminal cases. Susan compiled an internal database of these cases along with prosecutors' descriptions of what they understood to be victims' and witnesses' reasons for nonparticipation. As was the case with our analysis of investigative reports, ascertaining patterns in victims' and witnesses' decision-making regarding cooperation with prosecutors served as another form of research reciprocity.

Participatory approaches are rare in criminal justice settings, yet, when used, typically focus on the experiences of currently or formerly incarcerated people for whom this method "forces greater transparency, accountability, and fairness from those systems for the people who have disproportionately high system contact, but disproportionately little voice in system creation and administration" (Moore, Sandys, and Jayadev 2015). A small but robust body of literature documents how participatory research with currently and formerly incarcerated people can result in better research outcomes by emphasizing the perspectives of those with direct lived experiences of incarceration (Coyne 2018; Haverkate et al. 2019; Payne and Bryant 2018; Survived and Punished 2019). A Center for Justice Innovation (2022) brief, for example, notes how reentry program evaluations can benefit from including formerly incarcerated people and their family members in participatory research because their lived experience builds trust with participants while enhancing knowledge and perspectives. Writing of the multiple benefits of the "nothing about us without us" ethos underlying participatory methods with people in prison, researchers note how such work "can enhance findings and yield positive change by making reforms more accurate, credible, and useful" (Farrell, Young, and Willison 2021, 3).

One of the central-most goals of engaging in such participatory work is to uphold high ethical standards by shifting the traditional distribution of power from the researcher to those who have limited power to share their experiences with the general public as a result of their incarceration. Susan, who worked in prisons and jails for many years as a researcher and services provider, often wondered how our research might be enriched if we included defendants' perspectives as their cases proceeded toward acceptance of a plea offer or a trial. Defining the boundaries of community in participatory research ultimately requires shared goals and values among participants and, in the cases documented in this book, many defendants already wielded considerable power in their communities prior to their arrest by threatening, harming, and even murdering others. Had we included these defendants, our choice would have reinforced an extremely inequitable distribution of power in communities where guns and drugs allow some individuals to wield authority over others. This would have been contrary to the principles of participatory research and to our own professional ethics, as simultaneous research contact with both defendants and the prosecutors handling their cases might be misconstrued as influencing case outcomes. Nonetheless, we protected the confidentiality of defendants whose cases are featured in this book by not including their names or any information that would not have been publicly available through hearings or media reports about their cases.

Equitable Decision-Making and Mutual Accountability

Criminological research requires researchers to carefully consider their allegiances, in addition to traditional ethical issues such as informed consent, confidentiality protections, and participants' ability to withdraw from the research (Cowburn and Wahidin 2021). Adopting a participatory and ethnographic approach meant we understood from the start that our primary loyalty was to, as Hays put it many times in the course of our work together, "the pursuit of the truth." Yet it also encouraged us to deeply reflect on how to present the results of our work together beyond the obvious cautions against discussing sensitive information, such as trial strategy or case details, with anyone outside the office. Mutual accountability, for us, meant talking about how to use what we found to improve everyday office functioning. For example, one of Hays's decisions after implementing a new iteration of the Second Chance diversion court program was to ask Susan to interview all defendants who participated in this program to ascertain their perspectives on it.

Participatory research's fourth core value involves equitable decision-making and mutual accountability, which we ensured through Susan's regular presence at the District Attorney's Office and regular conversations with Hays about the work. Susan also attended criminal trials and other court proceedings, such as sentencing hearings, to observe dynamic interactions—procedural, interpersonal, discursive, and emotional—between the various actors that together form a courtroom community. To deepen their knowledge of how prosecutors', defendants', victims', and jurors' respective conceptualizations of violent crimes committed with a gun inform criminal trials, Susan and Brittany also reviewed trial transcripts in cases involving violent crimes committed with a gun.

After approximately seven months of our regular presence in the office, it became apparent that our collaboration might provide a model for both practitioners and academics, and we began to consider writing a book about the work. This raised a number of questions. How should we tell our story? How could we be sure to protect those we wrote about from unintended harms? Who would handle each aspect of the division of labor? Susan initially thought a creative nonfiction style would serve a dual purpose in protecting confidentiality and deeply engaging with the affective dimensions suffusing the administration of justice. Academic writing crashes into a brick wall at high velocity when its clumsy fingers attempt to grasp the deeply unsettling and intensely emotional human realities prosecutors navigate daily. There is so much that academic writing cannot convey. How it feels to sit breathing the same charged courtroom air as everyone who is present and riveted to the victim who, having just taken the stand, locks eyes with the defendant for a full minute as she testifies about the night he tried to kill her. Sitting at a computer listening to the air conditioner's whir, punctuated by the occasional police siren, surrounded by thousands of files antiseptically cataloguing life-transforming events: weapon, entry and exit wounds, cause of death. The delicately curved finger bones of a woman's corpse in evidence photos. Listening to a victim service officer attempting to convince a shooting victim to meet with prosecutors, as he shouts at her.

While Susan originally saw great value in a creative nonfiction book featuring composite characters whose actions would reflect patterns in cases and practices as a means to protect all participants' confidentiality, Hays and the Assistant District Attorneys strongly felt that we should use prosecutors' real names as a means to stand by their decisions and perspectives.

After developing the book's conceptual outline, and obtaining a book contract, our team designed an interview guide for prosecutors to supplement and clarify questions that lingered for Susan and Brittany after hundreds of hours of observations and informal conversations in the office.

Using real names and events posed some ethical challenges with respect to confidentiality, which we solved with an approach combining analysis of interviews using real names with analysis of de-identified cases, and a participatory writing process. We observed, and read detailed investigative reports about, hundreds of real cases of violent crimes committed with a gun that destroyed or irrevocably changed people's lives forever by causing permanent injury, putting them in constant fear about retribution—as a wise person observed outside the courtroom at a murder trial, "Just because the judge says it's over don't mean it's over"—or even took their lives. We could not morally or ethically reconcile the potential to unintentionally cause harm to anyone who gave us the tremendous gift of trust and total access.

Susan analyzed the interviews using an open coding method to ascertain themes, which she then juxtaposed with her long-term observations in the office to contextualize participants' statements. Working with prosecutors over an extended period of time made it easy for Susan to identify statements made in interviews that might be misconstrued and so required additional interpretation and contextualization. To ensure a truly collaborative final product, we engaged in a participatory writing process, which involved Brittany gathering the literature cited here, Susan writing the first draft, Brittany making comments and edits, followed by all individuals named in the book having two weeks to review the manuscript and make changes. We made this easy for those named in the book by recommending use of Microsoft Word's word search function to identify their names, although several prosecutors read the book in its entirety and offered thoughtful comments. After Susan made the minor edits suggested by those named in the book, Susan and Hays met for several hours each week to jointly edit the manuscript line by line, a process we repeated following the revisions recommended by two very helpful peer reviewers.

Flexibility in Responding to Ongoing and Evolving Needs and Priorities

Participatory research traditionally involves individuals and communities considered to be socially excluded or marginalized by virtue of their life circumstances. Yet we have found the participatory approach to be extremely effective in our collaboration because "it is not always possible (nor, indeed, desirable) to segregate people into dualistic categories of elite and non-elite or of powerful and non-powerful . . . issues of power have to be considered in a dynamic relationship" (Petintseva, Faria, and Eski 2020, 20–21). This reality corresponds with participatory research's fifth core value of flexibility in responding to the ongoing and evolving needs and priorities of all stakeholders (Goodman et al. 2018). For us, this value meant our team was always open to the possibilities of new projects and research questions. Our collaboration is ever evolving as colleagues present new ideas that build on the work we were already doing. As this book's analysis of gun cases progressed, we also recognized the value of systematically analyzing surveys mailed to jurors posttrial to assess their perceptions of their experiences. Likewise, reviewing trial transcripts emerged as a useful method to supplement in-person observations given the highly emotional-ized nature of courtrooms. Reading the verbatim transcripts provided a very different opportunity to analyze courtroom interactions from in-person observations. As our collaboration continues to grow and develop, we are currently conducting an evaluation of Hays's redesigned Second Chance diversion court program and patterns at work in domestic violence cases involving both male and female defendants.

Regarding the Work as Jointly Belonging to All Partners

For us, regarding all products of the work as jointly belonging to all part-ners meant agreeing early on that we would jointly review any materials prior to presenting or publishing due to our desire for accuracy and belief that multiple perspectives and interpretations ultimately make work stronger (Goodman et al. 2018). We found that over time our voices became unified, a process that became most apparent as we worked on the final stages of editing this book and we were able to anticipate each other's thoughts on particular issues with remarkable accuracy. Receipt of a grant from the RAND Corporation's National Collaborative on Gun Violence Research allowed us to hire a postdoctoral researcher, whose work statisti-cally analyzing the results of gun present cases helped illuminate patterns in these cases that provoked thoughtful discussion among prosecutors.

Criminological Reluctance to Engage with Community-Based Participatory Research

Despite our team's tremendous success with participatory research meth-ods and what we regard as the boundless potential for academics and prac-titioners to join forces in creating evidence-based policy and practice, this approach remains exceedingly rare among criminologists. There are three possible reasons for criminology's reluctance to engage with participatory methods. First, criminology remains dominated by quantitative methods and reliance on administrative data, a topic we discuss in greater depth in chapter 1, as part of the discipline's erroneous belief that such methods and data are somehow more objective than immersive qualitative methods. Nothing could be further from the truth, as failure to fully immerse oneself in the everyday contexts and life realities in which this "data"—which is typically documentation of the wreckage of people's lives as they proceed through the justice assemblage—is produced ultimately means failure to fully grasp its context.

Susan and Brittany both work in a Criminology and Criminal Justice department that prizes interdisciplinary research and, due to their respective disciplinary backgrounds in anthropology and geography, were at first shocked—and then mostly just amused—by the level of prejudice against qualitative methods in their adopted research field. In one extreme instance that Susan observed at the 2021 Southern Criminal Justice Association's annual conference, the editor of a prominent criminal justice journal announced in an unnecessarily loud voice to a room of anxious graduate students, "We refuse to publish qualitative research because it is not replicable." Yet how much of the human experience is replicable? To envision the nuanced human relations that surround and constitute crime and justice as somehow able to be fully represented in reductive statistical analyses is, in our professional experiences as researchers and practitioners, laughable at best and, ultimately, dangerous because it assumes researchers have the ability to render the complexities of the human experience empirically knowable—what Donna Haraway famously termed "the God trick of positivist science" (1988, 581)—with dire implications for law and policy.

A second reason for criminology's lack of engagement with participatory methods that Susan and Brittany have frequently heard from criminologists is the difficulty gaining access to criminal justice practitioners' everyday work environments. Yet at the 2021 and 2022 American Society of Criminology conferences in Chicago and Atlanta, Susan and Brittany sat in the front row of every presentation about prosecutors and noticed a conspicuous gap: not a single prosecutor in the entire venue. Instead, we heard lengthy explanations of prejudiced prosecutorial practices, or of efforts to document prosecutorial decision-making in databases designed to make the justice process more transparent. Prosecutors, it seemed, were not worthy of speaking for themselves and so did not warrant an invitation to the discipline's most well-attended conference. With such attitudes in place, it is perhaps no wonder that academics report difficulties gaining access to criminal justice research sites. Our project took place at a time when many law enforcement officers and prosecutors we spoke with took a dim view of public confidence in their work and were highly sensitive to the potential for further negative representations. This tense environment places the onus on researchers to prove themselves trustworthy and to emphasize the potential value of collaboration for all concerned, rather than just the researcher's own professional trajectory. Criminology, like many academic disciplines, has yet to make the shift from an extractive industry to a truly community-engaged venture.

Time is the third reason why participatory research remains rare in criminology. Despite the vibrant academic job market in our field due to widespread student interest and employability associated with a criminology and/or criminal justice degree, faculty face constant pressures to publish and obtain external funding. This extremely narrow definition of what success looks like—grants from specific funders, which require specific types of methods, and research published in specific types of journals, which in turn gatekeep by only publishing specific types of research—can actively discourage researchers from the time-intensive nature of participatory research. "That's the kind of thing that you do later in your career, you know, when you have more time," a junior criminologist explained to Susan with the kind of confidence that can only result from total ignorance about norms in other fields (and the extensive service obligations of tenured colleagues), including the reality that participatory research is common even for graduate student researchers in some areas of social science.

We note this both at the risk of sounding sanctimonious and with the caveat that only very lucky researchers get to build the kind of warm relationship we enjoy with Hays. After just a few initial meetings to discuss his deep concerns with violent crimes committed with a gun in our community, Susan expressed her desire to become a regular presence in the office, despite her expectation that Hays would respond with a long list of reasons why this would be impossible. Instead, Hays expansively waved his arms and shouted a welcoming "C'mon!" before immediately opening the internal file system on his office desktop to show Susan how to operate it. There is no doubt that our warm southern culture—with its emphasis on hospitality, community, relationships, and consideration for others—dramatically shaped this project from its inception. We hope that all the positive attributes of our southern culture shine through in the chapters that follow.

CHAPTER OVERVIEW AND STRUCTURE OF THE BOOK

Chapter 1, "Gun Present Cases," opens with a vignette featuring a prosecutor talking with a police investigator and deciding on appropriate charges for a violent crime committed with a gun to demonstrate the significant restrictions on prosecutorial discretion, the relational nature of violent crimes committed with a gun, and how individual prosecutors navigate both realities. This chapter argues that the presence of a gun performs legal, moral, ideological, and cultural work in criminal cases as they proceed from the incident itself through various stages, which, when a conviction is obtained, include investigation, arrest, arraignment, prosecution, and sentencing. The work of the gun occurs within demographic, residential, temporal, and environmental contexts that are profoundly relational in nature because victims and defendants typically share characteristics and know one another. A concise literature review encompasses research on violent crime in the South and notes the distinctions in material resources between investigations and prosecutions occurring in midsize cities versus those in larger metropolitan areas. This literature review concludes with a critique of criminology's heavy reliance on administrative data with the goal of suggesting the value of juxtaposing such data with methods, such as ethnography and participatory research, that illuminate the nuances of the law in practice.

Three thematic sections structure this chapter's findings section, which derives from empirical analysis of over one thousand cases of violent crimes committed with a gun prosecuted by the Tuscaloosa County District Attorney's Office. The first, "Guns' Symbolic Meanings at Crime Scenes," examines the meanings ascribed by defendants and prosecutors to guns used to commit crimes. The second, "Media versus Reality," explains prosecutors' perspectives on media representations of their work. The chapter concludes with Hays's advice to a new district attorney in the third thematic section.

Chapter 2, "Institutional Structures and Practices," opens with a vignette depicting a trial as an opportunity to guide the reader through how individuals engage with the institutional structures and practices analyzed in this chapter. Chapter 2 argues that the administration of justice takes place within physical, legal, and administrative structures that individual people must navigate through their interactions with others as they go about their everyday work of the law in practice. A concise literature review encompasses organizational sensemaking and legal and carceral geographies to speak to the routinized nature of these institutional structures and practices, as well as how individuals navigate them.

Three thematic sections structure this chapter's findings section, which derives from in-depth interviews and a year of ethnographic participant observation. The first, "The Orchestration of Institutional Logics," describes how institutional logics manifest in the justice assemblage through clinical markers and material practices both spatial and behavioral, including austere buildings that resemble places of worship, uniforms, badges, and ritualized forms of interaction in court. The second, "Rituals of Documentation," demonstrates how records, proceedings, and laws render the justice assemblage real by examining the possible criminal trajectories of a gun present case through the lens of institutional documents such as the felony report, motions, and other legal-administrative documents that individual investigators and prosecutors must use to render violent crimes committed with a gun legible to the justice assemblage. The third, "The Temporal Dynamics of Case Disposition," analyzes the nonstop march of time for state prosecutors as a case proceeds—as choices become crimes, bodies and everyday objects become state's evidence, and individuals become defendants, or victims/witnesses—and how prosecutors experience pressures associated with case disposition.

Chapter 3, "Relationships and Roles," opens with a vignette featuring a prosecutor reflecting on the continuum of relationships between prosecutors and defense attorneys as an opportunity to introduce the reader to the myriad ways that a case can fail if prosecutors cannot establish strong relationships of trust with victims and witnesses, make offers defendants do not accept, or do not convince a jury of the state's theory of a case. Chapter 3 argues that the everyday human interactions that comprise the administration of justice are situated within relationships and roles that, in turn, directly shape the investigation, prosecution, and disposition of a violent crime committed with a gun case. A concise literature review includes scholarly work from law and society, especially ethnographic work on courts, and the legal cynicism literature that (wrongly, in our view) depicts prosecutors as omnipotent.

Three thematic sections structure this chapter's findings section, which derives from in-depth interviews, analysis of trial transcripts, and a year of ethnographic participant observation. The first, "Political Will," emphasizes how prosecutors are fiduciaries obligated to act in the best interests of the public/the state by examining how ontological formations of political will coalesce around violent crimes committed with a gun and how, in turn, prosecutors formulate and conceptualize their decision-making in terms of the state's best interests. The second, "Criminal Justice Actors," analyzes prosecutors' overwhelming sense of besiegement within the justice assemblage by discussing their complex relationships with police investigators, defense attorneys, judges, and jurors. The third, "The Relational Context of Violent Crimes Committed with a Gun in Murder Cases," explores the demographic, relational, temporal, and environmental dynamics surrounding murder cases. A vignette, "What Doing Justice Means," engages with how prosecutors envision justice, how much punishment is "enough," and how much discretion prosecutors feel they actually have, even in egregious cases of violent crimes committed with a gun. The final section offers Hays's thoughts on the community as client, providing a transition to the final content chapter on prosecutors' moral and emotional worlds.

Chapter 4, "Moral and Emotional Worlds," opens with a vignette on the roller coaster of emotions that can accompany a hearing in court as a means to introduce the reader to how prosecutors balance the moral weight of their work with the value they believe their work has for others and their own understandings regarding popular understandings of their jobs. This chapter argues that individual prosecutors each have their own inner moral and emotional worlds that intersect with, and are simultaneously constituted by, the institutional structures and practices as well as the relationships and roles that comprise the justice assemblage. A concise literature review includes work on critiques of prosecutors, prosecutorial discretion, and moral injury.

Four thematic sections structure this chapter's findings section, which derives from in-depth interviews, analysis of trial transcripts, and a year of ethnographic participant observation. The first, "The Moral Weight of the Work," reports what the work of prosecution does to a prosecutor's sense of self, with specific attention to how prosecutors reconcile legal-institutional goals with their own individual orientations. The second, "Victims and Witnesses," and the third, "Defendants," explore how the moral weight of the work unfolds in the context of prosecutors' relationships with those most directly impacted by the administration of justice. The fourth, "Habituation," analyzes the process of individual socialization into the work of prosecution because although they are individuals, they are habituated to a work environment that requires particular behaviors, tasks, words, and perspectives.

The conclusion ends *Gun Present* by highlighting its big picture insights and contributions. Foremost among these is the justice assemblage with its focus on how relationships shape the law in practice and associated administration of justice, which we address alongside our recommendations for furthering criminology's place within the justice assemblage.

ADVICE TO A NEW PROSECUTOR

The first thing a visitor to prosecutor John Halcomb's corner office is likely to notice is the antique shotgun framed and mounted on the wall just above his desk. When the midmorning sun is high above the courthouse, John's window on the fourth floor shows its rays hitting the brick wall across the street in a brilliant triangle of light and shadow. The nonstop institutional whir of the air conditioner hums throughout the office, prompting many of the women to wear cardigans despite the outside heat of an Alabama June. Victim service officers, paralegals, and prosecutors glide in and out of offices on their way to court, meetings with victims and witnesses, and the myriad other tasks they must complete in a day. They periodically stop to embrace their colleagues and, still holding on tightly to each other's arms and gaze, ask about family members, summer plans, the progress of cases. It's a particular kind of southern scene.

"People in the office sometimes make a mistake thinking I'm pretty smart," John says with self-effacing charm, "but the only reason they think that is because I'm never further than a phone call away from knowing somebody who's going to know an answer that I don't know. And most things, I don't know." For John, whose job is to facilitate grand jury proceedings that determine whether a criminal case will proceed, the most remarkable aspect of his profession is its communal practice, something he has seen across a career in civil practice, family law, and now prosecution. "I remember distinctly all the lawyers who came in and went out of their way to help me when I was starting out," he explains. "The first thing I would tell a young prosecutor is 'Don't underestimate how many people that are out there that truly want to help you succeed.' Not only because they were there at one point in time, too, and they know what it's like to do their first trial or their first hearing or handle their first case for the first time and how horrifying that is, but also as lawyers, it is important for us to maintain the integrity of our practice and the confidence of the people out there. So, they're doing it for themselves, too. Never be afraid to ask because lawyers want to help you."

"In the workplace, you want to seem like you have it all together," prosecutor Maegan Smalley smiles from her meticulously arranged desk, her glamorous graduation and wedding photographs positioned toward the chairs for visitors to see. Many prosecutors in the office similarly display their personal photos, offering their visitors tiny windows into their humanity. "But if we had it all together," Maegan explains, "then we would all be the DA. I think a lot of attorneys, especially young attorneys—which even if you're fifty, if it's your first year practicing, you're still a young attorney—tend to want to not ask questions, because they want to seem like they know it all and don't need help. It's a pride thing. You got to put your pride aside and that'll definitely help with your stress level."

Chief Assistant District Attorney Paula Whitley's elegantly manicured hand automatically gravitates to the red Alabama Rules of Court book within easy reach on her desk as she laughs wryly and shakes her head about just how much recent law school graduates need to learn when they begin their careers as prosecutors. "People think 'Oh, you come out of law school, and you know all this law.' No! I keep the book on my desk and use it all the time, daily. There's not a case that walks in the door that I don't pull out the book to read the law because you can't absorb and retain everything, and there are always new things that you see that you didn't think about." For Paula, being practical and realistic about the limitations of human energy and the capacity to master enormous amounts of information is essential for new prosecutors. This can be difficult for newly minted lawyers who, as Paula puts it, "come in and think, 'Oh, well, I'm supposed to know all of this already,'" which, left unchecked, can lead very rapidly to frustration and exhaustion. "Open your mind," Paula advises, "to the fact that you don't know much of anything."

"We have the hardest job in the world," prosecutor Grace Prince intones with her characteristically intense sincerity, "but I truly believe it is the best job in the world because we are here for the community." Grace, like most of her colleagues, currently has over five hundred pending felony cases to prosecute, and the magnitude of this number is daunting to the point of abstraction. The Tuscaloosa Federal Building and Courthouse for the Northern District of Alabama is just a short half-mile walk from the Tuscaloosa County Courthouse, yet it could not be farther away in terms of workload. For a federal prosecutor here, a sizeable caseload generally means handling ten to twenty pending felonies. Sole responsibility for five hundred pending felonies forces new state prosecutors, especially those who are relatively recent law school graduates, to reconcile their understandings of themselves as highly efficient achievers with the reality that even the most skilled and experienced lawyer would struggle to manage such a large number of cases. "It is very hard to prioritize and to figure out what needs to be done now and what can wait," Grace explains, "because you think everything has to be done now."

"There are so many cases. So. Many. Cases," Susan says incredulously as she hands prosecutor Kymberly Porter a small mason jar of dried rose petals and catnip, herbal medicine she grows on her farm to alleviate headaches. "There are," Kymberly says, "and each one, it matters." Kymberly knows that no matter how much she might be struggling to find the time to finish her list of tasks and how exhausted she might be on any given day, her interactions with others and attention to her cases are life-changing, not just for defendants awaiting the resolution of their criminal case, but also for many victims and witnesses. "There's somebody who may end up being traumatized by what happened. There's somebody who needs you to speak for them," Kymberly explains, "and it's so very easy to get emotionally attached to your cases." This ease of emotional attachment presents both an additional source of stress and another reason to create a routine that allows time to recover from the constant barrage of human suffering and overwhelming workload.

Prosecutor Shadrian Gayles handles the everyday stress of prosecuting cases by, as he puts it, "compartmentalizing really well." For him, that means separating his work and home lives as well as the tasks he needs to complete to build the strongest possible cases. He envisions these tasks as a series of boxes to check: reading the felony report, talking to witnesses, gathering the state's evidence against the defendant, and then compiling plea offers for defendants in cases that settle or, for those that do not, wading into the swampy minutiae of trial preparation. For Shadrian, this box-checking approach also blunts the serrated emotional edge of communications with victims and their families, who may be just as distraught about the terms of the plea offer as they are about the defendant's impact on their lives. This is especially true when they learn that the plea will never contain the maximum possible sentence because doing so welcomes the risk of trial during which, as Shadrian says, "No matter how good the case is, something can go wrong and likely something will go wrong."

Prosecutor Thomas Marshall recently prosecuted a murder case that had two witnesses who gave statements to police that the defendant shot the victim. Both witnesses died in a car crash two months after the shooting. The defendant had an extensive history of violent offenses, but none of the approximately sixty people who were present could say for certain that the defendant shot the victim. "You have the weight on your shoulders of feeling like you have to do it," Thomas says of the pressure to successfully prosecute each case, "but sometimes you just can't and that's a big thing." Multiply this pressure times six hundred cases that span the gamut of criminal charges, from marijuana possession to murder, and then add to that, as Thomas puts it, "We are expected to have everything ready at a moment's notice." The volume of cases is matched only by the sheer diversity of these cases and how prosecutors need to transition between them rapidly and seamlessly in the course of the work week. As Paula advises, "They have to be able to, minute to minute, shift from 'Okay, well, this is somebody who has possessed a forged instrument,' and then the next thing, turn around be dealing with someone who was raped or injured or a child victim."

Yet this constant stress can also have a positive side, Thomas believes. "You will never get rid of the stress or the anxiety, but you have to rely on it and lean into it because me, if I'm not anxious or I'm not thinking about something, then I might be falling into a false sense of security about a case because you never know what that defense attorney is going to pull. You don't know if you're missing something." New prosecutors, in Thomas's view, should just "expect it to suck, so to speak." Prosecutor Corey Seale takes a sunnier view of how prosecutors move through the arc of experience in establishing their position within the justice assemblage, its institutions and structures, and the relationships and roles that animate them. "You are going to be thrown in and have a lot thrown at you," she gently explains in her warm West Alabama cadence, "but it's not always going to feel like that. It feels like it slows down. Nothing slows down. You are just operating at a fast pace, but it feels like everything slows down a little bit."

ADVICE TO A NEW DISTRICT ATTORNEY

Hays became District Attorney after nearly two decades as a criminal defense attorney. One of the first things he addressed was the fact that Alabama law allows people who have committed nonviolent felonies to legally purchase and carry guns, in sharp contrast to federal law, which prohibits all people with felony convictions from owning guns. Alabama only prohibits people with violent felony convictions from owning a gun, which, prior to Hays's tenure as District Attorney, impeded prosecutors' abilities to make criminal charges that reflected the severity of crimes involving a gun.

Prior to Hays becoming District Attorney, the presence of a gun at a crime scene meant so little that in felony marijuana and prohibited persons cases the routine was to plead guilty to the marijuana charge and dismiss the gun charge. Auto burglary charges, likewise, essentially functioned as throwaway charges despite the fact that in our jurisdiction auto burglars are almost always looking for guns to resell on the illicit market, thereby fueling future crimes. Today, with prosecutors using the tools already available in their prosecutorial toolbox, auto burglars remain in jail until a judge sets bond and routinely wear ankle monitors following their release from jail to prevent future burglaries, which typically take place in the middle of the night and victimize strangers, while funneling stolen weapons into the illicit gun trade.

Prosecutors face significant challenges in the wake of sentencing guidelines in drug and property crimes that make it difficult to send someone to prison. In any given case, there's a much narrower range of punishment if the defendant is a first-time defendant, and the guidance as to whether someone is sent to prison is that unless they have three prior felonies they cannot be sentenced to prison. For example, first degree robbery is a Class A felony with a statutory minimum sentence of twenty years in prison, but on that twenty-year sentence a split sentence ultimately may result in an offender only spending three to five years in prison even if they were acting in concert to threaten someone with a gun. The office regards three to five years in prison on a Class A felony as an inappropriate sentence, which means recommending one-third of time to serve or ten years to parole eligibility, whichever comes first. This makes the defendant potentially parole eligible in six years, with potential for twenty years of incarceration. Prosecutors derive no joy from putting people behind bars, but in reality, a group of people exist who pose such a threat to public safety that no one is safe while they remain out of jail or prison. Prosecutors must use the tools at their disposal within reason.

As a new District Attorney, Hays had to convince law enforcement to charge gun present cases 100% of the time because previously, due to the ubiquity of guns in Alabama, the presence of a gun at a crime scene counted for very little in terms of charging and sentencing decisions. In return, the District Attorney's Office self-reported case disposition to law enforcement and sent letters to victims with the same. A newly elected District Attorney who wants to implement a policy like gun present would need to resist apathy and inertia, Hays explains, because nature abhors a vacuum and defense attorneys and judges will fill that vacuum in prosecutorial leadership if a District Attorney does not.

"Be determined," Hays would advise a new District Attorney ready to implement innovative policies. "Why are you doing it? Because if you're not confident in why you're doing it, it won't withstand scrutiny. You have to have an understanding of why you're doing it, not because it's politically expedient." The support of law enforcement, as distinct entities also working for community safety, is really important. When Hays initiated the gun present policy, he reached out to the police chiefs, who are like-minded in their desire for a safe community and things done right.

Having a good relationship with law enforcement means that everybody is operating completely above board. Accordingly, law enforcement should be able to talk to any Assistant District Attorney, unless they are discussing a specific case to which they are assigned, so there can be no playing favorites. Emphatically, the office's effort has not been to have good relations with law enforcement, but the office's good relations with law enforcement are the result of law enforcement recognizing that public safety is consistent with cases properly moving through the system consistent with the defendant's rights and freedoms.

"We are not law enforcement's lapdogs," Hays explains of prosecutors' role as distinct from that of law enforcement in the justice assemblage. "Our ADAs are not going to the scene of crimes in the heat of the moment despite that law enforcement would love to have a lawyer on scene. We have different roles and must maintain our objectivity." This objectivity means protecting against unintentional bias that can create a problem, as propriety is essential to public safety. First and foremost, prosecutors must always respect our laws. Doing so requires recognizing the apolitical nature of public safety, and when this is done right, there is more agreement than disagreement and that transcends political, racial, socioeconomic, and any other potentially divisive line. Everyone wants a safe community.

1. Gun Present Cases

The on-call Assistant District Attorney (ADA) is nestled on the silty ocean floor of exhausted sleep, her arms extended as she slowly pulls her way upward to consciousness through the water's enormous weight. Brilliant light sparkles above her as she swims toward a dull buzzing sound and finally breaks the surface, briefly gasping for air before she wakes. Her phone pulses beside her, a steady heartbeat of sound and blue light illuminating 3:56 a.m. and the Tuscaloosa Violent Crimes Unit investigator's name on its screen. She cradles her phone in her palm as she walks into the hall to avoid waking her husband. As the prosecutor on call this week, she is the after-hours point of contact whenever investigators want to review the facts of the case to determine whether they have sufficient grounds to make an arrest on a particular criminal charge.

There's no voice for a few minutes after the on-call ADA answers. She hears the static of police radio traffic and the muffled voices of officers on scene in conversation amidst the high summer night chorus of cicadas, frogs, and crickets. Insects buzz around the blue and red glow of the patrol car's lights in her mind's eye. Although she has worked as a prosecutor for several years, she still feels a creeping sense of trepidation when she answers these calls. Any reasonable person would feel the same because her middle-of-the-night answers to the investigator's questions will determine whether officers arrest a suspect now, send a search warrant application to a judge seeking approval to collect additional evidence, or prepare materials for later presentation to a grand jury to determine whether or not probable cause for a criminal charge exists.

"Hello?" she says, her voice still creaky with sleep. "I'm so sorry to wake you," the police investigator begins, his tone suffused with the fast pace of adrenaline that courses through everyone at a murder scene. "We got two shooting victims, both transported to the hospital. Looks like one ain't gonna make it. Best we can tell this is another drug deal gone wrong." "Okay," she begins, wide awake as the adrenaline on scene reaches its spindly fingers through the phone. "Who was he shooting at?" "Well," the investigator continues, "he shot the two guys he was tussling with, but he meant to kill them." "How do you know that?" she asks, trying to determine whether the investigators have grounds to make an arrest for attempted murder. If the victim hospitalized with more serious gunshot wounds dies, that charge will likely be upgraded to murder.

The investigator sighs again. She can tell he is pushing against exhaustion, as adrenaline's sharp arc of energy gradually seeps away with the suspect in custody and victims hospitalized, to connect the slippery links of statements given by witnesses and the suspect and evidence collected on scene into the coherent chain of facts necessary to successfully prosecute the case. "Our suspect says he came over here to collect some money," he explains, "but the person who owed him wasn't here, so he demanded the money from the cousins of the guy who owed him. He says one of the cousins pulled a gun on him, but the only gun we have on scene is our suspect's. Now, the victims' neighbors, our witnesses, say our suspect was tussling with the cousins and screaming that he was gonna kill them both. They was midtussle when our suspect shot both cousins. Are we good to go on attempted murder? What charges you think fit?"

The on-call ADA takes a moment. She has two shooting victims, one of whom might not survive his gunshot wounds, statements from witnesses and the suspect to police, bullets, shell casings, the shooter's .357 Sig Sauer handgun collected and placed in evidence, and medical reports on the victims' injuries. With these aspects of the case in place, she is confident that police investigators can charge the defendant with attempted murder. Now she needs to decide if the suspect should receive additional charges. "You have an attempted murder with two victims," the on-call ADA tells the investigator. "Were any houses shot into?" "No ma'am," the investigator responds, "just a car with nobody in it. I'm fixin' to charge him with shooting into an unoccupied vehicle for that. Our suspect has priors, so we've got an additional certain persons forbidden to possess a firearm charge right there."

"Is he on probation? Or out on bond? Or in community corrections?" she asks, attempting to determine if the arrest report should read "judge to set bond," referencing a practice started in Tuscaloosa County within the past few years as an additional step in the office's gun present strategy to combat violent crime. This practice changed the decades-old local practice of setting bonds in every noncapital offense at the time of booking and requires instead that arrested defendants with guns see a judge before making bond. "No ma'am," the investigator says. "Okay," she nods, "so you are good to go with attempted murder, shooting into an unoccupied vehicle, and certain persons forbidden to possess a firearm. You stay safe." "Yes ma'am, you do the same. Thank you for taking my call," the investigator says. "You are so welcome!" she replies brightly as she walks into her kitchen to make a pot of coffee, the early morning sky just beginning to clear. No point in trying to sleep when she has five hundred other cases to prosecute.

Consider the realities facing the on-call ADA and the police investigator who called her at just before 4 a.m. to determine the correct criminal charges in this attempted murder case. To make an arrest on appropriate charges, they first needed to understand if the suspect was legally allowed to possess a gun, how the suspect used the gun in the commission of the crime, and whether the suspect had prior criminal convictions. This chapter accordingly argues that the presence of a gun performs legal, moral, ideological, and cultural work as criminal cases proceed from the incident itself through various stages, including investigation, arrest, arraignment, prosecution, and, when prosecutors obtain a conviction, sentencing. We use the phrase "the work of the gun" as conceptual shorthand for this legal, moral, ideological, and cultural work.

The work of the gun occurs within demographic, residential, temporal, and environmental contexts that are profoundly relational in nature because victims and defendants typically share characteristics and know one another. We situate the work of the gun within literature on violent crime in the South, violent crimes committed with a gun in midsize cities, and material differences between criminal investigations and prosecutions at the county level in comparison with the same in major metropolitan areas.

SITUATING VIOLENT CRIMES COMMITTED WITH A GUN IN THE DEEP SOUTH CONTEXT

"Now who here owns a gun?" Corey smiles warmly as her eyes scan the thirty prospective jurors assembled in the courtroom for voir dire in a case where the defendant claims he shot his brother in self-defense. All prospective jurors raise their hands except one, an elementary school teacher wearing a hipster beard and a bow tie. Corey's smile broadens at the prospective jurors' nervous laughter and continues, "Okay, we're in Alabama so let me rephrase. Who here *does not* own a gun?" The elementary school teacher glances furtively around the courtroom as he shyly raises his hand. Corey, who is from the small West Alabama town of Demopolis, is a kind person and wants her prospective jurors to feel welcome in the courthouse. She knows that, for most of the prospective jurors seated before her in carefully arranged chairs, this courtroom is an intimidating place that has pulled them away from job and family responsibilities. Some of them would rather not be here at all.

While Corey's warm demeanor is completely genuine, her job requires that she also be strategic in her interactions with these prospective jurors so that, in the brief time she has with them during voir dire, she can strike those she believes will be least favorably disposed to the state's arguments in this murder trial. She needs to understand her prospective jurors' beliefs about guns, and in which circumstances the people seated before her believe guns can acceptably be used, in order to make determinations about who she will strike. Yet she also needs to build a rapport with prospective jurors, whose impressions of her and her trial partner's credibility will inform their verdict. Corey opens with the question "We're in Alabama. Who here does *not* own a gun?" because, as she puts it, "That's just a good, easy segue to, 'Hey, this is what we're about to start talking about,' and it's light and funny because we are in Alabama. Most everyone is going to have a gun."

Corey wants to find and keep the prospective jurors who are either responsible gun owners or who do not own a gun because, in her view, these are the jurors most likely to find the defendant guilty of murder rather than accepting the defense attorney's argument of self-defense. Once she has those individuals noted on her mental list of desirable jurors, she wants to understand how the prospective jurors define responsible gun ownership. Some prospective jurors might regard the question Corey really wants to know the answer to—how do you define responsible gun ownership?—as too abstract, or even confrontational. So, Corey takes a different approach.

"When is it okay to shoot someone?" Corey asks, carefully adding, "Because there are times, by law, when it's completely okay." Responses to this question will provide Corey with insights into how prospective jurors might interpret the facts of this murder case. The facts of the case are simple: the defendant told his brother not to come to his house and, when the brother came over anyway, the defendant shot his brother to death from the front porch. What is in dispute and for the jury to determine is whether, as Corey and her trial partner are arguing on behalf of the state, the defendant committed murder because he came out of the house to shoot his brother rather than locking his door and calling police, or, as the defense attorney is arguing on behalf of his client, the defendant was in fear for his life due to his long history of fractious encounters with his brother.

"There are a lot of people in Alabama," Corey explains to Susan after the trial, "that are responsible gun owners who would think 'I told them not to come and if you come onto my property, I'm going to shoot you.'" Corey recalls a recent attempted murder case that required her to think carefully about how prospective jurors might apply their own understandings of their rights to the facts of the case. In this case, a juvenile defendant stole a vehicle whose owner left it running outside a gas station. The theft victim and his brother then began driving around to search for the stolen vehicle, which they eventually found with the juvenile still inside it. While waiting for police to arrive, the defendant and his brother blocked the juvenile inside the car and began shooting multiple times from both directions into the car. One of the bullets struck the juvenile in the head, and although he survived, he sustained significant lifelong injuries.

"I already know there are going to be people who think you can protect your property with deadly force," she explained to Susan as she prepared for voir dire in the case against the brothers who shot the juvenile car thief, "that you can shoot somebody who is trying to take an item, steal something from you. That you can shoot somebody who's just stolen your vehicle. That's not the law. So, I have to figure out, even if they're responsible gun owners, do they think you can shoot somebody for stealing your property? Because they really might. My granddad might think that." Corey faced the nearly impossible challenge of parsing out prospective jurors' deeply held beliefs about a highly politicized topic and ascertaining their abilities to apply the law to the facts of the case, all within the course of an hour or two.

As we attempt to situate violent crimes committed with a gun in Alabama's Deep South context, we are highly cognizant that we, like Corey, are working within historically fraught and culturally loaded terrain. Every ethnographer writes from a sense of the place that forms the substance of their work, and in our case, we are writing from "a mythologized land" (Waggoner and Taylor 2018) that is home to both spectacular art, most notably in the form of our region's myriad lush southern writers, and terrible stereotypes about racism, poverty, and vigilante justice. Our experiences include both the warm southern hospitality of courthouse colleagues who genuinely care for one another and the horror of southern "I'ma shoot you from my front porch" family feuds that end in murder cases. Alabama-born author Margaret Renkl describes our region as so "bound up in both beauty and suffering that it isn't possible to untangle one from the other" because our state is characterized by both "terrible darkness and . . . dazzling light" (Renkl 2021).

The Deep South is a culturally distinctive region defined by "how people relate to the world around them" through manners that prioritize concern for others, local agricultural and food production traditions, particular accents and pronunciations, and ambivalence regarding the historical role of race and racism in shaping southern identities (Cooper and Knotts 2017, 15). Historians and social scientists emphasize how ambivalence surrounding southern identities stems in part from the northern culture industry's actively myth-making the South as a permanent Other through popular cultural productions that caricature the region as a rural anachronism (Cobb 2005). Such northern popular cultural representations of southern people include those of "southern mountaineers as backward, lazy, dumb, and unable to cope with the modern world" (Inge 1989, cited in DeKeseredy 2014, 180) alongside the dissolute grandeur associated with mythologized notions of the "southern lady" associated with chivalry and grace (Waggoner and Taylor 2018).

Criminology has historically replicated this cultural ambivalence in studies of rural southern crime, most notably in enduring scholarly debates centered on the role of the so-called "southern culture of violence" or "southern culture of honor" in perpetuating high rates of violent crime in the South relative to other parts of the United States. These debates first emerged in the late 1960s to explore connections between widespread gun ownership, high poverty rates, punitive religious beliefs, and cultural values that legitimize violence as a reasonable retaliatory response to insult (Ellison 1991). This body of work collectively argued that Southern Appalachia, an area that includes our part of Alabama and is historically associated with Scots Irish migration and herding economies, has significantly higher rates of argument-related homicide than the rest of the region; this research finds that conservative Protestants tend to express greater tolerance for defensive and punitive violence and tend toward dichotomous morality (Andreescu, Shutt, and Vito 2011). Yet homicide rates are much higher among southern blacks—78.75% of murder defendants and 77.5% of murder victims in our community are black—than among southern whites, and some scholars suggest that this culture of pride and honor is pervasive among southern blacks (Lee, Thomas, and Ousey 2009).

Another critical cultural explanation for higher rates of violent crime in the South posits that defensive attitudes and heroic convictions concerning family, property, and self may be related to the notion of violence as an acceptable reaction to insults of honor among both men and women, as homicides perpetrated by women occur more frequently in the South than in the rest of the United States (D'Antonio-Del Rio, Doucet, and Chauvin 2010). Researchers suggest that the culture of honor was a response to weak southern institutions and that this culture has accordingly faded over time (Grosjean 2014), with some scholars finding no relationship between southern residence and defensive gun use (Copes et al. 2014). Nonetheless, region continues to be an important predictor of carrying a gun for self-protection, with southerners and westerners more likely to carry a gun for this reason (Felson and Pare 2010b), and southerners much more likely than their northern peers to become victims of gun homicides and assaults (Felson and Pare 2010a).

Southern beliefs about violence are a product of their cultural context. For example, a Louisiana study found that cultural scripts condoning violence are evident across a broad cross-section of the rural population and appear most likely when people perceive that the police or other agents of the law are unavailable or slow to respond due to rural communities' isolation, when individuals perceive that they or their family members are in danger from a defendant, or if they perceive there is a risk of revictimization by the defendant (Lee and Ousey 2010). These rural southern findings are in sharp contrast to literature that finds strong associations between rural group cohesion and low homicide rates across the United States, as did a study of 3,130 US counties (Kowalski and Duffield 1990). Argument-based aggravated assaults are more prevalent in southern counties with higher levels of poverty, unemployment, and familial instability (Thomas, Medaris, and Tuttle 2018). Rural criminological research in this vein emphasizes the importance of cultural scripts, context, and perceptions about possible alternatives in southerners' decision-making about violence, describing "culture as a strategy of action" (Lee and Ousey 2010, 905), that is most salient in the presence of others in ways that are more likely to result in escalation and firearm violence (Lantz and Wenger 2020).

Despite the cultural ambivalence and stereotypes that pervade representations of the Deep South in both research and popular culture, the subfield of southern criminology has remained exclusively confined to the study of the Global South. Southern criminology focuses its analysis on the marginalization of social experience and knowledge production in the Global South relative to the North, with criminological theorizing firmly situated in the Global North (Lee and Laidler 2013). Southern criminologists recommend a "decolonial option" that dismantles universalizing narratives about the Global South as backward and underdeveloped (Dimou 2021), stereotypes that apply to the US South as well. Conducting "ethnography of the periphery" in the Global South, these researchers argue, has great potential to illuminate the tensions that surround crime and justice (Xu, Laidler, and Lee 2013).

GUN CULTURES

Given this fraught cultural terrain, why study the dynamics of how defendants use guns to commit crimes in a midsize Deep South city and risk reinforcing stereotypes about our region? We argue that contextualizing the justice assemblage's approach to gun cases in our jurisdiction within literature on violent crimes committed with a gun in midsize cities, US gun cultures, and southern gun cultures offers important insights on how these forces intersect at the ground level. This approach supplements our ethnography of the periphery (Xu, Laidler, and Lee 2013) as we explore the dynamics of crimes involving guns outside the major metropolitan areas that dominate mainstream news media.

Shootings and other crimes involving guns in midsize cities are rarely cited in national media reports and, as a result, are a silent crisis. The number of crimes committed with a gun in the greater Birmingham area, which includes Tuscaloosa County, where we live and work, is disproportionately high relative to overall population size when compared with other areas of the United States with similar population sizes. The Birmingham Police Department estimates that the greater Birmingham area has the second-highest homicide rate in the nation when adjusted for population size, and most of these murders involve guns (Archibald 2021). Beyond the Tuscaloosa-Birmingham metropolitan region, Alabama has the fifth-highest firearm mortality rate (CDC 2021a) and the second-highest rate of violent crimes committed with a gun in the nation (EveryStat 2021). Violent crimes committed with a gun increased 37% in Alabama over the past decade compared to the national average of 17% (EveryStat 2021). These statistical trends reflect broader regional patterns of violent crimes committed with a gun prevalence in other southern states, including Mississippi, Louisiana, Arkansas, and Tennessee (CDC 2021a).

What explains such high rates of violent crimes committed with a gun? Sociologists who study gun culture examine the diverse cultural meanings and beliefs associated with guns and their role in society. Sociologists have explored demographic differences in gun ownership, how cultural meanings associated with guns impact social institutions, the relationship between gun ownership and personal well-being, and the relationship between gun ownership and identity (Dowd-Arrow, Hill, and Burdette 2019, 2021; Hill, Dowd-Arrow, Burdette et al. 2020; Hill, Dowd-Arrow,

Davis et al. 2020). Guns are deeply rooted in US culture, yet the meanings attached to guns nevertheless vary greatly across geographical locations (e.g., urban and rural) and identities (e.g., gender, race, ethnicity, political affiliation).

The presence of a gun plays a central role in the likelihood of a conflict escalating into a fatality, which in turn relates to how social constructions of masculinity contribute to the use of guns to commit violent crimes. Sociologists suggest that meanings ascribed to gun ownership are profoundly gendered, including among women who associate gun ownership with freedom from the threat of potential victimization (Kelley 2021), and for poor and working class men disenfranchised by economic precarity, the symbolic ability to protect oneself and one's family (Janoff-Bulman 2009). Investigations of the relationship between race and gender ideologies, gun ownership, and gun policy preference have provided mixed results. In a study titled "What Guns Mean," sociologists found that gun owners associate guns with rights and freedoms, personal identity, and feelings of confidence rather than fears about crime and victimization (Warner and Ratcliff 2021). Guns are part of both cognitive schema and sensory experiences that jointly produce the ways in which people who carry guns think about and physically use guns, making gun ownership a social process that unites sentiments about risk and safety with sensory experiences of comfort and pleasure in carrying and shooting guns (Yamane 2017). As researchers make strides in identifying patterns and trends among gun owners and motivations for gun ownership, growing evidence refutes the assumption that gun owners are a homogenous group. For example, stark divides in gun control attitudes exist even among law-abiding gun owners along political party lines, as guns are powerful political symbols (Burton et al. 2021).

Studying gun cultures may help identify predictive factors of gun ownership. Results from the Guns in American Life Survey, for instance, challenge monolithic understandings of gun ownership by revealing important similarities between those who believe they would never own a gun ("never-owners") and those who believe they might someday own a gun ("maybe-owners"). Maybe-owners demographically resemble never-owners, who tend to be women and lower-income people residing outside a rural area, yet these maybe-owners also resemble owners in identifying as conservative, Republican, and with children in the home (Kelley and Ellison 2021). Results reveal that individuals who experienced past victimization are more likely to be open to owning a gun to protect themselves against violence, including hate crimes (Combs 2021). Gun ownership tends to be cyclical in nature, with those who have previously owned a gun more likely to buy another one, which differentiates gun owners into those who are long-term owners and those who are occasional owners and indicates that attitudes about guns and gun ownership are fluid and can change over time (Shapira, Liang, and Lin 2021).

Sociological advancements in gun research acknowledge the lawful use of guns as normative in many contexts (Steidley and Yamane 2021). Accordingly, *how* we study guns and the frameworks we use to explore issues involving guns is a social process that can impact the development of attitudes about guns. Attitudes about guns develop through processes of active socialization that are, in turn, influenced by political beliefs, participation in shooting as a recreational activity, and/or being a victim of a violent crime committed with a gun (Shapira, Liang, and Lin 2021). Gun cultures, then, are an amalgamation of individual attitudes about guns filtered through unique experiences and relationships that can change over time. Although the production of knowledge about guns informs the interlocking political, institutional, and cultural systems that shape understandings of guns (McMillan and Bernstein 2021; Carlson and James 2021), such knowledge production must also analyze locally embedded meanings of guns, known as "firearm localism" (Lynch et al. 2018). Firearm localism reveals the nuances of the diverse gun cultures that inevitably exist within communities, even within the most pro-gun areas, and can help better inform strategies to reduce the use of guns to commit violent crimes while also respecting lawful gun ownership as a normative behavior.

Most research on gun cultures focuses on attitudes and beliefs among white gun owners or takes a race-neutral approach by referring to "gun owners." Yet what does research suggest about attitudes and beliefs among black gun owners, who are the majority of victims and defendants in our jurisdiction's gun cases? Public health researchers note how "little is known about the patterns of household gun ownership among Black Americans" (Hemenway and Zhang 2022). The sole article estimating these patterns draws on Centers for Disease Control and Prevention survey results indicating that 44% of the adult white male population and 26% of the adult black male population live in homes with guns; the South had the highest rate (over two-thirds) of black men living in homes with guns (Hemenway and Zhang 2022). Urban and rural patterns of living in homes with guns is similar for black and white men, with 22% of black men and 37% of white men in metropolitan counties living in homes with guns and 41% of black men and 63% of white men in nonmetropolitan counties living in homes with guns (Hemenway and Zhang 2022). However, we suspect these numbers are higher because such survey results—which rely on participants' willingness to complete the survey—likely do not include data from individuals who use guns to commit crimes or who are legally prohibited from owning a gun as a result of previous felony convictions.

While regional and race-specific beliefs and attitudes may inform gun cultures, almost all gun owners share a common belief in their right to defend themselves. Gun ownership was common among black leaders and participants in the civil rights movements in 1960s Alabama and Mississippi, which is generally known for its nonviolent strategies of passive resistance yet nonetheless relied on black gun owners who guarded, patrolled, and defended themselves against white supremacist violence (Cobb 2014). Armed self-defense was critical for black civil rights organizers in Mississippi and throughout the Deep South, where local law enforcement often supported racist segregation (Umoja 2013).

Important similarities and differences exist among contemporary gun owners by race. For example, a Detroit study of men who legally purchased and carried firearms found that both black and white men connected their desire to own a gun with postindustrial declining wages and downward social mobility, and a desire to protect wives and children (Carlson 2015). A national survey that examined firearm carrying by region found that, in the South, 19% of white men and 17% of black men carried guns, in contrast with 8% of northern white men and 13% of northern black men; rates of gun carrying for northern white women were especially low at less than 1%, and 4% for northern black women, in contrast with approximately 6% of both southern black and white women (Felson and Pare 2010b). A national survey on gun policy preferences found higher rates of support for banning all handguns among blacks and Latinos (41%) than whites (19%), and much higher support for the creation of a federal database of all gun sales among blacks (86%) and Latinos (78%) than whites (67%) (Filindra and Kaplan 2017), likely because of the disproportionately high levels of crimes committed with guns in black communities.

Research indicates that many guns used to commit crimes have been obtained illegally. For example, a survey of primarily black men incarcerated for violent crimes in Chicago's Cook County Jail found that most obtained firearms from acquaintances, with 60% of those guns obtained by purchase or trade with others in their social network and one in seven participants reporting selling guns (Cook, Parker, and Pollack 2015). These illegally obtained firearms also appear in cases of homicide, which is the leading cause of death among young black men between the ages of fifteen and twenty-four, and most of these homicides are committed with firearms (Richardson et al. 2016). A Baltimore hospital trauma unit study of black males hospitalized after being shot, stabbed, or beaten found that 58% had previously been hospitalized two or more times for similar injuries (Richardson et al. 2016). Of these violent crime victims, those most likely to have been hospitalized multiple times were those who had previously been in a fight or used a weapon in the past year, regarded disrespect as justification for violence, and served jail or prison time (Richardson et al. 2016). To understand these dynamics more fully, it is helpful to turn to a discussion of how this violence manifests in midsize cities like ours around the country.

VIOLENT CRIMES COMMITTED WITH A GUN IN MIDSIZE CITIES

Research on violent crimes committed with a gun in midsize cities, while relatively limited in comparison to similar research in major metropolitan areas, provides important insights into the dynamics of such violence, particularly with respect to illegally acquired firearms. For example, a study of firearm- and nonfirearm-related homicides in 226 US cities found that greater availability of illegal guns correlates with higher firearm homicide rates in conditions of structural economic disadvantage such as pervasive poverty, unemployment, income inequality, and residential segregation (Semenza et al. 2021). For example, a Louisville, Kentucky, study found correlations between the prevalence of violent crimes committed with a gun and residence in redlined poor and predominantly black neighborhoods (Benns et al. 2020). These racial disparities are also evident in shooting injuries involving children in Birmingham, Alabama, where black children are most often injured in shootings intended to harm another person and white children most often injured after a person unintentionally fires a gun through improper handling (Senger et al. 2011).

Concentrated disadvantage at the neighborhood level, which is defined by a high proportion of people living in poverty, limited positive community support networks, and a high density of predominantly black female-headed households (Wehrman 2010), correlates with high numbers of fatal shootings in midsize cities. For example, a study of criminal nonfatal shootings in Indianapolis, Milwaukee, St. Louis, and Detroit found that nonfatal shootings are more geographically dispersed than fatal shootings and typically involve defendants who are younger, have less extensive arrest records, and are in the process of committing a robbery at the time of the shooting (Hipple et al. 2019). In Detroit, shootings occur less frequently in public parks in comparison with other locations, although shootings that do occur in public parks happen in areas with more tree cover (Breetzke et al. 2020). A St. Louis study found that high rates of aggregated lead exposure at the census tract level were associated with high rates of violent crimes committed with a gun, homicide, and rape (Boutwell et al. 2017). Risk terrain modeling revealed that Baton Rouge, Louisiana, homicides occur most often in areas with large numbers of blighted properties and convenience stores (Valasik, Brault, and Martinez 2019).

Such overwhelming evidence of these correlations between concentrated disadvantage and fatal shootings has led many researchers to regard shootings in midsize cities as a public health problem. A study of New Orleanians who committed suicide with a gun found that half had experienced a past trauma, including family members killed by homicide (Ramchand et al. 2018). Conceiving of crimes committed with a gun as analogous to a communicable disease suggests that the frequency with which fatal shootings occur could be reduced by changing social norms and community attitudes (Butts et al. 2015) in communities of color with low levels of trust in police and justice processes more generally (Goodwin and Grayson 2020). In a study of victim cooperation in nonfatal gun assaults in Indianapolis and St. Louis, for example, 43% of victims did not cooperate with police, although white victims with serious center mass gunshot wounds were more willing to cooperate with police than nonwhite victims, who were not significantly more cooperative with police even when seriously injured (Hipple, Thompson, and Huebner 2019).

The public health approach to violent crimes committed with a gun has shown promising results in midsize cities by operating with the presumption that community norms, attitudes, and beliefs are central to both the prevalence of shootings and their prevention. For example, attitudes and norms that condone or even endorse violent crimes committed with a gun are predictive of being arrested or shot among young men in high-violence communities in Baltimore (Milam et al. 2018). As an effort to change such attitudes and norms, the CeaseFire model originally developed in Chicago relies on the expertise of community outreach workers, known as violence interrupters, to mediate potentially violent interpersonal conflicts before they lead to a shooting by separating the potential shooter, and peers who may encourage the shooter to fire a gun, from the potential victim and persuading all parties involved to resolve the conflict peacefully with the goal of preventing both violent crimes committed with a gun and toxic cycles of retaliation (Whitehill et al. 2014).

Three Baltimore sites that implemented the CeaseFire program experienced a reduction in homicides in one site, a reduction in nonfatal shootings in another, and a decrease in nonfatal shootings in the third alongside an increase in homicides (Webster et al. 2013). Targeted interventions in New Orleans, in the form of police meeting with individuals known to be involved in activities they believed lead to violent crimes committed with a gun, such as gang disputes, resulted in a decline in targeted violence in the form of gang violence, young black male homicides, and violent crimes committed with a gun (Corsaro and Engel 2015). The premise underlying such targeted interventions is that the risk of violent crimes committed with a gun decreases when police make an individual involved in criminal behavior aware of the charges they will face if that behavior escalates to violent crimes committed with a gun.

Far less is known about how shooting cases proceed through the justice assemblage in midsize cities. While District Attorney's Offices in major metropolitan areas such as Chicago, Philadelphia, and San Francisco have prioritized making de-identified case disposition records accessible online to improve public confidence in the criminal justice system (Stageman, Napolitano, and Buchner 2018), hesitancy to make this information public remains the norm in rural areas and smaller-to-midsize cities in combination with a relative lack of citizen oversight (Gordon and Huber 2002). This lack of citizen oversight, which may also be a sign of greater trust and confidence in prosecutors relative to major metropolitan areas, often correlates with more politically conservative voting districts.

These realities are further complicated by the reality that significant material differences exist between criminal investigations and prosecutions at the county level in comparison with law enforcement in major metropolitan areas, which tends to be more bureaucratized, specialized, and better resourced. These material differences include resources (e.g., salaries, technological equipment and expertise, staff); training (e.g., departmental ability and interest in sending officers/staff attorneys to professional development opportunities and conferences); and specialized units devoted to particular types of violent crime (e.g., homicide, sex crimes). This is significant given that high rates of homicide clearance are associated with strong community policing presence, collaboration with external agencies, and innovative culture (Carter and Carter 2016). Likewise, these reduced material resources may slow down or hinder criminal justice and legal processes in addition to indirectly facilitating capitalization on these operational inefficiencies by those who break the law. Rural and midsize cities, particularly in the Deep South, have become transit hubs for firearms trafficking into larger metropolitan areas in regions with stricter gun control laws, further complicating the legal geographies of violent crimes committed with a gun (Robinson, 2021).

SOME REFLECTIONS ON PARTICIPATORY METHODS AND ADMINISTRATIVE CRIMINOLOGY

As we discussed in the introduction, one of the major contributions our team's work makes to criminology lies in its immersive participatory methods. This chapter deals primarily with data Susan collected from the internal case management system at the Tuscaloosa County District Attorney's Office with the goal of helping prosecutors understand patterns in crimes involving guns. In so doing, our work might be regarded as veering quite close to the maligned subdiscipline termed administrative criminology. Coined by criminologist Jock Young in the mid-1980s, the pejorative phrase "administrative criminology" broadly refers to scientific methods' application to the refinement of criminal justice practices at the expense of attention to the social causes of crime (Hough 2014). Critics characterize this work as narrow in scope, lacking in scholarly value, and performed to serve the state's agenda (Mayhew 2016).

Conservative in orientation, this approach to criminology focuses on practical solutions to reducing or preventing crime, rather than focusing on the socioeconomic causes of crime (Matthews 2014), and accordingly faces widespread criticism from academic criminologists who dismiss it as disconnected from the realities of defendants' lives and lawbreaking (Cullen 2011). In writing of the split that occurred between practitioners and academics at Berkeley's School of Criminology in the 1970s, which actively collaborated with criminal justice practitioners, Koehler (2015, 532) cites one of her participants as noting, "Criminology had become politicized to the point where it really wasn't taken very seriously by the public safety establishment anymore."

It is vitally important to us, as a participatory research team, to mutually respect one another as part of a focus on what Hays frequently characterized as "the pursuit of the truth." For us, pursuing the truth meant compiling a database that accurately depicted the realities at work in the over one thousand cases involving guns prosecuted during Hays's tenure as District Attorney. This chapter accordingly explores two key aspects of these cases: the versatility in the use of guns at crime scenes and the versatility of guns' meanings at crime scenes. Data that forms the basis of this chapter would, for many criminologists, constitute the totality of a study, which gives us pause to reflect on what we would have missed had we not engaged in a participatory approach, with Susan present for many hundreds of hours to observe unfettered the nuances of everyday working life at the District Attorney's Office.

There are three major aspects of the law in practice that Susan and Brittany would have completely missed had they confined their study solely to collection and analysis of administrative data. First, we would not have witnessed the frenetic pace, enormous workload, and very high expectations facing Assistant District Attorneys if Susan had not spent so much time in the office. "This is a hard job," Chief Assistant District Attorney Paula Whitley explained. "This is not an eight-to-five job because sometimes you're in court eight-to-five. Then the real work gets done on nights and weekends." Failing to observe these on-the-ground realities would have completely obscured the realities of the law in practice in these cases, including how individual prosecutors manage what many readers will likely regard as prosecutors' excessive and even unmanageable workload.

Second, focusing solely on administrative data would have left huge gaps in our knowledge about habituation into the work of prosecution. Since so many Assistant District Attorneys were relatively recent law school graduates, Susan was able to watch Hays and Paula mentor them as a group every week as they mastered the nuances of prosecuting cases. This mentoring, in Susan's interpretation, involved highly specific ways of thinking about arguments and supporting evidence that, in turn, dramatically shaped our own approach to evidence-based arguments presented throughout the book. For example, one morning when Susan was talking with prosecutor Thomas Marshall about a witness who did not want to participate in the defendant's prosecution, she asked, "What do you think is going on with this witness?" Thomas looked at Susan quizzically for a moment before responding with a brilliant clarifying question: "Are you asking me what I know, or what I can prove?" This distinction, while seemingly subtle, is critical to the everyday work of prosecution.

Third, an exclusive focus on administrative data collection would have obscured the complex relationships between prosecutors, defendants, victims, and witnesses from our research view. Overhearing witnesses and victims who are, whether from fear or more commonly from simple disinterest, unhelpful because unwilling, and subsequently watching prosecutors understandably frustrated in response quickly made us aware of the absolute wrongness of academic critiques of prosecutors as all-powerful. For some of these victims and witnesses, assisting with the prosecution of someone who played an important role in their lives was a choice they were unwilling to make, irrespective of the severity of the crime. Emotions could accordingly run high when it became apparent that all efforts to persuade victims and witnesses to participate had failed, or when trial preparation was actively in progress. It was only while writing this book that we began to realize how ignoring the role of emotions in the justice assemblage effectively means erasing the fact that human beings—not abstract automatons—carry out the everyday administration of the law in practice, including the symbolic meanings guns have at crime scenes.

GUNS' SYMBOLIC MEANINGS AT CRIME SCENES

A key aspect of the legal, moral, ideological, and cultural work of the gun involves the versatility of its symbolic meanings at crime scenes. "The gun changes the dynamic," Susan often heard prosecutors say as they talked through their cases. The gun is itself a relational symbol and an actor, irrespective of its use, in the events leading to its carrier's arrest and subsequent entry into the justice assemblage. The gun has important relationships to the justice assemblage and to the law, and often these relationships have significant temporal components, as the meaning of the gun changes significantly depending on when and how its carrier engages it, as well as where and with whom they do so.

Susan experienced this temporal dynamic firsthand when she was still living in snowbound Wyoming and counting down the days until her move to her newly purchased farm in subtropical Alabama. While writing at home one subzero April afternoon, Susan felt delighted when she saw a phone number with a Tuscaloosa area code. She picked up on the first ring. "Ms. Susan," her Tuscaloosa insurance agent began in an uncharacteristically forthright tone, "did y'all know there was a bad break-in at y'all's place?" The agent had just completed the police report review of the risk assessment process insurance brokers undertake before issuing new homeowner policies. Police photographs momentarily arrived in Susan's email inbox depicting her soon-to-be home as a crime scene: the previous owner's glass gun cabinet smashed to pieces with a tire iron, his guns conspicuous in their absence, the home's back door meticulously pried open by city people who failed to understand how breaking a window would be a much more efficient and less labor intensive way to intrude on a country home.

A wildlife camera captured black-and-white, but nonetheless clear, images of intruders breaking into another farmhouse a few miles down the road using the same method to steal guns. Eventually the police investigation revealed that a group of young men from Bessemer, a troubled Birmingham suburb, studied the schedules of the farmers and other rural people in Susan's dispersed community because they knew that an overwhelming majority of people in rural Alabama have guns at home.

As Susan sits writing at this moment, she can see the indentation on the back door where the burglars used a crowbar to force entry into the house when the previous owner was at work. As soon as the burglars stole the previous owner's guns, these firearms made a symbolic transition in the eyes of the law from legally owned possessions used for recreational hunting and self-protection to stolen property intended for resale in the illicit gun trade.

Guns stolen in property crimes quickly enter the illicit gun trade outside the purview of state and federal laws, and accordingly, police commonly recover these stolen guns at new crime scenes. Officers typically use the federal National Crime Information Center (NCIC) to check the serial numbers of firearms recovered at crime scenes; if a property crime victim has reported a gun as stolen, NCIC relays this information to the officer. Sometimes police recover stolen guns during misdemeanor arrests, such as the third-degree receiving stolen property case where officers made a traffic stop and discovered a small amount of marijuana, improperly registered license plates, and a Smith and Wesson M&P .40 caliber handgun confirmed stolen from Northport, a city just north of Tuscaloosa. As we will see, guns are powerful objects precisely because their material and symbolic meanings emerge—and sometimes shift—in context.

Our review of felony reports marked "gun present" indicated how guns typically perform one or more of five types of symbolic work at crime scenes by (1) granting the person holding the gun tremendous (albeit temporary) power; (2) serving as a proxy for money; (3) dramatically increasing the potential for rapid escalation into lethal violence; (4) demonstrating the intention of the person holding an altered gun to evade police or commit lethal violence; and (5) serving as an illicit badge of authority. These five types are not necessarily mutually exclusive, as guns themselves are inert objects with symbolic meanings defined by their context. For example, a victim in a second-degree theft case whose 9mm Taurus handgun was stolen from his business's counter told police he typically left the gun visible "to deter criminals," effectively transforming the gun from a symbolic power-giver to a proxy for money on the illicit market. Similarly, in a second-degree theft and larceny case, a victim reported her sister's boyfriend took the victim's Ruger LCP .380 pistol in the glove compartment of her car without her permission and then told the sisters he threw it away because they were attempting to get him charged with another crime. Here we see the gun symbolically transformed from a gun as an illicit badge of authority used for self-defense to a power-giving tool for incrimination.

Gun as Power-Giver

In the first type of symbolic work the gun performs at a crime scene, the gun grants the person holding it immediate power to threaten or take what they want—cash, property, drugs, sex, revenge, life—from another person. While this power is symbolic and accordingly may not be readily apparent, it is obvious to people who use guns to commit crimes, victims of these crimes, and police investigators who review suspects' social media accounts to see if their posts may contain evidence to move forward with a case. Consider the first-degree stolen property and unlawful breaking and entering case where the young men who stole guns and cars from an apartment complex posted photographs of themselves dramatically displaying the stolen guns while seated in the stolen vehicle. In another social media example, the Fugitive Task Force was attempting to convince a suspect with six first-degree robbery warrants to leave a residence when a bail bondsperson showed the lieutenant on scene a social media post of two men, including the suspect, posing with multiple handguns and a long gun just forty-five minutes prior to the officers' arrival. Social media photographs in the first case appeared as state's evidence against the young men, while the photographs in the second case provided sufficient cause for the lieutenant on scene to activate the special response team, which convinced the suspect to willingly leave the residence.

The gun's symbolic power and authority is also evident because sometimes the gun does not even exist, yet the illusion or intimation of its presence nonetheless grants the person pretending to hold it power. For example, in a second-degree assault case, police responded to an apartment complex shooting where the victim, who did not want to cooperate with prosecutors, was shot in the shoulder after he held an item under his shirt to fake the appearance of holding a gun and demanded money and marijuana from the man who then shot him. With this symbolic power and authority so granted to the person carrying (or pretending to be carrying) it, the gun communicates to all present on scene, "Now I have your attention."

The gun's attention-getting power is apparent in a menacing and first-degree burglary case in which a woman forced her way into the victim's home armed with a knife and handgun. She used the gun to smash a hole in the wall before demanding to see the victim's young daughter about a school fight with her own daughter before the woman pushed her out of the home. It is likewise evident in a discharging firearm into an occupied vehicle case in which a woman accused her man of infidelity and stole his watch, prompting him to shoot into her car to, as he told police, "scare her into giving the watch back." In a reckless endangerment and discharging firearm into an occupied vehicle case, a couple attended a sports game with a friend who had been drinking heavily for several days, and when the couple returned home later that night following a dispute in which the friend told them they were no longer welcome, he fired a Browning X-Bolt .243 Winchester rifle at the couple, shattering their windshield.

When the gun emerges on the scene, its material and symbolic presence shifts the social dynamic by forcing everyone present to make an immediate decision about what to do next. A second-degree robbery case, for instance, featured three men who contacted the victim on social media under the pretext of selling him a phone, and then took him to an ATM to withdraw money. After the victim realized that the phone was locked and protested, one of the three men handed a black rifle to a back seat passenger who told the victim to strip, at which point the victim jumped out of the car and ran into a bar, only to realize his phone and wallet were gone. In a first-degree robbery case, two men approached a driver seated in his vehicle at a gas station; one asked him for change for a twenty-dollar bill and the other showed the driver his .22 caliber pistol, demanded that he step out of the car, and then stole his vehicle.

Guns are especially evident as symbolic power-givers in violent crimes, which span a gamut of harm caused to another person, including assault, domestic violence, attempted murder, kidnapping, manslaughter, and rape, and the relationships between defendants and victims likewise vary from strangers to intimate partners or family members. Violent crimes also include engaging in threats, harassment, or extortion with a gun, with potential charges including reckless endangerment, criminal mischief, extortion, and discharging firearm into an (un)occupied dwelling, building, or vehicle.

Guns may emerge in violent crime cases as emotive retaliatory responses for an undesired outcome, as in a second-degree assault case with a defendant who pulled out a handgun in an illegal gambling venue and shot the victim following an argument. Violent crimes involving guns often blur the distinction between victim and defendant because both are involved in illegal acts when the gun emerges during the escalating dispute. For example, in a first-degree kidnapping and robbery case, two victims who visited a mobile home with the intention of selling methamphetamine were greeted at the door by four defendants who bound their hands, covered their eyes with duct tape, and beat them with a gun and a bat before driving them to a remote location where the victims escaped.

Guns are also symbolic power-givers in cases where they serve as communication tools designed to convey a warning to an individual or the community more generally. The latter occurred in a discharging firearm into an unoccupied building case where police responded to a scene with a black-clad shooter firing several rounds of ammunition into the air from a pistol before retrieving a semiautomatic rifle from his home, firing thirty rounds into the air, and then running back inside. After obtaining a search warrant, police entered his residence and recovered two rifles propped up by the bed, a black Hi-Point .45 semiautomatic rifle with a loaded magazine containing ammunition similar to the shell casings found on the street outside, and a Marlin .22 rifle, along with eight loose .380 live rounds, a box of sixteen Federal .45 ammunition, a box of thirty-eight 9mm Luger ammunition, and a clear bag containing an American Eagle box with thirty-eight rounds of ammunition.

Guns also function as symbolic power-givers in property crimes—such as burglary, robbery, theft, receiving stolen property, or breaking and entering—which typically occur between strangers. "You have one more time or I will shoot you," a masked man charged with first-degree robbery said as he and his codefendant pointed a shotgun and a handgun at a restaurant manager as he attempted to unlock a safe with shaking hands, the floor already strewn with shattered glass and shell casings. The gun may also be used to both assault and threaten, as occurred in a case where the codefendants pulled the victim from his vehicle and struck him in the back of the head with a small handgun and threatened to shoot him if he did not hand over his phone, shoes, gold chains, and the several thousand dollars he was carrying.

Yet guns do not always achieve their intended symbolic effect as power-givers, especially in instances where the victim does not regard the gun as sufficiently threatening to end the encounter in favor of the person holding the gun. In one example where the victim met an unknown person in a strip mall parking lot to exchange a cell phone for marijuana, the victim chased after the man holding both the gun and the victim's cell phone until the man jumped into his girlfriend's waiting car and told her to flee the scene because of his outstanding warrants. Here we see the gun failing to achieve the goal of the person holding the gun when the recipient of its threat refuses to recognize the gun's symbolic power.

Gun as Proxy for Money

The second type of symbolic work performed by the gun at a crime scene is as a proxy for money through its use as a valuable trade item. In these instances, the gun is an object of value in illicit trade outside the state's purview. A man who promised his friend a Ruger AR-15 rifle as collateral for bonding him out of jail until he could repay his bond stole the firearm from his former roommate's house. His friend promptly gave the gun to his brother, who kept it until the father of the man he bonded out of jail arrived on scene and pointed his own gun at the man and his friend to demand the valuable rifle back. Sometimes individuals trade stolen guns for illicit drugs, as in a second-degree theft case where a man stole a pistol from the employer who paid him to do odd jobs, traded the gun for drugs, and then, in a state of extreme anxiety, stole his employer's car and fled to a neighboring state, where local police apprehended him.

Illicit gun deals are fraught with risks for both seller and buyer. In a first-degree robbery case, the victim attempted to purchase a Glock 19 9mm pistol from a man he met on Snapchat, but when the victim and the seller met for the transaction, the seller robbed the victim of $280 after aiming the gun at his head, leaving the scene with both the gun and the money. Officers who responded to a burglary call in which three pistols were stolen from the victim's car in a receiving stolen property case located one of the firearms, a Taurus Judge, in a pawn shop database four days later, after a woman pawned it at the request of her boyfriend, who bought it from a friend for a hundred dollars.

Individuals frequently steal guns from family members, intimate partners, and acquaintances to resell them on the illicit market. In a third-degree burglary case, a man left a social gathering organized by a woman and her friends at their apartment complex's pool to break into her apartment and steal her Israeli Military Industries Desert Eagle 9mm pistol, along with cash, her passport, and her social security card. A certain persons forbidden to possess a firearm case with a man under investigation for a separate theft of property case led to the man confessing that he stole a relative's SPR 100 12-gauge shotgun, Bryco Arms .380 caliber pistol, and a .410 shotgun and pawned them at various locations in Tuscaloosa. A third-degree burglary victim advised police that his daughter, who had recently stayed with him and was frequently, as he put it, "in trouble" for stealing, might know something about the theft of his 9mm pistol and $11,000 in cash.

Some of these cases include blurry boundaries between guns "borrowed" from friends or family members and then either resold or never returned. In a second-degree theft case, a victim reported that a friend asked to borrow his PSA AR-15 rifle due to an altercation he had at "the club," and when the victim refused, the man took the firearm anyway and said he would return it the next morning. When the victim filed a police report after he did not, the man told police he sold the gun. In another second-degree theft of property case, the victim allowed a friend to borrow his 9mm Hi-Point handgun for work, but the friend did not return the firearm despite the victim asking for months. Investigators found the gun at a pawn shop and learned the man pawned it shortly after borrowing it from the victim.

One of the most common ways guns enter the illicit gun trade in our community is through car break-ins in which the victim and the person who commits the burglary do not know one another. In one unlawful breaking and entering motor vehicle case, surveillance video recorded five men smashing the window of a car in a bar parking lot and stealing a pistol. An unlawful breaking and entering victim who was passing through Tuscaloosa during his family's cross-country move had numerous personal items stolen from his vehicle, along with a suppressor and Legion and Ruger firearms. Sometimes these car break-ins are highly organized, as occurred in a spate of seventeen separate incidents with multiple personal items stolen, in addition to a Ruger model P85 9mm, a box of Remington 9mm bullets, a Smith and Wesson Shield 9mm, a Ruger LC9S 9mm pistol, and two Ruger magazines.

Burglaries of unoccupied homes are another way defendants illicitly obtain guns. In a third-degree burglary case, police responded to a call about a break-in with bloodstains throughout the unoccupied residence, followed by a second call about a bleeding man knocking on the door looking for work after he and his girlfriend were evicted from a backyard shed owned by a woman with dementia, and when he was told none existed, walking down to the railroad tracks. Police located the man along the railroad tracks, and he told police he and his girlfriend had been walking to Walmart when they saw the vacant mobile home, where he cut himself on broken glass breaking in and took a 12-gauge shotgun, .22 rifle, and pellet gun, along with copper wire, a suitcase, a phone, a purse, $5,000 in gold coins, and household items such as hedge clippers. He then became anxious about having the stolen guns and left them by the railroad tracks.

Gun as Escalating Potential for Lethal Violence

The third type of symbolic work performed by the gun at a crime scene involves the potential for rapid escalation into lethal violence at a crime scene, with the gun's presence looming as it changes relational dynamics between the person holding the gun and others on scene. Consider the meaning of the gun in a case where a man received first-degree domestic violence, attempting to elude police, second-degree receiving stolen property, tampering with physical evidence, and resisting arrest charges after he forced his way into his ex-girlfriend's room and began screaming at her, hitting her with a closed fist, kicking her, and threatening to kill her while chambering a round into a stolen handgun pointed at her and ejaculating on her. The next day the victim met with police to sign a warrant, and when pursued by police, the man sped away, threw the handgun he stole in a car break-in out the window, lost control of the vehicle, and drove into a ditch, where police arrested him.

Guns present in fraught, impassioned domestic scenarios pose an imminent threat of escalating violence, particularly when the gun changes hands among multiple individuals who are fighting and have limited firearm safety knowledge. In a first-degree burglary case, officers arrived at a residence on a domestic dispute call where the female victim had been in bed with a male when her boyfriend began banging on her bedroom door and arguing with the man in bed, who insisted he did not know the female victim was in a relationship. The boyfriend then attacked the victim, leading the man who had been in bed with her to separate her from her assailant, who pointed a handgun at the other man before the female victim snatched the gun away from him and left the residence.

In a second-degree domestic violence assault case, police responded to the victim's residence after a person she was texting with called 911 to advise dispatchers that a man struck the victim in the head with a handgun after they had been arguing all night about their mutual jealousy of one another. The couple told police that they argue frequently and, perhaps because the man was a convicted felon prohibited by law from possessing a firearm, the couple insisted to police that he struck her with a back scratcher, although police located a Ruger LCP .380 and two 6-round Ruger magazines in the room. In a first-degree burglary and third-degree domestic violence/criminal mischief case, a woman who has children with a man she had been in a relationship with for several years broke into his home with a loaded 9mm Jimenez Arms pistol and took his cell phone. The male victim took the gun from the defendant, emptied the bullets, and returned it to her in exchange for his cell phone, at which point she used the gun to break the window of his truck.

Gun cases in these fraught domestic scenarios demonstrate how police, prosecutors, and offenders continuously reimbue meaning into guns as extraordinary objects that elicit extraordinary responses or changes to situations. This is particularly evident when police discover guns present in the home when 911 callers request police presence to settle an interpersonal dispute. Officers who responded to a complaint from a man about an unwanted guest in his residence found that the caller, who had an active arrest warrant on a failure to appear charge for a third-degree theft of property case, was also in possession of Xanax, a Ruger 9mm pistol, a 9mm magazine, bullets, and an Anderson Arms AR-15 rifle. In a similar instance, officers responded to a man's residence on a menacing call and located two loaded Taurus 9mm handguns, one in the man's car and one in tucked inside a pink Crown Royal bag in his residence.

These violent domestic incidents that escalate into brandishing or using a firearm are typically unplanned, as in the attempted murder case where the victim's boyfriend threw a knife at her from his front door when she approached his residence. She then pepper sprayed him, at which point he ran out of the residence armed with his .357 Sig Sauer handgun and fired several rounds in her direction. Here we see the gun emerging as a symbolic equalizer in response to an assault with a less harmful weapon (pepper spray). The lethal potential of guns is inherent in symbolic threats such as those made in cases where one party uses a gun as a tool of punishment with the implied threat of actually firing the gun. For example, in a second-degree domestic violence assault case, a woman struck the victim in the head with the base of her SCCY 9mm handgun following an argument about his staying out the night before and failing to contribute to their shared childcare responsibilities.

During an impassioned altercation between intimate partners or family members, guns can also very rapidly transform from a symbolic into an actual threat of gunfire and even lethal violence, as occurred in a manslaughter case where a woman accidentally shot her boyfriend in the head while trying to wrest his gun away during a fight. These cases also demonstrate the threat of lethal violence implied by brandishing a gun as a tool to instill fear or achieve acquiescence with a threat beyond pain or injury by foreshadowing death. This dynamic is evident in a case with multiple violent felony charges—attempted murder, second-degree assault, and shooting into an occupied vehicle—where a man brandished a gun during an argument with the woman driving him, prompting her to pull into a high school parking lot and push him out of the car, at which point he grabbed her by the hair, pistol whipped her across the face, and began shooting. Likewise in a first-degree burglary case and assault case, a man and his family members attacked the victim when she attempted to retrieve her identity documents from their formerly shared home, causing her to flee to her mother's house while pursued by the man and his family, who then entered the victim's mother's house without permission and slashed the victim with a knife, pepper sprayed and punched her, and then brandished a handgun while promising to return and "shoot the house up."

Guns present with quantities of illicit drugs also pose an imminent risk of rapid escalation into lethal violence, particularly when intoxicated people are within reaching distance of firearms. For example, in a trafficking methamphetamine and failure to affix tax stamp case, mobile home occupants refused entry to police executing a search warrant, and after an officer used a battering ram to force the door open, a physical confrontation ensued between the officer and one of the residents. After the resident was hand-cuffed, officers breached the bedroom door to find the two remaining residents using methamphetamine near three rifles, with an additional shotgun and rifle stored outside the bedroom. Likewise during a probable cause search following an officer-initiated traffic stop, officers located a loaded Ruger .357 GP-100 revolver wedged between the driver's seat and the center console, a plastic grocery bag filled with various ammunition types in the rear pocket of the passenger seat, and a Palmetto Arms AK-47 7.62 rifle with an empty magazine in the trunk, along with a backpack containing a digital scale, sandwich bags, various types of ammunition, an empty Glock handgun magazine, and two mason jars of marijuana.

Gun as Demonstrating Criminal Intent

The fourth type of symbolic work performed by the gun at a crime scene is as a demonstration of criminal intent, whether through firearm alterations or carrying despite legal prohibitions. Firearm alterations indicate the intentions of the person carrying the altered gun to evade police detection and/or commit lethal violence by intensifying the gun's capacity to kill. In a certain persons forbidden to possess a firearm and possession of a short-barreled rifle or shotgun case, for example, police executed a search warrant on a mobile home where an individual was asleep on the porch with a pistol in his lap. While searching for the wanted subject, police located a Stevens 94 20-gauge sawed-off shotgun near a bag of methamphetamine. In a possession of a short-barreled rifle, possession of firearm with altered identification, and possession with intent to distribute methamphetamine case, narcotics agents entered a motel room where a man was sleeping next to a quantity of methamphetamine, more than fifty used syringes, and a sawed-off shotgun with the serial number scratched off, which he later told police he purchased for sixty dollars. In a possession of an altered firearm and possession with intent to distribute case, police arrived on a domestic dispute call to find a man choking his mother-in-law and holding a sawed-off shotgun to the 911 caller's head in a mobile home because they would not allow him to use their car to go to work. The man then brought the officer a duffle bag containing marijuana, cocaine, methamphetamine, and pills he said he was holding as collateral for a $600 loan he made to a friend and told police he found the sawed-off shotgun and a hand grenade at his workplace.

Altered serial numbers, which make a gun untraceable through the federal NCIC system, likewise symbolize the intentions of a person carrying an altered firearm. In a possession of firearm with altered identification case, an officer executing a search warrant encountered an individual concealing a weapon that, when the officer removed it from that individual, had the serial number scratched off. In a case with charges including certain persons forbidden to possess a firearm, possession of a controlled substance-cocaine, first-degree unlawful possession of marijuana, possession of firearm with altered identification, and fourth-degree receiving stolen property, police executed a search warrant at the defendant's residence for his two distribution of controlled substance warrants and seized six firearms: a Glock 19 9mm pistol, Walther PPX 9mm pistol, Masterpiece Arms 9mm handgun, Tanfoglio handgun, Smith and Wesson M&P semiautomatic pistol, and Raven Arms MP .25 caliber semiautomatic pistol.

At a transitional housing facility, officers were in the process of administering breathalyzer tests when they saw a resident run to his room, retrieve a loaded 9mm firearm from under his mattress, and place it in his waistband. Officers could not determine whether the pistol was stolen through the NCIC database because the gun's serial number had been filed off, resulting in both certain persons forbidden to possess a firearm and possession of a firearm with altered identification charges. In a possession of firearm with altered identification and third-degree burglary case, officers responded to the victim's complaint of two men burglarizing his shed to find the men attempting to steal an air conditioner and copper wire, and a silver Stallard Arms 9mm pistol with part of the serial number drilled through on the front seat of a truck that belonged to one of the defendants.

People who carry guns despite legal prohibitions on their doing so also demonstrate criminal intent and accordingly face charges of certain persons prohibited to possess a firearm as a result of previous felony convictions. These charges almost exclusively occur during contact with police, whether during a traffic stop or at the scene of a newly committed crime that may or may not involve use of the gun, such as the case where officers initiated a traffic stop for failing to signal, and after smelling marijuana, searched the vehicle and found crack cocaine, methamphetamine, marijuana, and a loaded Taurus G2 pistol, which the defendant claimed to have purchased for one hundred dollars on the street, in a container under a pair of pants. In another case, officers observed an intoxicated driver with a felony criminal record asleep through four cycles of lights at a major intersection with a

Hi-Point JCP .40 caliber handgun and magazine in the car. In yet another officer-initiated traffic stop for failure to signal, officers noticed a box of shotgun shells in the door pocket, and when searching the vehicle, a stolen Hi-Point .45 caliber handgun with a 14-round single stack magazine in the defendant's vehicle's center console that the driver said he purchased for $150 from a friend, along with a Mossberg 12-gauge shotgun he bought from another person whose name he claimed not to remember.

Certain persons forbidden to possess a firearm cases also follow interactions with police during controlled buys with assistance from cooperating individuals, as in the trafficking cocaine, failure to affix tax stamp, and certain persons forbidden to possess a firearm case where police provided a cooperating individual with $1,100 to purchase 29.5 grams of cocaine in a home improvement store parking lot. The defendant, who had a Taurus 9mm on the driver's side floorboard between his legs, advised police that the gun belonged to his wife and that he only agreed to meet the cooperating individual to resell the cocaine back to the cooperating individual after the defendant's "stripper party" was cancelled. Unsurprisingly, certain persons forbidden to possess a firearm cases are also common during search warrant executions in drug cases, where firearms almost always appear in addition to possession of a controlled substance or trafficking in illegal drugs charges.

A gun may also be carried on the person of an individual apprehended as a suspect in another crime and then determined to be a certain person forbidden to possess firearms, as happened when officers on patrol observed several young men flee during a business check. When police recognized and searched one of the young men as a suspect in another crime, they found he was carrying a Smith and Wesson M&P Bodyguard .380 and a digital scale. Possession of a gun by a person with a previous violent felony conviction is itself sufficient grounds for arrest and criminal charges. Police typically recover stolen guns while investigating other crimes that may or may not involve the use of a gun. For instance, police responded to a scene following a 911 call from neighbors who reported hearing shots fired and people screaming and then located a disassembled AR-15 rifle reported stolen in a burglary in the bedroom of the resident male who had prior felony convictions.

Gun as Illicit Badge of Authority

The fifth and final symbolic work performed by the gun at a crime scene involves the use or presence of a gun to convey authority, whether immediately in the context of a heated altercation or as a normalized expectation in drug sales due to the enhanced risk selling drugs presents for becoming a victim of crime, particularly robbery or assault. In some of these instances, the gun is a fear-provoking instrument that speeds up gratification for the person holding the gun by dramatically concluding the conflict. "Do they want to die?" a woman screamed in the parking lot of a discount store at two women, with whom she had a long multiyear history of disputes and arranged to meet for a fight before firing her handgun into their car and following them to a nearby gas station when they attempted to flee in a discharging firearm into an occupied vehicle and reckless endangerment case. In a similar case of discharging a firearm into an occupied vehicle, two women met outside an apartment complex to fight in front of an audience of their friends, and when one of the women got into a car to leave the scene, the other woman fired multiple shots in her direction, with one bullet striking the victim and another hitting a bystander watching the altercation from a nearby apartment.

The use of a gun as an illicit badge of authority to dramatically end a conflict is also evident in infrequent road rage incidents involving guns. In a case where the defendant was charged with second-degree assault, discharging a firearm into an occupied vehicle, and reckless endangerment, the victims were driving through a convenience store parking lot when another driver almost collided with their car, at which point the driver began shooting at them with a long gun. In some other instances, multiple parties in a road rage incident fire their weapons, such as in a reckless endangerment case where the defendant was accused of flashing his vehicle's lights and shooting at the victim, who then stopped his car, removed an AR-15 rifle from the trunk, and then fired into the air before getting back into his car and driving away, pursued by the defendant who shot a .40 caliber rifle at the victim from his vehicle.

While the gun is either fired or clearly visible to the victim in each of these examples, crimes such as rape and extortion may rely solely on the threat of the gun's presence. In a first-degree rape case where a family member's boyfriend sexually assaulted the victim in her home, the victim was further terrorized because she saw her assailant with a gun immediately prior to the assault even though he did not use the gun to threaten her. In another first-degree rape case, an unknown male assaulted the victim in her apartment complex hallway after pushing an object against her head from behind and threatening to shoot her. A first-degree extortion case included men who contacted a victim on social media to exchange nude photographs with him, and when he complied, one of the men then texted the victim a photograph of himself brandishing a handgun and demanded several thousand dollars not to publish the photographs, even calling in a bomb threat to the victim's workplace when he did not comply with the defendants' demands.

Guns also symbolically function as illicit badges of authority in drug crimes, which include a wide range of offenses, including unlawful possession, possession with intent to distribute, trafficking, and driving under the influence. Guns present at crime scenes that result in arrests on these charges typically have one of four inert roles at the crime scene: present in the residence where police are executing a search warrant, present in the residence when police are called to the scene for another reason, carried by the person arrested, or present in the car of a person arrested during a traffic stop. The symbolic meaning of the gun as an illicit badge of authority is particularly apparent in drug crimes because of the contextual transfer of meaning surrounding the actions surrounding the gun in these cases. For example, as part of the gun present policy and its premise that the presence of a gun changes the dynamics of a crime, a person who is carrying a gun lawfully with a person in possession of a controlled substance will result in the arrest and detention of the person in possession of the controlled substance but not the arrest and detention of the person with the gun. The person in possession of the controlled substance will remain in jail until they make bond, which is set after they see a judge. In all gun present crimes, the amount of time to be served additionally in jail or prison depends on the severity of the crime involving a gun.

"I must be the brokest drug dealer y'all ever arrested," said a man officers found in possession of a Glock 17 9mm, sixty-one grams of marijuana, and a digital scale during a search warrant execution and subsequently charged with first-degree unlawful possession of marijuana and third-degree receiving stolen property. Felony reports of search warrant executions often depict the domestic nature of small-time drug sales, complete with baking scales, Pyrex measuring cups, and bedroom dresser drawers with firearms and ammunition tucked into old T-shirts or hidden behind a washing machine. During one search warrant execution resulting in the defendant receiving possession of a controlled substance, possession with intent to distribute cocaine, and first-degree possession of marijuana charges, a woman answered the door holding a baby and told narcotics officers that she knew drugs were in the residence but was unaware of any guns, although officers located a Brescia Brevello 6.35 caliber firearm, a Hi-Point .45 caliber firearm with loaded magazine, a loaded .380 magazine in a top dresser drawer in the bedroom, and a Planters nuts can of .45 ammo in the bedroom closet.

Much like bullets loaded in a chamber, potentiality overpowers the absolute in the investigation and prosecution of drug cases with guns present as an illicit badge of authority. Police often recover multiple firearms in drug cases, irrespective of the amount of controlled substances on the scene. A possession with intent to distribute and failure to affix tax stamp case revolved around twenty-one grams of methamphetamine found in a plastic jar wrapped in electrical tape in a black plastic bag, a set of digital scales hidden in a pile of clothes, and a small amount of methamphetamine on top of a cable box. At this scene, investigators also found a Steyr .22 caliber rifle under the bed, a Remington 7600 .270 caliber rifle, a Remington 1100 12-gauge shotgun, and a Taurus Ultralite .38 caliber pistol wrapped in cloth standing up in the closet. In another unlawful possession of controlled substances case, officers located 1.5 pounds of marijuana, two MDMA pills, one Xanax bar, and one oxycodone pill, along with the defendant attempting to throw an AR-15 rifle out of his bedroom window. During a West Alabama Narcotics Task Force search warrant execution resulting in unlawful possession of a controlled substance, third-degree receiving stolen property, and first-degree stolen property charges, officers located a stolen Glock 19 handgun, a stolen Taurus .38 revolver, and 9mm bullets, along with a large amount of cash, digital scales, and illicitly possessed prescription drugs.

Guns often function as inert yet symbolically powerful objects in drug crimes because of their obvious presence despite not being brandished or fired. For example, guns may be carried by the person arrested on drug charges at the scene, such as in the example of a trafficking marijuana and carrying a concealed weapon case where police accompanied a postal inspector who delivered a seven-pound package of marijuana mailed from California and then arrested the man who accepted the delivery with a Taurus GLC 9mm with twelve rounds of live ammunition, including one in the chamber, in his pocket. In a possession with intent to distribute cocaine and first-degree marijuana possession case, officers conducted a knock and talk after surveilling a residence subject to multiple police complaints for selling drugs and observed a strong odor of marijuana smoke and saw a film of smoke inside the residence. "I'm smokin' weed with him," the resident who answered the door with a Sig Sauer handgun in his front pocket informed police when asked what he was doing, and officers located a 9mm handgun lying on the bed next to a pile of cash. Guns are inert but symbolically powerful in all of these instances, which accounts for the extensive attention gun cases receive in the media.

MEDIA VERSUS REALITY

We conducted this research at a time when shootings were in the news every day in all forms of news media. Mass media was also saturated with crime shows perversely marketed as "entertainment" to an anxious public, which in turn formulates its opinions (and votes) on criminal justice issues based on partial and often inaccurate information (Grubb and Posick 2021). Critics have warned against turning justice processes into a spectacle for decades, noting the potential for superficial media coverage to undermine public confidence in the law by transforming the practice of law grounded in logic into legal strategies akin to advertising and public relations (Sherwin 2002). Prosecutors, like their peers across the United States, are saturated with these images when they leave work. Forced to confront negative and even grossly inaccurate media representations of their work, prosecutors cannot help but reflect on the ongoing circulation of stories about crimes involving guns between media, the public, and the everyday realities of the justice assemblage.

"The realities of it are people think that we have unlimited funds," said Assistant District Attorney Shannon Lynch when I asked her how media representations impact her work as a prosecutor. Prosecutors' work is made much more difficult by the impact of television crime shows' inaccurate depictions of all-powerful prosecutors with unlimited resources. These include representations of prosecutors as able to mobilize technology that can, as Shannon colorfully put it, "get fingerprints off an eyeball," when such technology is either unaffordable or simply does not exist. Such media also drastically distort the time line from arrest to trial in most cases so that, as Shannon observes, prospective jurors often have seen movies or series where prosecutors are "trying a rape case where the victim still has a black eye," in contrast to the reality that cases often take years before they go to trial.

Prosecutor Corey Seale echoes Shannon's concerns about how media inaccuracies negatively impact their work by creating unrealistic expectations among prospective jurors. "The media," Corey explains, "create a really high burden, especially in the forensic evidence sense. People expect DNA on everything, and people expect fingerprints and people expect this high level of stuff that if it's there, great. And I'm not saying I wouldn't love to have that in all of my cases, but that's just not reality. And if we have all that, that case isn't going to trial, so the case you're going to get is the case where we don't have the fingerprint that matches this defendant on the murder weapon that says, 'He did this.'" Here Corey contrasts inaccurate media representations with the reality that a defendant with indisputable evidence of his guilt is likely to accept a plea offer rather than risk a potentially longer sentence following a jury trial.

It is no coincidence that prosecutors in our study faced the challenge of confronting inaccurate media representations at a time when most media outlets lack the resources or the gumption to do real investigative journalism. The public faces an enormous vacuum with respect to thoughtful and politically neutral investigative journalism on issues related to crime and justice. "I would say almost ninety percent is inaccurate," prosecutor Maegan Smalley said of the few local media accounts that feature trials, which journalists who report on them rarely attend in their entirety. As Maegan says of these journalists, "When they come to preliminary hearings, things they will report are not correct. And then I think that gets the public in a stir . . . like we're not doing our job."

Prosecutor Grace Prince shares Maegan's frustrations, noting that the average person believes that "if it's reported by somebody, it must be fact. Like in our trials, the media will come for ten minutes and then it's a full-blown news article. I'm like, 'You don't know, you weren't there, you got ten minutes and you're thinking out of context.' People take that as fact. That's just what people do now. There are no repercussions for the reporters that report these 'facts' that are just grossly inaccurate." Susan witnessed this tendency firsthand during her extensive trial observations, when journalists would arrive with cameras toward the end, film a few minutes of interviews, and rapidly leave the scene.

The result of this bleak media landscape is that most people receive their "education" about crime and justice from dramatized representations in movies or series, which forces prosecutors to engage with these inaccurate representations every time they interact with prospective jurors or with people who criticize the current state of justice. "I wish more people were interested in the truth," Corey says wistfully as she lists the questions that she wishes critics would ask prosecutors. "What are people in prison for? What are people getting denied parole for? What is their charge, not just their name and how long they've been in prison, what is the charge that they're in there for? I think people would be surprised with the actual answer. I think the answer would be very different from the skewed perspective that they've been given based on whatever popular opinion of the moment is."

For some prosecutors, inaccurate and politically motivated media representations of their work is a symptom of the much deeper problem facing a society in which many socially disconnected people rely on snippets of information rather than deep critical thinking about complex issues, and impassioned emotions supersede meaningful action. Research indicates the pervasiveness of these realities even among criminal justice students, who typically report significant perspective shifts when they have the opportunity to engage with real-world criminal justice settings. For example, students who engaged in a virtual tour of a juvenile correctional facility, which included audio recordings of incarcerated youths talking about their experiences, reported increased empathy and support for rehabilitative programs (Miner-Romanoff 2014). Active learning techniques, such as correctional institution tours, speakers with criminal justice experience, and narrative and film analysis, likewise challenged assumptions students brought to the classroom (Rockell 2009). Reflective journals of visits to correctional facilities have also been shown to be particularly effective in helping students deeply engage (Wesely 2021).

The interplay between popular culture and personal experience is perhaps even more pronounced among the general public, leading one prosecutor to attribute inaccurate media portrayals of the criminal justice system to "a cultural thing right now where personal accountability is at an all-time low." Prosecutor Ben McGough uses the example of the gun present policy of mandatory jail time for anyone arrested for a crime at which a gun was present as a real and meaningful effort "to do something about the runaway violent crimes committed with a gun that we have here. And if everybody, everywhere across the country would try to do something, instead of just giving speeches, we could affect some change." Ben echoes all the prosecutors in the office in expressing the sentiment that "we're not just throwing people away. The people that we lock up are doing the things we say they did, and they deserve the punishment that they get."

Prosecutor Grace Prince initially felt compelled to tell everyone in her social circle about how she fairly and impartially prosecutes cases, a feeling that was intensified during former police officer Derek Chauvin's prosecution and subsequent murder trial. "All that I was seeing on social media was that the system was flawed," Grace explains. "Everyone in the system was racist, and that included me." Grace contrasts this popular perception with the everyday realities of her work, noting, "When I look at a felony report, I don't see their race. . . . When you get the case report and the facts and they run it down, they're giving you the facts, they don't talk about their race. I don't know. I got to go search it. I got to see them in court. I don't look at that stuff. In the beginning I was superoffended, and I would make it a point to tell people about my job . . . [but now I realize] the best way that I can prove them wrong is to do my job and do it well, and to not stop doing my job."

These negative media representations of prosecutors create a toxic feedback loop whereby, as Corey explains, "What's put out there is the bad, and then that's what the public sees and that's what they come to expect." Corey describes her frustration when, during a relaxing evening at home with her husband, a Netflix series called *The Staircase* piqued her interest.

This interest quickly shifted to profound horror as Corey grew increasingly upset with the series' depiction of flagrant prosecutorial misconduct as status quo. "There has become a market for villainizing law enforcement and prosecution," she says. "A prosecutor doing a good job is not necessarily good TV. So that doesn't really make the news all the hard work that goes into it to get the right result is not that interesting. So, I think what you see are where people get it wrong, where law enforcement gets it wrong, where prosecutors get it wrong."

This toxic feedback loop has direct implications for what happens in the courtroom. Prosecutor Kymberly Porter describes a voir dire jury selection that exemplified media's powerful impact on prospective jurors. "There was an outspoken juror, incredibly outspoken. And each time she would speak, it would be these long monologues," Kymberly explains. "'Statistics say this. Statistics say that. This is generally how black women are treated,' and all of this. And so that was a bigger barrier. And then, on one of her last monologues, if you will, she mentioned that we should defund the police, and got a round of applause. And, so, I'm looking around at my venire, like, 'Oh, this isn't at all the jury I want. Oh, my gosh. How do I strike everyone?'" Kymberly experienced the repetition of language propagated by media—specifically, "defund the police"—noting that "I had never heard that phrase before the media started to say that . . . all I could do was to pay close attention to the people who seemed to agree the most and strike those people . . . you're stuck with what you have."

Chief Assistant District Attorney Paula Whitley, who previously worked as a public defender, says that she feels most community members are still supportive and respectful of prosecutors' everyday work, yet she does sometimes feel the seepage of media discourse into courtroom discussions. "I do hear it when jurors are answering questions and when they are questioned after a jury verdict is reached," she says. "I do hear that they don't always take a police officer's word as being the truth. And that's okay. I mean, they're humans just like everybody else, but it is an interesting phenomenon to me to see that kind of breakdown of trust which, in my experience in our community, is completely unfounded. I've worked on both sides of the criminal justice system. And I do not see a current problem within our law enforcement community of any intentional stereotyping or anything other than a true desire to get cases not settled but solved."

Corey actively attempts to combat negative and inaccurate perceptions of her work by informing prospective jurors if a case settles immediately before or right after voir dire, as well as informing jurors of case outcomes or asking the judge to do so. "I want people to get a clearer picture of how things work," she says. "A lot of stuff today from both sides can be skewed towards conspiracy theories. And I think that can be really dangerous too, because instead of just looking at facts and law and what have we proven, we're putting in this idea of there's this behind-the-scenes conspiracy, no matter what side, defense or prosecution, no matter what it creates this idea of like, 'Oh, well, could this have been the alien from Mars?'"

For Corey and her fellow prosecutors, the central message she would like to convey to the public is just how hard prosecutors work to administer justice in all cases. "When that means dismissing cases, that's what we're doing," she explains. "When that means advising law enforcement, 'You don't have enough to make an arrest,' that's what we're doing. Us doing our job and getting it right is not just we get the result we want, it's that we are trying to make the right call based on law and facts every single time, no matter which way that goes."

THE VIEW FROM THE DISTRICT ATTORNEY

Hays implemented the gun present policy as a District Attorney who is passionate about both the need to end crimes committed with guns and to uphold the rights of law-abiding gun owners in a region where guns are ubiquitous. "Responsible gun ownership absolutely entails knowledge of how to safely carry, store, and use guns," Hays explains, "and how much can you legislate that?" Mimicking the grip on a firearm, Hays moves his index finger slightly and says, "That quarter-inch movement can send out a bullet that's not coming back." Hays is aware of guns' deadly potential and used to correct other people on the shooting range, knowing that these corrections could save someone's life. Yet basic principles of responsible gun ownership—knowing your target and what's behind it, not pointing at anything you don't intend to shoot, keeping your finger off the trigger— are irrelevant in cases where guns are present at crime scenes.

As part of his gun present policy's emphasis on responsible gun owner- ship, Hays would like to see prohibited persons charges extended to all felons alongside sentence enhancements for those who commit crimes using, for example, rifles that shoot pistol rounds with bottleneck cartridges that drive bullets at higher velocity. Such weapons have additional power to propel bul- lets through a wall or a window, creating additional dangers to public safety when used to commit crimes. For Hays, 99.9% of all firearms are owned by law-abiding people whose rights are upheld through such approaches, which operate in tandem with diversion and employment opportunities at well above average hourly wages offered to all first-time nonviolent defendants.

"I can't raise other people's children," Hays explains when Susan asks how he would respond to those who might criticize gun present as a reactive policy. "I'm tasked with prosecuting criminal conduct." He situates the gun present policy within office-wide initiatives to protect public safety. "This is also a place where felons come for jobs," he says. "We want everyone to succeed. We are the progressives in fact. We honor our laws. First-time nonviolent defendants have diversion that lifts them up. No one is beyond redemption, and we work hand-in-hand with community to get people jobs. I care about criminals with guns. No gun buyback or law ever stopped someone who wanted to get a gun. We try to create disincentives for criminals to carry and misuse guns. From our prosecutorial perspective, people stealing guns get significant punishment to keep the community safe. There's a human element here of people who find power in guns, who see them as a means to an illegitimate end."

For Hays, the real solution to the problem of violent crimes committed with guns lies in stigmatizing the misuse of guns in community. The solution does not lie in restricting law-abiding gun owners' abilities to own firearms. This stance required making the underlying goals clear from the outset. "There was a concern amongst some that gun rights groups would be against it," Hays explains, "but I knew they were wrong because they're for responsible gun ownership. There will be people who want to take political shots and so create a political target, i.e., if I speed and I've got my turkey gun I'm going to go to jail. We've been very intentional about making it clear that's not the case. I encourage anyone who can do so legally to have a gun. If you can afford all the guns, do it! But if you have dope in the car with those guns, stand by because you'll be arrested. Those arguments of 'You're trying to take my guns away' are not self-supporting."

"In the courtroom we tell stories, have a theory of the case," Hays explains, "so it was important in getting the word out that we capture its intention. I created gun present stamps for the cover sheet of the felony report so defense attorneys knew their defendant was going to jail. I'd been a nineteen-year career defense attorney and I came to career prosecutors and said, 'Trust me, we're going to do it one hundred percent of the time and no defense attorney is going to ask, 'Does he have to go to jail?' I sent a letter to the chiefs, made a public service announcement, weekly arrest reports highlight cases in red with guns present. Law enforcement adopted it. How funny that a former defense lawyer did this! If anybody says, 'Oh, he just walked into this,' understand our battles have been myriad in the courthouse. I didn't walk into a well-functioning machine with lawyers who had the same shared idea about what is a desirable result. We're proud of the efforts of our office seeking to protect the public and protecting the rights of defendants."

"We're process oriented, not results oriented," Hays says, which means that defendants who use guns to commit crimes are not surprised when they have to serve jail time following their arrest. "You don't mess around with Tuscaloosa County," Hays explains, noting of these innovative approaches that "you have to do it consistently and without fail, consistently analyze all cases the same no matter your like or dislike of the other side or the defendant."

2. Institutional Structures and Practices

"Let us talk about desperation," Assistant District Attorney Ben McGough slowly intones in his honeyed South Alabama drawl as he rises from his wooden chair to face the jury. Outside, the air has the warm, burnt quality of late summer. Ben looks every bit the polished southern lawyer ready to make his closing arguments. He has been waiting patiently for his turn while listening to the defense attorney, whose job is to uphold his defendant's constitutional rights. Prior to speaking, Ben has been closely observing everything the defense attorney does during closing arguments, including his obliviousness to the jurors' obvious discomfort when he theatrically mimicked swinging a large weapon several times up and down between his legs while attempting to impress its awkwardness and, in the process, managing to only look extremely awkward himself. "Ladies and gentlemen," the defense attorney said to the jury before sitting down to end his closing argument, "my client was a desperate man that day."

Now the defense attorney is seated, periodically glancing toward the prosecutors who are eagerly watching Ben from the benches that line the courtroom on the judge's right. "Let us talk about desperation," Ben repeats, immediately getting the jurors' attention with his down-home cadence and calm demeanor that makes them feel as if he might be casually conversing with them on the front porch rather than in the courtroom at a second-degree assault trial. Momentarily shifting his gaze from the jury to point a long arm, index finger extended, toward the defendant and his attorney, Ben positions himself just feet from the jury box. "He's desperate for you to believe he's not guilty. A man in his position has two choices: to admit that he's guilty or get a defense attorney to convince you to believe that he's not guilty."

Ben pauses momentarily and moves a few feet to engage with the jurors on the other side of the box, making eye contact. "Let us talk about a defense attorney's job," he continues, again raising his right arm to point in the direction of the defendant and his attorney. "His job is to stand between you and what this guilty man did. Throw some dirt on top of it. Throw some leaves on. Set it afire to make some smoke. Your job is to see past that smoke to that guilty man sitting right here today." Emotional static in the courtroom feels tuned just off frequency, making Ben the sole focus of everyone's attention as he continues talking to the jury as if he has known them for years. His analogies are intentionally vivid, and all present in the courtroom are picturing the scene Ben is expertly painting for us.

For Ben, the defense attorney's "smoke" entails contextualizing the defendant's actions in a way that will garner the jury's sympathy for the defendant. Hence the defense attorney's argument, in this case, that the defendant was "a desperate man" when he viciously assaulted the unarmed victim. Ben's expert redirect to describe the defense attorney's case as desperate emphasized the hollowness of that argument. While some defense attorneys might take offense at Ben's analogy, it is a highly effective technique to engage the jury.

In this case, the court has already heard from a witness Ben located by questioning witnesses listed in the felony report shared with the defense attorney during discovery. Ben has already proved in court that the witness's testimony is false by calling another witness to testify to that fact. To remind the jury of the witness's false statement, Ben chooses to appeal to Alabama cultural values that prioritize family above all other things by telling a story about his own family to illustrate the fallibility of memory. "My parents were high school sweethearts," Ben continues, "and they met when my mama was riding her horse in a pair of shorts. My daddy says they were green shorts, and my mama says they was yellow, and to this day they cannot agree on the color, only that my daddy thought they were too short for a young girl and that she had nice legs." Most of the jurors are smiling at Ben now. "See," Ben says, "that's the thing with memory." After the judge reiterates instructions to the jury and adjourns, members of the jury deliberate for twenty minutes before returning with a guilty verdict.

Ben's polished performance demonstrates the theater of trial, where prosecutors and defense attorneys both engage in storytelling to convince jurors of their arguments. Language is everything at trial. As Katie Kitamura notes in her brilliant novel *Intimacies*, about the International Criminal Court in The Hague,

> Linguistic accuracy was not enough. Interpretation was a matter of great subtlety, a word with many contexts. For example, it is often said that an actor interprets a role, or a musician a piece of music. There was

a certain level of tension that was intrinsic to the Court and its activities, a contradiction between the intimate nature of pain, and the public arena in which it had to be exhibited. A trial was a complex calculus of performance in which we were all involved . . . our daily activity hinged on the repeated description—description, elaboration, and delineation—of matters that were, outside, generally subject to euphemism and elision (Kitamura 2021, 15).

As Kitamura notes, it is never enough for participants at trial to state the facts of the case. They must engage in thoughtful, evocative storytelling in order to bring the case to life for the jury as part of an iterative performance that includes, and affects, everyone present. Prosecutors take the lead in storytelling on behalf of the state. An extraordinary storyteller like Ben will make each and every juror feel what the victim felt at the time of the crime. In a shooting case, he will want the jurors to feel the fear the victim experienced when they first realized the defendant shot them and their death was imminent, the immense suffering that preceded their death as their life force spilled out onto the sidewalk, their lungs slowly collapsing under their own weight as the victim gasped for air. He will also want the jurors to grasp the callous disregard the defendant showed for the victim, all accompanied by enormous projections of entry and exit wounds, bodies torn apart by bullet wounds.

Repetition can be a very effective strategy for accomplishing this goal because it can leave powerful emotional messages unsaid, without the prosecutor forcing his or her point too strenuously upon the jury. Ben's repetition of the phrase "let us talk about desperation" redirected the defense attorney's claim of self-defense by emphasizing its hollowness. In a domestic violence murder trial Susan observed, Grace Prince took a similar strategy in repeating the defendant's chilling statement—"I'm gonna get her"— before he murdered one victim and attempted to murder a second. "I'm gonna get her," Grace forcefully recited during both her opening and closing arguments, clearly enunciating each word as her eyes scanned the jury box to gauge their reactions. The reality of the defendant's deliberate, calculated actions congealed in the jurors' minds as Grace and Shadrian alternately recounted for the jury the numerous steps—including traveling from his residence, stopping at multiple red lights, getting a child to let him into the residence where he no longer had a key, and then walking up a flight of stairs—the defendant took before he entered the bedroom and fired his weapon. Listening to the cold deliberation of the statement "I'm gonna get her" again and again, jurors quickly realized the absolute wrongness of the defense attorney's claim that the defendant committed a crime of passion.

Yet these theatrical, performative elements of trial that so captivate jurors are the product of prosecutors' exhaustive preparations for trial. The jury is rapt as they watch and listen to expert storytellers like Ben because he has spent countless hours preparing to hold their attention. Ben's mind is completely occupied with every possible eventuality as he prepares for trial. "I tell folks all the time, I prep a case [for trial] for at least a week, I like two weeks," Ben explains. "By the time you get there [to the courtroom], the hard part's over." As Ben prepares for trial, he is first and foremost considering the law and the facts of the case, but also how he will go about the storytelling that will convince the jury of his theory of the case.

"Get a hook," Ben says, his voice deepening for emphasis on the importance of this word to his point as he lingers over its vowels. "Revenge, jealousy, to get their [jurors'] minds where you want them to go, and you better be able to prove it." Ben knows that this storytelling starts during voir dire and will continue through closing arguments. "What we say in opening isn't evidence, but it is a promise," he says, repeating, "you better be able to prove it." Ben loves voir dire because it is the part of the trial where he gets to have the most meaningful direct interaction with the jury. When Ben is in trial preparation mode, nothing else matters to him.

"I only care about fourteen people in the world when I'm in trial mode: my twelve jurors and two alternates," he says. Ben is not concerned with anyone else during these preparations because he knows his case is well-prepared, and so his single-minded goal is to convince the jury of his argument based on the facts of the case and their intersection with the law. "When I'm in bed at night, at the gym, at home, I'm thinking about them," Ben says of the jury. These thoughts can become obsessive if a prosecutor cannot set clear mental boundaries around the limits of their imaginations about jurors' thought processes.

In Ben's view, much of the case has already been resolved by the time he first walks into the courtroom, leaving the jury as his primary focus. Before the trial even begins, Ben already knows whether his evidence is admissible and he has done everything he can to prepare his witnesses to withstand scrutiny in court. Details the witness might share beyond the facts of the case are immaterial at this point, he explains. "She saw the light, the car was blue," he says of a witness in a recent trial. "I don't care what else she says as long as she doesn't waver."

Ben's single-minded focus on jurors renders other participants' presence of little relevance to him. He stares off into the distance if a defendant tries to make eye contact and does the challenging internal work necessary to avoid taking on the emotions of the victim's family, because doing so would mean personalizing the case. A prosecutor needs distance from victims and their families to do their work effectively. As he sits in the courtroom, he is listening to the defense attorney and what he or she is saying, but his primary focus as he listens is on how he might redirect the defense attorney's line of questioning and, in so doing, his or her theory of the case to sway the jury in the state's favor.

"Most people," Ben explains, "they don't know the most important skill in a trial is redirect. I ask my witness questions for five, ten minutes, and the defense attorney questions my witness for twenty and the most important skill I have is to decide if redirect is necessary and then, in as few words as possible, help the jury understand why it's wrong." To accomplish this goal, Ben closely observes how the jury is reacting from voir dire forward, because while their job is to apply the law to the facts of the case, jurors are also making decisions through the lens of their own experiences and beliefs about the world, which means they are also watching both the prosecutor and defense attorney closely through this lens.

Courtroom scenes like this one vividly illustrate the relationships and roles, which we discuss at length in chapter 3, and the moral and emotional worlds, the subject of chapter 4, that animate the justice assemblage's institutional structures and practices. The ceremonial aspects of court are central material aspects of the institutional structures and practices that render the justice assemblage real in place, space, and time. For example, prosecutors, victims, and victims' families are seated to the right of both the judge and jurors, with defendants and their families seated to the judge's and jurors' left, separated by their relationship to the justice assemblage just as the families of the marriage partners are at a wedding. The practice of all present rising to stand when the judge and jurors enter and exit the courtroom and the resemblance of the courtroom's layout to an austere church likewise visually communicate the courtroom as the justice assemblage's ceremonial space.

The courtroom's physical space itself is deliberately designed to promote solemnity and discourage disruption. Its solemn atmosphere forces mindfulness of bodies and actions among all present. Poor acoustics in its sharp-cornered wooden spaces means that a dropped pen in the back row can magnetize everyone's unwanted gaze, and any talk must be in whispers. Rigid benches force good posture in all but the most deliberate slouchers. Minimalist institutional decor defines the room: a wall clock with ticking hands, gleaming wood panels lining the walls, a metal seal featuring an outline of Alabama's borders, neat and rectangular until they hit the southwestern coastal chasm of Mobile Bay nestled between Mississippi and Florida.

The courtroom rigidly separates individuals into neat boxes according to their role within its broader rectangle. The judge's bench is centrally located at the uppermost center of the rectangle, separated from the rest of the courtroom by the elevated bench itself as well as its solid wood, which extends all the way to the floor to obscure all but the judge's upper body. The witness stand is immediately to the judge's left, where the witness, like the judge, is the visual focal point for everyone in the courtroom, with the court reporter's workstation located immediately below and near tables for prosecutors and defense attorneys. A barrier with a gate for entry separates the attorney tables from the spectator gallery's two rows of long benches separated by an aisle. Jurors must also open a gate to enter the jury box, where they sit in chairs riveted to the floor. The bailiff sits outside the jury box to assist with courtroom actors' entry and exit. This spatial choreography, and the interactions that take place within it, help render the justice assemblage real.

SITUATING PROSECUTORS WITHIN THE JUSTICE ASSEMBLAGE

Prosecutors occupy a unique position at the beating heart of the justice assemblage as fiduciaries tasked with upholding the democratic administration of justice by prioritizing criminal justice considerations over other public policy interests (Green and Roiphe 2020a). These criminal justice considerations rely first and foremost on the notion that the prosecutor's client is the state. As Hays explained to Susan, "A defense attorney's job is to seek the win, but the prosecutor's job is to seek justice. We are hired guns for no one."

This chapter illuminates the complexity of prosecutors' unique position by arguing that the administration of justice takes place within physical, legal, and administrative structures that individual prosecutors navigate through their interactions with others as they go about the everyday work of the law in practice. Grounded in scholarly work from institutional logics scholars, as well as legal and carceral geographies, analysis presented here focuses on the routinized nature of these institutional structures and practices while carefully attending to the ways that individual prosecutors navigate them.

As legal scholars Sepulveda and Wilenmann (2022) note, prosecutors' modalities of work—their ways and means of doing justice—derive from immediate practical considerations as well as formal and informal influences. These practical considerations include the resources, such as (perhaps especially) time, that can be invested in a case, the type and amount of information used to interpret the case, and working relationships between individuals involved in the case. In addition to these practical considerations, prosecutors' modalities of work also derive from both formal influences, most obviously criminal law and legal culture, and informal influences, such as office culture and organizational arrangements (Sepulveda and Wilenmann 2022).

Relationships to other actors within the justice assemblage are critical to prosecutors' modalities of work, rendering their role within the justice assemblage essentially collaborative and relational. At a very basic relational level, workshopping trial narratives with colleagues prior to sharing them with prospective jurors during voir dire is a core aspect of how prosecutors prepare for trial by crafting and refining the story that surrounds their theory of a particular case (Offit 2021). At a more abstract level, prosecutors' political legitimacy derives from their relationship to the community as its protectors (Degenshein 2022). These relationships emerge within, but also constitute the institutional structures and practices that shape, the justice assemblage.

Organizational Sensemaking

The justice assemblage is fundamentally comprised of relationships, yet it also shapes those relationships through institutional structures and practices enacted daily by individual prosecutors and other actors in the justice assemblage. To understand how the justice assemblage takes shape through these institutional structures and practices, we engage with scholarly work on organizational sensemaking. This body of literature attends to the ways in which organizations rely on the formation and maintenance of distinct cultural practices to coordinate the diverse interests and working styles of individuals within the organization. Taken together, these organizational cultural practices form a unique institutional logic, a "set of material practices and symbolic systems including assumptions, values, and beliefs by which individuals and organizations provide meaning to their daily activity, organize time and space, and reproduce their lives and experiences" (Thornton, Ocasio, and Lounsbury 2012).

Researchers who study organizational behavior as it pertains to cultural understandings of justice and fairness offer insights into how individuals engage with institutional logics in the course of their everyday work. Such scholars have underscored distinctions between organizational conceptions of justice, defined as adherence to rules of conduct and fairness, and individual moral assessments of this conduct (Goldman and Cropanzano 2015), emphasizing the inherent and ceaseless dialogue between individuals and the organizations of which they are a part. Organizational behavior scholars also indicate the relational nature of moral character for individuals in the workplace. Cohen and Morse (2014) argue that moral character comprises the individual motivation to consider the impact of one's actions on others, the ability to self-regulate one's behavior, and envisioning oneself as a moral person.

Individuals certainly develop their understandings of morality and fairness based on their own life experiences, yet organizational culture directly impacts individual experiences of, and beliefs about, the workplace. This impact is particularly significant in criminal justice workplaces, which require extensive collaboration between individuals within a hierarchical social structure with a finite set of options for resolving cases. For instance, deputies who regard their supervisors as organizationally fair report feeling more motivated and safe, and they experience a greater sense of public support than their peers who believe their supervisors are unfair (Nix and Wolfe 2016). Such correlations between perceptions of fairness and justice and workplace experiences, in turn, have direct implications for public safety, as officers who feel unmotivated, unsafe, and unsupported are far less likely to be able to perform their jobs effectively than their peers who feel the opposite.

Organizational sensemaking involves "the practical activities of real people engaged in concrete situations of social action" (Boden 1994, 10). Organizational behavior researchers find that organizational sensemaking occurs through discourse that translates events and circumstances into a comprehensible narrative, acts of political legitimation that render organizational beliefs and values real through official documentation, operational filters through which individuals interpret their experiences within the organization, and fostering shared identities to facilitate collective action (Brown, Colville, and Pye 2015). Over time, the accumulation of shared organizational experiences leads to the creation of schemas through which individuals make sense of new events, a process that occurs both consciously, through concrete decision-making, and unconsciously, via the interpretation of events through the lens of experience (Steinbauer, Rhew, and Chen 2015).

Anthropologist Mary Douglas famously observed that constructing institutions entails "squeezing each other's ideas into a common shape in order to prove their legitimacy by sheer numbers" (Douglas 1986). Organizational sensemaking consists of processes geared toward the production of specific outcomes, yet the sensemaking process is also dynamic because ambiguous events set its interpretive gears into motion (Sandberg and Tsoukas 2015). Prosecutors routinely confront ambiguous events as they study the felony report, speak with police investigators, decide on appropriate criminal charges to file, and develop the theory they will use to prosecute the case. They rely heavily on institutional structures and practices, as well as their and their colleagues' knowledge and experiences, as they translate these ambiguous events into actions legible to the justice assemblage.

Sensemaking also occurs in courts, in criminal investigations, and in the individual rationalization processes violent offenders use to explain their actions to themselves and others. Understanding courts and criminal justice agencies by using an inhabited institutions perspective allows us to regard institutions as animated by agentic individual actors whose interactions collaboratively produce case outcomes (Ulmer 2019). The inhabited institutions perspective rejects the concept of a monolithic Fordist criminal justice system that uniformly processes indictments into adjudication by reminding us that court participants are ultimately responsible for interpreting criminal law and policy. For example, a study of municipal court interactions between judges, bailiffs, and defendants explored how each type of courtroom actor initiated positive, negative, and negative-complimentary (e.g., "I know you can do better") emotion cycles designed to influence case outcomes (Scarduzio and Tracy 2015). Studies of courtroom workgroups—which include all the individuals involved in the criminal trial process—likewise indicate how relationships between the various workgroup members impact case outcomes (Metcalfe 2016; Portillo et al. 2013; Young 2013).

Police investigations are also highly social processes that engage in sensemaking as officers interact with each other, suspects, witnesses, victims, prosecutors, and, if testifying in court, jurors and judges (Hällgren, Lindberg, and Rantatalo 2021). Homicide investigations likewise employ social processes as police officers work together to determine, eliminate, or charge suspects through organizational sensemaking practices that include criminal law, scientific expertise, and their collective professional experience (Brookman et al. 2020b). Crime scene investigators use sensemaking to mitigate the potentially damaging psychological effects of routinely witnessing death and suffering, such as managing their thoughts, using visualization, sharing emotions and responsibilities, and knowing their limits in potentially traumatizing work situations (Sollie, Kop, and Euwema 2017). Violent offenders likewise engage in sensemaking through the construction of explanatory narratives that attribute their violent criminal behavior to its context and time (Hochstetler, Copes, and Cherbonneau 2017). In all these instances, sensemaking is part of a momentous group effort to render violence intelligible.

Geographies of Law, Violence, and the Carceral

The justice assemblage is an organizational effort at sensemaking that materializes in institutional structures and practices that take shape in the form of administrative documents and courtroom proceedings. To understand how the justice assemblage makes violence legible through its institutional structures and practices, we engage with geographers' theoretical conceptualizations of the emplaced nature of law, violence, and the carceral. This body of work emphasizes the materiality of the justice assemblage through analysis of the physical sites that sustain the relationships comprising the justice assemblage.

Legal geography examines how individuals, place, and the law co-constitute one another by drawing attention to the central role of place within the law in practice (Bennett and Layard 2015). Geographer David Delaney uses the term *nomosphere*—from *nomos*, the ancient Greek word for law—to describe "the spatio-legal expression and the socio-material realization of ideologies, values, pervasive power orders and social projects" (Delaney 2010). Legal geographers have explored, for instance, how courtroom architecture, courtroom arrangements, and the orchestration of physical actions during trial convey silent messages about the law in practice through its material manifestation (Jeffrey 2019). Legal geographers have also examined the spatial dynamics of jurisdiction and discretion by analyzing "where, when, and to whom various institutions are permitted to speak the law" (Kahn 2017).

Violent geographies examine the spatial dynamics of violent victimization, with a focus on how particular physical locations become associated with violence in the popular imagination. By considering place as a relational assemblage, scholars of violent geography emphasize how violence is always experienced and mediated through broader cultural understandings of material spaces rather than isolated to highly localized and embodied experiences within those material spaces (Springer 2011). In this line of thinking, violence is a geography of being, an inherent aspect of the human social, political, and ontological condition that "is embedded in the flesh and bones of our world" (Laurie and Shaw 2018). The politics of fear, threat, and risk also surround the production of space, prompting researchers interested in violent geographies to explore the role that fear of violence has in planning and anti-violence measures (Abu-Orf 2013).

Carceral geographers examine how spaces of confinement materialize and intersect with broader socio-legal structures. For example, researchers have explored how time and space manifest in prison settings where incarcerated people's perceived control over time, and the life-course more generally, sharply differs from the experiences of people in the free world (Moran 2012). Carceral geographers have also explored how efforts to reduce the numbers of people who are incarcerated by promoting community-based endeavors for juveniles may serve only to create prison-like conditions within the community for juvenile defendants (Brown 2014).

In what follows, we build on these bodies of literature to explore how three aspects of institutional structures and practices render the justice assemblage real. First, we detail the orchestration of institutional logics by describing how cases move procedurally through the justice assemblage. Second, we examine the rituals of documentation that render gun cases legible to the justice assemblage. Third, we analyze the temporal dynamics of case disposition by exploring how prosecutors navigate the nonstop march of time as cases proceed through the justice assemblage. We conclude with a vignette that provides a window into the philosophical reflections about the nature of justice that accompany many prosecutors' thoughts as they go about their everyday lives.

THE ORCHESTRATION OF INSTITUTIONAL LOGICS

Cases proceed through the justice assemblage from criminal charge to adjudication in a chronological manner shaped by legal administrative procedures, case load, and court dockets. Following the steps prosecutors take in these cases helps illuminate the orchestration of institutional logics that constitutes the justice assemblage's institutional structures and practices. Assistant District Attorney Kymberly Porter considers three preliminary questions when she first evaluates a felony report after a paralegal delivers it to her from a police investigator. Did a crime occur? If so, how bad was it? What proof does she have? As she considers these questions, she begins to engage with a set of administrative-procedural steps.

Kymberly is well aware that charges, accusations, or warrants sworn out do not necessarily mean that a crime actually occurred, especially in misdemeanor cases. "Any Joe Blow off the street can come up to the courthouse and say such-and-such happened and sign a warrant," she explains, "and now someone has a warrant out for their arrest." Kymberly pays close attention to whether the facts alleged match with the crime that has been charged. Once she determines her belief that a crime occurred, her attention shifts to the degree of the criminal activity in terms of its severity. "You can have the exact same charge," she says, "but some facts are just much worse than others."

The facts of the case can indeed vary wildly among defendants with the same charge. First-degree robbery, for example, generally means that the defendant is accused of robbing a victim with a gun or other deadly weapon. A first-degree robbery case might involve accusations that a defendant showed a gas station clerk the gun tucked into his waistband and then demanded that the clerk give him all the money from the cash register. Yet a first-degree robbery case could also involve a defendant accused of dragging a victim from their car, slamming the victim's body to the ground, and pointing a gun in the victim's face while threatening to pull the trigger if the victim does not hand over their valuables. Both are examples of first-degree robbery, but the facts of the case in the second example demonstrate far greater harm to the victim than in the first instance.

Next, Kymberly considers the proof that she has that the defendant committed the crime. "There are plenty of instances where prosecutors know what happened, the victim knows what happened," she explains, "but there isn't much proof of what happened." After Kymberly determines the severity of the crime based on the facts of the case and the proof she has that a crime actually occurred, she examines the defendant's criminal history. Does the defendant have a long record of committing similar types of crimes? Or did the defendant make a terrible decision and otherwise live their life according to the law? Kymberly's colleague Grace Prince takes a similar approach to her initial case review of the indictment. Once she determines that the charge is correct, Grace notes, "I make sure that the facts fit the law; where they intersect is the proper charge," and reviews the defendant's criminal history and age.

Office practice sharply contrasts with pervasive media and cultural representations of "plea bargaining" that depict prosecutors' plea offers to defendants as a means to expedite huge numbers of criminal cases through sentencing. This incorrect understanding regards plea offers as a negotiation, rather than a fair and systematic process reliant on careful, meticulous analysis of facts and law. For example, a fair and systematic analysis of facts and law will not allow a defendant who commits an act consistent with a serious robbery charge to plead to a lesser offense in order to increase the likelihood the defendant will accept the plea offer on that lesser charge. Instead, a fair and systematic analysis ensures that prosecutors prioritize the law and the facts of the case and pursue conviction of the defendant on the appropriate charge to the best of their abilities.

A plea offer is not a negotiation in an office that demands propriety and integrity of all prosecutors. For example, a prosecutor handling the case of a habitually violent defendant whom most reasonable people would regard as a serious danger to public safety cannot manufacture facts to justify a lengthier prison sentence. A weak case in which facts and law do not come together against this habitually violent defendant remains a weak case irrespective of the defendant's criminal history.

Deciding how the facts fit the law is a challenging task at best, as it involves a conceptual abacus of sentencing guidelines, criminal history, and offense type along with facts, circumstances, past histories, and, of course, interpreting and applying the law within the justice assemblage's institutional structures and practices. We use the term *abacus* to evoke the ancient counting device that slid beads mounted on a metal frame up and down to calculate amounts. Listening to prosecutors talk about how they determine appropriate offers using a combination of sentencing guidelines, prior offenses, and other factors often felt much like observing someone using an abacus, the beads shifting up and down the metal frame to determine totals. For example, a defendant with several felony property- or drug-related priors who has no history of violence or resisting arrest, for example, would fall near the middle of the recommended sentencing range. A defendant with numerous robbery and assault priors involving guns, conversely, will likely receive a plea offer on the higher end of the recommended range, especially if there are additional serious charges such as eluding, resisting arrest, or leaving the scene of an accident with injury.

Circumstances—both the defendant's individual circumstances and the circumstances that surrounded the defendant's commission of the crime— are important for prosecutors to consider as they develop a plea offer, but facts and law are the first point of intersection in determining the correct charge, followed by an analysis of the threat posed to public safety as long as the defendant remains in community. Public safety is also a motivator for prosecutors as they formulate plea offers, but this consideration is secondary to facts and law. While prosecutors are not social workers, they do consider the circumstances of the case. Did the defendant stick a gun in the victim's face? Did he pull the victim's hair? Answers to these questions can help determine if there were aggravating factors that warrant consideration in the case. Yet a prosecutor may also review a felony report of a case that law enforcement initially charged as attempted murder, only to determine that the facts and law intersect at first-degree assault. The same can be true in cases of trafficking versus possession, with the distinction determined by the amount of controlled substances in the defendant's possession. Likewise, the distinction between first-degree assault and attempted murder is intention. Prosecutors ask themselves a series of questions as they make these determinations. What do they think the facts suggest? And of the evidence, what of it are they able to admit at trial, because if witnesses have changed their stories, prosecutors must reconsider what, if anything, they are able to prove now.

Law is a rule of conduct enforced by penalty, and prosecutors carefully evaluate the elements of a crime to determine what the facts of a case must satisfy to prosecute the case. Statute defines the elements of a crime so that, for example, murder is statutorily defined as "with the intent to cause the death of another person, he or she causes the death of that person or of another person." A prosecutor's task is to break apart the different elements of the crime that he or she needs to prove in such a case. For second-degree stalking, for example, the elements of the crime include the facts that victim told the perpetrator to stop, defendant harmed the victim, defendant intentionally acted, defendant repeatedly acted, or the defendant initiated contact.

Prosecutors utilize this conceptual abacus to render the defendant's actions legible to the justice assemblage. The inherently shifting nature of this conceptual abacus is why Chief Assistant District Attorney Paula Whitley never initially approaches a case from the premise that it will settle. Instead, she asks herself many of the same questions as her colleagues Kymberly and Grace do. What can we prove? What are the elements? What is the proof? What does the law say every single time? Like her colleagues, Paula's motivation is community safety and so in each case with a gun present she wants to understand how the defendant allegedly used the gun in committing the crime. "Was someone hurt or threatened to be hurt?" Paula asks of each crime with a gun present. "Because that's the most frightening thing that people can face." Once Paula's case develops to the point that it appears it will settle, she shifts her focus to ask, "What is a reasonable settlement that will accomplish our goals of punishment, community safety, and moving on to the next case?" These questions are inherent to the conceptual abacus that shapes prosecutors' everyday decision-making.

Prosecutors must understand the gun's role in the crime itself to accomplish their goals, and as we discussed at length in chapter 1, guns have tremendously versatile material and symbolic roles at crime scenes. "If the gun's an element of the crime, we're going to offer you at least a year in prison," prosecutor Shadrian Gayles explains of cases involving defendants with previous felony convictions who are carrying a gun when arrested on new charges, "because of the societal implications of you having that weapon. You're not doing anything legitimate with a stolen gun. You're not going to the local Walmart to buy a pistol to go murder someone in a club fight." Most guns used to commit violent crimes are illegally obtained through robberies and burglaries and/or used by people with felony convictions legally prohibited to own a firearm, which, following Shadrian's point, emphasizes the likelihood that the person obtaining a firearm illegally has the intention to also use the firearm to commit a crime.

In cases involving defendants with lengthy criminal histories, particularly when those histories involve violence, prosecutors making plea offers after using facts and law to determine the correct criminal charge are likely to be more concerned with a defendant's previous criminal history than with the intricacies of the crime with which they are currently charged. "In order for you to be willing to settle this already," Shadrian says of a hypothetical defense attorney reviewing a prosecutor's plea offer for a defendant, "your guy is likely already toast in some capacity. So, we likely already have either some more serious charges in another county or you have so much stuff stacked up here that it's like, 'Yeah, I know he's going off to prison for a while, just make the offer, we're going to take it.'"

Each prosecutor's extremely large workload of five hundred-plus felony cases necessitates prioritizing the preparation of plea offers or trial preparation by call docket, as determined by the judge presiding in the prosecutor's assigned courtroom. "Because we have such a large number of cases, I'm primarily docket-driven," Corey explains regarding how her judge's court schedule (dockets) determines the scope of her priorities. Multiple dockets exist along a regular schedule, with Mondays dedicated to pretrial hearings, Tuesdays for youthful defendant cases in which the judge decides whether to grant a defendant youthful defendant status that yields multiple benefits to a defendant—including sealing the defendant's criminal record and setting the max sentence at three years for any crime—and Wednesdays for call dockets in which parties report on the status of cases and assist with scheduling.

All felony prosecutors have a docket week every month and then a week to prepare for trial, although motion hearings, pleas, and other court appearances significantly impact their ability to prepare for trial week. Trials occur eleven months of the year, meaning that this cycle is nearly nonstop for prosecutors throughout the year, with each case settling or trial concluding followed in rapid succession by preparation for another trial or court appearance. Corey is accordingly "working from, 'Hey, I have this going on next week,' so here are all the cases on my docket. Let me look at all of those and make sure discovery's been sent out and offers have been sent out. And then we're in a good place where we can make a decision if the case is going to trial or if it's going to settle." Prioritizing a multifaceted set of simultaneous tasks to handle numerous cases is made both easier and more challenging by the docket.

Per Alabama law, prosecutors have fourteen days to provide discovery following a motion filed in court by the defense attorney. The Tuscaloosa County District Attorney's Office is unique in separating the discovery process from the court process because the Office has maximized efficiency by creating a completely separate system from the dockets for providing discovery. The Office sends discovery before a defense attorney files a motion, expediting the review for diversion in the Second Chance program for defendants accused of nonviolent crimes. The Office is unique in its highly efficient discovery process, in that while it may take five months for a case to get on the docket, discovery goes to the defense attorney as soon as it is ready, which is typically within two weeks of its preparation by law enforcement.

Grand jury and paralegals both rely on receipt of this felony report, and grand jury occurs within two to four weeks of arrest. Discovery generally happens at same time a case is being heard by the grand jury although these are two completely separate processes that both require the felony report to proceed. Once a grand jury has determined sufficient grounds exist for the charge, a prosecutor prepares a plea offer, at which point the defendant and his or her attorney can either decide to accept the offer and move to a sentencing hearing or reject the offer and go to trial. This schedule is highly efficient but also extremely challenging because it means that prosecutor has little control over the order in which she or he handles the cases, a reality in sharp contrast with the widespread misperception of prosecutors as all-powerful. The order in which cases appear on the docket is almost exclusively determined by the judge.

Prosecutors rely jointly on their review of state statutes and, particularly for nonviolent crimes, the Alabama Sentencing Standards developed by the Alabama Sentencing Commission (Alabama Sentencing Commission 2023) in formulating plea offers. "If it's a low-level drug case, and there's not a lot of criminal history," Corey explains, "then I, off the top, know that I'm going with the lowest I can go, which is a thirteen-month suspended sentence and twenty-four months of probation." Her offers will be similar in lower-level property crime and drug cases with defendants who do not have lengthy criminal histories. She examines each defendant's priors carefully, including more serious misdemeanor priors such as resisting arrest, attempting to elude, and possession of a pistol without a permit. For offenses that fall under state sentencing guidelines, her plea offers must be limited to the recommended range, so Corey utilizes the conceptual abacus of the sentencing guidelines, criminal history, and offense type to make her decision.

Prosecutor John Halcomb enjoys reading statutes to determine what the law's conceptual abacus will allow in prosecuting cases involving defendants with long histories of criminal charges in gun and drug cases. For example, charged independently, possession of an altered firearm is a Class C felony with no prison time, yet when combined with drug charges, a separate non-guideline statute stipulates that a sawed-off shotgun or a handgun with a scratched-off serial number becomes a B nonguidelines felony that could result in a two-to-twenty-year prison sentence. John now includes this language in his indictments because, as he says, "If you utilize that statute in the combination of the two, you've got a controlling B, which kicks out any guidelines and this person ... we're getting them out [of society] before they kill somebody because those folks, they're not safe people."

Cases that are subject to the sentencing guidelines significantly increase a defendant's likelihood of accepting a plea offer given their relative laxness of consequence, both in sentence duration and whether or not incarceration is possible upon a conviction in comparison with the historical statutory ranges of punishment. As one prosecutor explains of those cases, "I'm usually pretty confident we're most likely not going to try this case unless someone tells me, 'Hey, you have this suppression issue' or there's some kind of evidence or search issue." Violent crimes present a murkier scenario that leaves this prosecutor considering numerous questions: "When we go to trial, how's this going to work, and what do we have and what do we not have? And how's this going to play to a jury? And what's my victim like? And what are my law enforcement officers like?"

Yet, as part of the conceptual abacus prosecutors use in making plea offers, as prosecutor Thomas Marshall observes, the sentencing guidelines still allow for the exercise of discretion in terms of whether prosecutors recommend defendants serve a prison sentence. Thomas explains that a defendant "might be a prison recommendation" according to the guidelines, "but if the reason they're an 'in' [prison recommendation] is because of ten worthless check convictions from twenty years ago, I'm going to call the investigator." Thomas will ask the investigator who compiled the felony report, and hence has a deeper knowledge about the defendant, a series of questions to determine the appropriate offer. Is the defendant a person whom police frequently encounter in criminal investigations? Do police suspect that the defendant is involved in criminal cases, but they lack sufficient evidence to file charges? Is the defendant someone with a criminal history who lived a law-abiding life for a while and then slipped up?

Facts and law accordingly come together in multiple complex ways as prosecutors decide on the appropriate charge. "I'm going to follow the guidelines," Thomas says adamantly, "but where I have discretion, as much as I can, I use it because we are all people at the end of the day." Corey likewise exercises discretion as part of the conceptual abacus of formulating plea offers. "For a violent Class A felony where a gun was used the [statutory] minimum is twenty years in prison," she explains, noting that judges can still opt to sentence under the voluntary sentencing guidelines to less time. "The law has created a good, or as close to good as it can get, system for limiting your options," she says. If Corey is uncertain about how the other defendants were treated, she also searches Filemaker, the office's internal case management system, to review settlement offers in similar cases and then discusses how the prosecutor responsible for the case handled it.

The gun itself, of course, likewise impacts both the type of criminal charges and the plea offer the defendant receives. Prosecutor Maegan Smalley asks the police investigator if the defendant was carrying a stolen gun, if they carried additional magazines—"because I think that's alarming, if you have a loaded gun and three magazines"—if the defendant had a valid permit, or if they bought the gun on the street. "Guns seem to be very mobile and get passed around a lot," observes Chief Assistant District Attorney Paula Whitley, a fact that prompts her, like her colleagues, to ask investigators if they recovered the gun used at the crime scene and, if so, whether it has a serial number that links it to other crimes. Prosecutor Beth Crutchfield, likewise, asks officers involved about the type and number of guns, and ensures that they have sent all relevant evidence, including shell casings, for forensic examination.

The immense work of trial preparation begins to loom large in prosecutors' minds when it becomes apparent that a case may not settle via plea agreement. Prosecutor Ashley Ross begins envisioning how jurors will react to the case and crafts her approach in response. She first considers the number of times she will say the words "the gun" in her opening arguments, and asks herself, "How is somebody going to react to a gun being there, especially in the South where gun presence and gun ownership is very common?" She also asks herself, "Are you going to have people that see it as a big deal, that this was a felony being committed with a gun or somebody that's like, 'Okay, well, it's whatever.' So, to me, it's how can I build this case? How strong can I build this case? What am I looking for to go forward? What are elements of this case that are going to make it stick out to jurors?"

Ashley begins to think about her witnesses as trial approaches, and these may include individuals who saw the gun or who heard gunshots. Even if the witness can only testify to hearing gunshots from their location relative to the crime scene, such details may be able to persuade a jury that the defendant fired the gun a certain number of times. Corey wants to start from the beginning when preparing for trial, particularly with police investigators who she will call to testify in the case. "Prepping for trial, I want to know every single thing," she says. "How'd you get there?" she will ask the officers. "What time did you get there? What'd you do when you got there? . . . Are you sure that's what time? Are you sure that's where you found it? That kind of thing." She pushes the investigators to answer her questions in multiple ways to make sure she understands every aspect of the case and how the jury will process the investigators' testimony. "I need to feel comfortable that every single thing you're saying is actually what happened and how it happened because a long time has passed," she tells the investigators, some of whom are testifying about events that occurred years prior. "So we're going to work out all those kinks ahead of time in great and exhaustive detail."

"Jurors are always thinking about what you don't have, essentially," Shadrian sighs, and offers an example of the kind of kinks that can appear at the last minute in trial, such as when police were unable to recover the gun and thus it is not in evidence and investigators were not prepared to describe it fully. In one successful case, police apprehended the defendant after a lengthy chase only to discover he had disposed of a black revolver that officers had previously seen him carrying. Shadrian used the investigators' testimony to help the jurors visualize the missing gun in their minds. "What kind of gun?" Shadrian asked the officer, who replied, "Oh, a black revolver, looked like a six shooter and it was black." The officers' observations became the testimony for the case. Shadrian has also used the same technique with witnesses. "Oh, he stuck a gun in my face and said, 'Give me your money,'" Shadrian says, playing the part of both witness and prosecutor. "He stuck a gun in your face. What kind of gun? 'Oh, it was one of those with the clip on.' Oh, with the clip. Was it big? Was it long? 'It was decently long.'"

For Shadrian and his colleagues, trial preparation is a paramount step in the orchestration of institutional logics as a case nears adjudication because it involves speculating on how a host of actors in the justice assemblage—witnesses, judge, jurors, defense attorneys, and sometimes victims—will react to aspects of the case. Especially with jurors, Shadrian says, "The more information you can give them about the thing that's missing, the better for us."

RITUALS OF DOCUMENTATION

The justice assemblage's institutional structures and practices materialize through rituals of documentation that, in turn, render the assemblage real through the legal-administrative documents that individual investigators, prosecutors, and other assemblage actors must use to render cases legible to the justice assemblage. These rituals of documentation are themselves powerful assemblage actors that record each collective assemblage step taken in a criminal case through the creation of legal documents, proceedings, and other evidence of the administration of justice. This section accordingly focuses its attention on the felony report as the primary set of documents that prosecutors use to initiate and guide a criminal case through the justice assemblage.

"I've gotten to the point," Corey says, "where I can read through a felony report and sort of issue spot." What is the primary issue? Factual? Emotional? Seeing things that are strong or weak may not be obvious at first. The issues she might spot range widely, beginning with facts beyond change in the case. For example, it is one thing for a felony report to note that a defendant opened the door before he entered the door into a residence. This fact is obvious even without video evidence of the defendant opening the door to the residence. Yet there are many ways that a door can be opened. Prosecutors attempting to prove a fact beyond change—as opposed to claiming to know what happened in a case without disproving all alternatives—risk losing credibility before a jury if a defense attorney emphasizes these alternatives at trial.

Consider two extremely different cases in which issue spotting well in advance helped Hays make decisions that resulted in winning a case. In the first case, the defendant, an astronaut, had just returned from a cruise when he stopped in Tuscaloosa en route to pick up his son in Louisiana, drank a bottle of wine, and took ten generic Ambien. He left his motel room door open with his wallet and his luggage inside, traveled 100 mph down the road, hit a family going 65 mph, and ejected two little girls as the car rolled multiple times. His blood wasn't taken until hours later and so his blood alcohol concentration was zero. For Hays, the most important issue to focus on in this case was the defendant's wallet left on the motel room table behind the open door, because his actions showed his state of mind by indicating he didn't know what he was doing. The real wrongfulness in the case centered on when the defendant drank his wine and took Ambien together, which is where Hays would have started discussing the case during voir dire.

The second case, which initially resulted in a mistrial, was a sexual assault case with a black male defendant and white female victim. Video evidence showed the defendant following the victim, DNA evidence revealed sexual contact had occurred between defendant and victim, and additional evidence proved he shot into her staircase after he raped her. The Friday before the trial started, prosecutors learned the defense's theory was that the victim consented and then later accused the defendant of rape because she did not want to admit to having sex with a black man. Hays advised prosecutors in the second trial to talk with the victim's friends who saw her after the sexual assault occurred and who could testify to the level of her distress and trauma. These kinds of issues are critical to succeeding in a case.

Corey's review of the felony report typically includes over one hundred scanned pages of completed checklists, typed statements, investigators' handwritten observations, and evidence photos, alongside other documents that together comprise the viscera that collectively entail the facts of the case. For Corey, the felony report's combined elements communicate clear messages. What issues will she face in prosecuting this case? Will these be pretrial issues, such as a battle she'll need to fight with a defense attorney at a suppression hearing in which a judge will ultimately decide what evidence to include at a potential trial? And then, if she wins the suppression hearing, will the case settle when the defendant and the defense attorney recognize the increased likelihood that a jury will find the defendant guilty if the evidence is presented?

With these questions in mind, consider the mistaken belief that prosecutors have an easy job because they have tremendous resources provided by the state, including law enforcement support. This mistaken belief regards prosecutors as emboldened by an all-powerful state, as if all prosecutors need to do is present the felony report in making their case to the court. The reality, in fact, is that the felony report is just the beginning of the process prosecutors follow as they prepare their cases. Prosecutors in our jurisdiction have great confidence in law enforcement, yet prosecutors also understand how their role in the justice assemblage is distinct from that of law enforcement. The felony report compiled by law enforcement usually gets prosecutors pointed in the right direction, especially considering that 90% (and more, in murder cases) of defendants plead guilty, yet prosecutors must do more investigation following their review of the felony report.

Prosecutors routinely meet day after day to determine what happened in the minutiae of a case, and while each prosecutor may handle their review of the felony report differently, every prosecutor needs to be extremely familiar with the facts detailed in the over one hundred pages of a typical felony report in a serious violent crime involving a gun. A prosecutor may only focus on facts contained in 10% of the felony report because those facts are most pertinent to the case, but the prosecutor must prepare to present all the facts of the case to the court if necessary. Shooting cases are typically complex. Scientific evidence and witness statements collected by police typically gets prosecutors headed in the right direction, but it is just a start.

Prosecutors effectively begin a new investigation as they review the felony report, which they regard as an outline of the case. Simply put, law enforcement creates the roman numerals of the outline, but prosecutors flesh out the letters and numbers listed beneath to substantiate their theory of the case. It is the prosecutors' final work product that convinces the jury, which is comprised of a group of almost random people, that someone is guilty of a serious crime. Reviewing the felony report also tells prosecutors whether they are likely to face difficult issues at trial. For Corey, this means asking a series of questions as she reads. Is her case weak on identity witnesses? She reviews the felony report documents with a view to what her case is missing, and these elements guide her plea offer to the defendant. "If I see gaping holes," Corey notes, "that's an area where I need to take that gaping hole into consideration whenever I'm making an offer."

To understand how these material aspects of the justice assemblage frame and interpret criminal cases as part of the justice assemblage, this section analyzes how the felony report documents each step in the justice assemblage's handling of a hypothetical shooting death in which the state charges the defendant with murder. These cases typically include greater detail and length than, for example, felony reports in auto burglary cases, and accordingly allow for a more thorough examination of the mundane administrative processes—which we term rituals of documentation—through which the justice assemblage transforms individual actions into criminal charges.

In a typical shooting case resulting in a murder charge, the felony report contains thirty-three documents. Here we consider the means by which an event becomes a crime and the institutions, relationships, and individuals that enable that ontological shift by exploring three aspects of each document. To accomplish this goal, we present a word picture of the felony report. First, we examine how the narrative facts of the case emerge through each document's content. Second, we explore the relationships between the individuals who create each document in their respective professional roles. Third, we analyze the specific actions that each collaboratively created document authorizes in the case.

The felony report's first section is a black-and-white cover page featuring the scales of justice with the name of the police agency responsible for its creation on the top, along with the statement "For presentation to the Tuscaloosa County District Attorney's Office for Grand Jury." In all shooting cases, especially those resulting in serious injury or death, this agency is the Tuscaloosa Violent Crimes Unit, a collaborative effort between investigators at the Tuscaloosa County Sheriff's Office and the Northport,

Tuscaloosa, and The University of Alabama Police Departments. This document features a twelve-digit case number that will follow the case until resolution; offense date; names of the investigator, victim, and defendant; and the charge listed in bolded font in the lower middle. Here we have the basic points of contact involved in the case, the agency that conducted its investigation, and the investigator's authorization to proceed with criminal charges against the defendant. Although all the documents featured in the felony report present the same information, they do so in a different format and style.

Ben conceptualizes the felony report as analogous to a beautiful southern home's subfloor that supports polished oak floorboards. "That stack of paper is not your case," he says of the felony report as he expansively waves his arms toward a group of imaginary witnesses, "because your case is out here." So, while the felony report is extraordinarily important to the case, it is just the beginning of prosecutors' development of the theory of a case.

Section Two, the felony report list, is a black-and-white checklist that the investigator assigned to the case completes by hand, checking each box in ink for nine distinct types of evidence collected at the crime scene. The investigator checks boxes under "Ballistics" to record whether police collected firearms, shell casings, and projectiles at the crime scene, and whether the ballistics report from a crime lab is included in the felony report. Under "DNA Evidence," the investigator checks a *yes or no* box to indicate if police collected evidence on scene and whether the forensics report is included in the report. "Fingerprints" has boxes to check for latent prints lifted and inclusion of the subsequent forensics report. "Autopsy report" is either preliminary or complete, with the option to include a toxicology report from the medical examiner. "Medical records" are likewise requested or included. "Crime scene unit" indicates the police agency used and whether their report is included. "Video evidence" includes images of the crime scene, defendant, and other relevant aspects, along with a box to note whether investigators placed each type of image into evidence. "Telephone records" has boxes for subpoenaed or included, and "911 recordings" has a single box to check if included. Here we have the investigator's synopsis of all the material evidence collected at the crime scene, which prosecutors will evaluate to determine if the case should move forward to prosecution on the charge noted on the cover sheet or take a different action. In cases that go to trial, jurors often want to see video and DNA evidence, making more checked boxes predictive of a stronger case.

Section Three, the felony fact sheet, includes two pages of typed text in list format, beginning with the Tuscaloosa Violent Crimes Unit case number. There may be another law enforcement agency—such as the Tuscaloosa Police Department or the Tuscaloosa Sheriff's Office—case number attached to the report if officers from another agency responded first to the scene only to realize its severity and contact the Violent Crimes Unit. The felony fact sheet lists the defendant's name, address, place of birth, date of birth, social security number, home phone, sex, race, height, weight, eye and hair color, and previous criminal record, and then does the same for the victim. The charge, date, time, and location of the crime follow, along with a note regarding whether force was used or threatened. This section provides a first glimpse of some of the actors in the particular justice assemblage surrounding the case under scrutiny.

Also noted in Section Three is any stolen property, including its description, value, and if recovered, where, when, and by whom. The investigator notes the date, time, and person who notified police, the first officer on the scene (and names of others who arrived at other times), and names of those who transported the victim and defendant from the scene. Arrival dates, times, and name of the responding violent crimes investigator feature here, along with the date, time, and location investigators Mirandized the defendant and sought the defendant's statement, as well as whether or not witnesses were present. Whether the defendant's statement was recorded, the type of recording, and its file location, as well as who did the recording, is also noted. The name of the officer who took photographs at the crime scene is also included, along with the date, time, weather, and temperature. The header "legal information" includes the defendant's name, charge, warrant number (composed of the year plus four randomly generated digits), warrant issue date, execution date, and signature of the person who executed the warrant. "Lineup information" includes the defendant's name, date, location, and witnesses, along with the investigating officer's signature, name, four-digit officer identification, department address, and telephone number. Here the narrative facts of the case begin to emerge more strongly in the investigator's account through initial documentation of its demographic, relational, temporal, and environmental dynamics. The assemblage thickens and we begin to understand how many actors shape how the criminal event itself will be reimagined as the case unfolds.

Section Four, the one-page Tuscaloosa Violent Crimes Unit synopsis, lists the case number, charge, and names for the investigator, victim, and defendant. The synopsis that follows concisely summarizes the time, date, location, and content of the initial call to police and what officers found when they responded. It then summarizes the suspect's statement in response to the investigator's questions, witnesses' statements, warrant and date obtained, arrest date, and the outcome of arrest. Here prosecutors begin to get a sense of the substantive ways in which the case began its entry into the justice assemblage as well as how actors involved in the crime—specifically, the defendant and witnesses—engaged with the justice assemblage through their initial statements made to the 911 dispatcher and to investigators questioning them. Their modes of engagement provide important context regarding how the case may proceed; for example, a witness to a murder who refuses to give a statement or answer any questions is less likely to actively participate in prosecution than a witness who calls 911, speaks to investigators on scene, and then later provides a lengthy statement at police headquarters. Nonetheless, it can't be stated strongly enough that initial assistance is no guarantee of future cooperation.

Section Five, the Tuscaloosa Violent Crimes Unit felony report witness list, varies from two to four pages in length and begins with the case number followed by addresses and phone numbers for both the defendant and victim. Each witness is numbered followed by their name, race, address, date of birth, social security number, sex, driver's license number, employer, and work/school address, and what each witness can testify to in the case. Some of these documents feature lengthy lists of police officers who were on scene, with few other types of witnesses. Typically, police are the primary witnesses, either in cases where the shooting occurred in a residence with only the defendant and victim present and there are no witnesses to give statements about whether the defendant and victim have a history of domestic violence, or in cases where witnesses claim to have seen nothing. While this document compiled by investigators authorizes prosecutors reviewing this document to contact listed witnesses, a prosecutor reviewing a list comprised primarily of police officers may see, as Corey put it, "gaping holes" where other witnesses should be in ways that might compromise a prosecutor's ability to succeed in the case. Witnesses, then, are crucial to the justice assemblage in the eyes of both prosecutors and jurors, and in most instances larger numbers of justice assemblage actors willing to participate makes a much stronger case.

For Ben, the witness list is one of the most important aspects of the felony report. He says, "I tell new prosecutors, 'You've got your base-level case. If you have ten witnesses, you put in ten pieces of evidence.'" By questioning witnesses, who are the real substance of the case beyond the felony report, Ben has consistently been able to find at least one piece of evidence in each case that does not feature in the felony report. "That's what's going to carry you," Ben explains. "Police do a good job, but they're trained to do police work. They see the case differently. We get the report, we know where to start." For Ben, this means if he sees five witnesses in the report, he has the chief victim service officer and the office investigator subpoena these witnesses immediately. "I start adding to my subfloor by putting my oak on top," Ben continues with his analogy of building the structure of the case. "Here's my witness, then I get other witnesses." Ben's reference to oak, the strongest and most valuable part of the subfloor, again emphasizes witnesses' centrality in the justice assemblage.

Section Six, the case report, opens with a case number followed by a two-to-three-page narrative summary of events that focuses on facts beyond change in the case. These are the facts that, irrespective of interpretation or line of argument, cannot be altered. For example, this document summarizes events that occurred in the following chronological order: 911 call, police arrival on scene, police investigation and evidence recovery on scene, questioning of suspects and witnesses, identification of additional witnesses and summaries of their statements, where and how police apprehended the suspect, type of guns recovered, medical determination of cause of death, and DNA swabs and exam for prints. The document concludes with a statement that evidence—such as bullet projectiles, DNA swabs, handguns, and ammunition—will be sent to the Alabama Department of Forensic Sciences for examination. If we imagine the justice assemblage as a web, these are the silk strands holding the actors together in a movable but immutable state.

Here the facts beyond change juxtapose the chain of investigative events (i.e., 911 call, police arrival on scene) with science (i.e., forensic examination), thereby deepening the association between the emerging narrative facts of the case and evidence collected by the individuals creating the documents that together comprise the felony report. For example, a concise case report statement might note that while the body was undergoing autopsy, the "bullet was removed and turned over to investigators," noting a fact beyond change that prosecutors will use while crafting their case on behalf of the state.

Section Seven, the Alabama Uniform Incident/Offense Report, is a densely lined black-and-white form of approximately three pages, including narrative, with space to populate with information about the crime and those involved. It lists the originating agency's identification number, which is seven digits preceded by the letters *AL*, report date, time, type (incident, offense, or supplement, including date), nine-digit agency case number, name, and section (i.e., police beat number). Under the header "Event," the form lists types of incidents or offenses (i.e., felony/misdemeanor, attempted/completed), degree (i.e., first, second, etc.), uniform crime reporting code (a series of numbers developed by the FBI; for example, attempted murder is 9999), state code/local ordinance (e.g., 13A-4-2 is attempted murder), and place of occurrence. Boxes can be checked to indicate involvement of any of the following: alcohol, drugs, or computer equipment; adult or juvenile gang involvement; and hate/bias motivation.

Section Seven also includes physical descriptions of the crime scene, including check-the-box options for point of entry (i.e., door, window, roof, other), method of entry (i.e., forcible, no force, attempted forcible), lighting (i.e., natural, moon, artificial exterior, artificial interior, unknown), weather (i.e., clear, cloudy, rain, fog, snow, hail, unknown), and location type (i.e., terminal, bank, bar, church, commercial, construction, highway/street, hotel/motel, jail/prison, lake/waterway, etc.). It additionally features information on victim type (i.e., individual, business, financial [bank], government, religious organization, society), fill-in-the-blank sections for property crimes (description, value, loss code, i.e., destroyed, stolen, etc.). The form's administration section asks for case status (i.e., pending, inactive, closed), if the case has been entered into NCIC or CJIC, case disposition (i.e., cleared by juvenile arrest, cleared by adult arrest, unfounded, exceptional clearance, administratively cleared). Exceptional clearance boxes are available in cases where the suspect/defendant is dead, prosecution declined/other prosecution, extradition denied, victim refused to cooperate, juvenile (no custody), or death of victim.

Section Seven also includes the reporting officer's name and identification number, followed by the victim's name, address, phone number, employer/school, occupation, address, sex, race, ethnicity, language, height, weight, date of birth, age, and social security number. The officer completing the report can check boxes to indicate if the case involved multiple victims or law enforcement victims, whether defendant was known to victim (and, if so, how, by indicating a relationship code; e.g., 24 is the code for ex-wife), the type and description of weapons used, place of occurrence, type of injury (i.e., internal injury, severe laceration, minor injury, other major injury, loss of teeth, unconscious), circumstances (i.e., homicide or assault), and whether the victim received treatment for assault or rape. Suspect information includes the same information as is recorded for the victim, with additional information on alias, hair color, eye color, complexion, whether the suspect is believed to be armed, clothing description, distinctive marks (i.e., scars, tattoos, amputations), and whether the suspect is arrested, wanted, or part of a dual arrest (e.g., in a domestic violence case). For each witness, the form records sex, race, date of birth, address, phone number, and social security number. Section Seven ends with a brief narrative of thirty or so lines concisely describing the incident. This document, which will be shared with the Federal Bureau of Investigation through the Universal Crime Reporting system, documents the investigator's report of facts in the case. While this section may seem dull and administrative, it sets the scene of the crime and provides the vital context prosecutors will bring to life for jurors if the case goes to trial.

Section Eight, the Alabama Uniform Arrest Report, resembles the incident/offense report by similarly sorting information into tightly grouped boxes that rest on one another. A black column on the left labeled "Identification" lists originating agency number (ORI), case number, agency name, case name, and defendant name and alias, alongside space to enter defendant's sex, race, ethnicity, height, weight, eye, hair, and skin color, scars, marks, tattoos, amputations, place of birth, social security number, date of birth, age, home address, and phone number. The black column on the left titled "Arrest" spans the following fill-in-the-blank information: location of arrest, sector (i.e., police beat), if the officer made the arrest for the officer's jurisdiction (and, if not, the name of the out-of-state agency), arrestee's condition (i.e., drunk, drinking, sober, drugs), whether arrestee resisted arrest, any injuries to arresting officer, whether arrestee was armed (and description of weapon if so, i.e., handgun, rifle, shotgun, other firearm, other weapon), charge one (i.e., "murder" in bold font) with additional boxes to check (i.e., felony, misdemeanor, attempted), state code or local ordinance, warrant number, date issued, UCR code (i.e., 905 is murder), and the same information following for charge two (i.e., burglary). The final black columns on the left side collect information on the vehicle (i.e., information on make and model, seized and where impounded), juvenile (how disposed, released to parent/guardian), release (date/time, releasing officer name, agency), personal property released (y/n), agency address, agency division, and remarks (e.g., any injuries at time of arrest). Here we have the investigator's detailed account of the circumstances surrounding the defendant's arrest, which documents an individual's movement to a new stage in the justice assemblage. This movement, of course, marks a critical ontological transition because the individual is no longer just a person of interest to the justice assemblage but a defendant whom the state accuses of a crime.

Sections Nine, Ten, and Eleven—the complaint, deposition and charge sheet, and arrest warrant—are documents signed by a judge or magistrate and an investigator that together comprise a chain of events leading to the defendant's incarceration in jail. Section Nine, the complaint, includes the agency number, warrant number, and case number, along with a statement from the judge that the investigator, referred to here as the complainant, believes there is probable cause to believe that the defendant "whose name is otherwise unknown to the complainant, did within the above named county and did on or about ＿＿ (date), with the intent to ＿＿＿ (i.e., cause the death of another person), he causes the death of ＿＿＿ (victim name) with a gun in violation of ＿＿＿ (statute #) against the peace and dignity of the State of Alabama." Section Ten, the deposition and charge sheet, is likewise signed by both the judge and investigator and lists the charge, code, warrant number, agency case number, and ORI number, along with the defendant's and victim's names, addresses, dates of birth, race, sex, height, weight, hair and eye color, and a concise paragraph-long description of the case (e.g., "at approximately Y p.m. the TVCU responded to Z address in ＿＿ on a shooting . . ."). Section Eleven, the arrest warrant, likewise signed by the complainant (investigator) and magistrate/judge authorizes any law enforcement officer in Alabama to arrest the defendant on the charges stated in the complaint and deposition. These sections formalize the documentation by creating an official record of these details, and the actors named within become materially and symbolically bound both within and together in the justice assemblage.

As they review the felony report, prosecutors frequently consult Alabama code books to determine the elements of a crime a defendant is charged with committing. The law in practice is an interpretive act, and often this interpretation involves lengthy discussions among prosecutors and with the District Attorney. While we were editing this book, Hays frequently paused to take phone calls or speak in person with Assistant District Attorneys who wanted to consult with him about appropriate charges. In this way, legal practice is very much a collaborative endeavor. Susan routinely watched Hays put his reading glasses on to pore over Alabama code in response to prosecutors who asked a wide range of questions about how to apply law to the facts of a case. In this way, assemblage actors are always moving and coming into contact with one another. Tethered together by facts beyond change, the assemblage is dynamic rather than a linear path from arrest to prosecution.

Section Twelve, a single-page form titled "The Rights of a Person Being Interviewed in Tuscaloosa County," includes the date, name and title of the officer who Mirandized the defendant, and the name, sex, race, date of birth, address, and phone number of the person being interviewed. The five points of the Miranda warning follow: the right to remain silent; anything you say can and will be used against you in a court of law; you have the right to talk to a lawyer and have him present with you while you are being questioned; if you cannot afford to hire a lawyer, one will be appointed to represent you before any questioning, if you wish; and you can decide at any time to exercise these rights and not answer any questions or make any statements. "Do you understand each of these rights I have explained to you?" asks the form under the word *Waiver*, next to a space marked for the defendant's and a witness's (usually the investigator's) initials, and signature, along with the date and time. Here the investigator and defendant jointly confirm that due process is underway in the defendant's criminal case, which could otherwise become grounds for dismissal.

Sections Thirteen, Fourteen, and Fifteen feature individual statements, which are usually approximately two pages long, from defendant, victim (if victim is alive), and witnesses assembled by a Tuscaloosa Violent Crimes Unit investigator. Each includes a name, address, social security number, driver's license number and state, date of birth, telephone number, height, weight, eye color, hair color, place of employment, work address and work telephone, and name, address, and phone number for next of kin. This is followed by a paragraph typed by the investigator that summarizes what each individual shared, typically concise statements such as "X advised that she did not see the shooter. X said she heard a loud pop sound followed by a man screaming." The defendant's name, along with the date, time, and location (e.g., interview room 2), follows, along with the date, time, and name of the investigator who Mirandized the defendant. Here the relationships comprising the justice assemblage begin to expand, as witnesses, victims, and defendants each give their own version of events, and becomes more complex, as prosecutors face the difficult task of interpreting these statements in conjunction with the facts beyond change in the case. These documents show how actors can enter and exit the justice assemblage at different junctures of the process, whether willingly or unwillingly.

Sections Sixteen, Seventeen, and Eighteen pertain to the collection of evidence. Section Sixteen, the Tuscaloosa Violent Crimes Unit Evidence List, opens with the case number followed by numbered items that include the date, time, description (e.g., wallet, cell phone, black .38 caliber revolver, .38 caliber bullets × 4, victim's body), and location where investigators located each piece of evidence. Section Seventeen, a consent for taking of gunshot residue kit, informs the defendant of the constitutional right to refuse without a search warrant or court order, is signed by the defendant, the investigator, and a witness, with the address where the kit was taken and results (positive/negative) noted with investigator initials. Section Eighteen, the firearm examination form, includes agency, case number, victim, and investigator; firearm make, model, caliber, and serial number; whether the firearm was processed through NCIC, swabbed for DNA, and processed for fingerprints; and, if applicable, had the serial number restored.

For semiautomatic weapons, the form requests information on make, model, caliber, serial number, hammer position (if applicable), whether cartridge/cartridge case was recovered from chamber, status (fired/unfired), magazine capacity, and number of cartridges recovered from magazine; for revolvers, the form requests the same with additional information on cylinder rotation, cylinder cartridge capacity, and number of cartridges recovered from cylinder. Here the justice assemblage, through the work of the investigator and, subsequently, forensic scientists, documents the chain of evidence, a record of who collected the evidence, and where they did so.

Prosecutors reviewing these sections will travel to visit the examining scientist to understand how best to depict the case in court. This involves asking a series of questions. Where are the shell casings, what does that mean? How do we know this bullet was taken out of that guy, fired out of that gun? Ben prosecuted a case with a defendant who claimed he put a gun to the victim's chest and the gun "just went off," yet testimony in court from a firearms expert confirmed this was impossible, with the defendant firing the weapon. Consultations with scientific experts who analyze the evidence are vital to case success.

Sections Nineteen through Twenty-Two pertain to the documentation of the chain of custody, which refers to the control and transfer of evidence from a crime scene to another location, in this case the Alabama Department of Forensic Sciences. Section Nineteen, "Evidence Submission," includes the case type, county of offense, investigating agency, investigating officer and email, agency case number, and mailing address; submitting agency, phone, duty hours, submitting officer and email; charge; date of offense; and type, with options for "suspect" or "subject" (victim), along with space to enter name, sex, race, and date of birth. A few sentences describe the crime and evidence recovered, along with a description of evidence submitted (including location of recovery), list of evidence (e.g., gun, swab), type of service requested—DC (drug chemistry), FA/TM (firearms/toolmarks), FB (forensic biology), FD (fire debris), or TX (toxicology)—and instructions to seal all evidence along with the completed form prior to submission. Separate evidence and custody receipts request the same information, along with signatures from the person delivering and the person receiving it. Evidence bolsters the facts beyond change prosecutors tether together in the justice assemblage. As the amount of evidence increases in amount and credibility, the justice assemblage thickens and becomes more effective.

Section Twenty, the "Laboratory Evidence Release Form," notes the lab case number and lists the items (e.g., "One (1) sealed envelope containing fingerprints described as: collected by X"), and is signed by the individuals delivering and receiving the evidence. Section Twenty-One, "Evidence Receipt of Body," includes the day, date, time, case number, decedent's name, date of birth, age, race, sex, location, and name, agency, and title of the person releasing and receiving the body, along with a box to check indicating that the person receiving the body received it in a zippered, closed body bag sealed with the seal number. It also includes funeral home name and phone number, notes to record personal effects with the body, and signatures for the individual delivering and the person receiving the body. Here we see careful documentation of the chain of custody as evidence, including the victim's corpse, is transported from law enforcement to forensic scientists for examination and back to law enforcement for appropriate transfer. Even in murder cases, which by definition begin with a justice assemblage actor's death, the decedent remains part of the assemblage. Corporeality is at the core of the justice assemblage, so even in death the body remains a silent but central actor in the justice assemblage.

Section Twenty-Two, "Report of Autopsy," includes the Alabama Department of Forensic Sciences case number; the victim's sex, race, length, and weight; and date, time, and county of death. It provides a final diagnosis (i.e., gunshot wound), cause of death (i.e., gunshot wound), manner of death (i.e., homicide), evidence of injury (i.e., paragraph describing wound and passage of bullet), and external examination that reviews each body part and evaluates each as remarkable or unremarkable. It notes if postmortem X-rays were taken or toxicology tests administered and, if so, the results. A section titled "Logistics" provides the statutory authorization for performing the autopsy, identification of body by law enforcement, and persons present at the autopsy, and lists evidence (i.e., photographs, radiographs, fingerprints, palm prints, DNA cards, hair, blood, vitreous, tissue, projectile, buccal swab). A sketch of the body, with wounds marked, is signed by the state medical examiner, with a statement indicating that "tissues and evidence will be disposed twelve months from the date of the original report unless alternate arrangements are made prior thereto." This section speaks for the decedent as their body tells the story that is taken up and given new life within the justice assemblage.

Sections Twenty-Three through Twenty-Eight deal with the search and seizure of property and document the procedures the state undertakes to obtain additional evidence in accordance with the law. Section Twenty-Three, "Application and Affidavit for a Search Warrant," is a brief one-page document filed by a Tuscaloosa Violent Crimes Unit investigator in court. It generally includes a paragraph-long description of the crime with a few concluding sentences that request a warrant to search for specific evidence in a specific location. "Your affiant shows that based upon the above and foregoing facts and information," the application and affidavit read, "he has probable cause to believe and does believe, that the aforesaid property is concealed upon the aforesaid persons, property, and/or vehicles and is subject to seizure and makes this affidavit so that a warrant may issue to search the aforesaid persons, property, and/or vehicles." At this point, a judge or magistrate reviews the application and opts to either issue or decline a search warrant to gather further evidence in the case.

Section Twenty-Four, "Search Warrant," is a document signed by a judge or magistrate that authorizes any law enforcement officer in Alabama to search a specific location—such as a residence—and seize specific property, such as a vehicle or firearms, for example, or property generalized to include "any items of relevance to murder." This document, which includes a warrant number, notes the relevant Code of Alabama statute the investigator applying for the search warrant believes the defendant violated and references Rule 3.8 in the Alabama Rules of Criminal Procedure, which pertains to search warrants. The subsection "Search Warrant Return and Inventory" is a document signed and dated by the investigator who conducted the search warrant that either checks a box indicating that no property was found or seized, or checks a box that describes the seized property (e.g., bullet projectile, cellular phone, bloodstained shirt), and verifies that the investigator left an endorsed copy of the inventory taken at the scene of the search in accordance with Rule 3.11(a) Alabama Rules of Criminal Procedure.

Section Twenty-Five is a receipt signed by a duty judge acknowledging receipt of the search warrant inventory and designating a named investigator to hold the inventory in the investigator's possession for use in court or to deliver for examination or testing. The judge sets bond and determines probable cause in cases postarrest, but this process is separate from the process of obtaining a search warrant. Section Twenty-Six, compiled by the police agency (usually the Tuscaloosa County Sheriff's Office Investigative Services) is handwritten by the investigator on scene and includes the investigator's division (usually the Violent Crimes Unit), officer in charge, where the warrant was served, officers present, individuals present at location warrant was served, and items seized (e.g., victim/body, cell phone, seven bullet projectiles). Section Twenty-Seven, which requires no warrant, is the "Tuscaloosa County Violent Crimes Unit: Form for Consent to Search Vehicle and/or Premises," which lists date and location, along with a defendant's and a witness's signature on a statement authorizing investigators to search their residence and seize personal property.

Section Twenty-Eight, "Tuscaloosa Violent Crimes Unit Property Release to Owner," includes the date, time, and type of property (e.g., social security card, Medicaid card), along with the name, signature, phone number, and address investigators released the property to once they determined it was not relevant to their investigation. Throughout the search warrant–related documents, we see multiple actors in the justice assemblage—including defendants, witnesses, investigators, and judges—collaborating to collect additional evidence that they believe will support the narrative facts of the case and strengthen the link between actors.

Section Twenty-Nine, the "Crime Scene Log," documents the names, professional titles, and rationale for presence (e.g., medical, investigation) for all individuals at the crime scene. Section Thirty, the "Tuscaloosa Violent Crimes Unit Photo Log," lists each photograph line by line, along with the date, case number, location, victim, photographer-investigator's name, and description (e.g., address, backyard), followed by photos labeled with corresponding numbers (e.g., IMG_001). Section Thirty-One, the "Computer-Aided Dispatch" (CAD, which provides brief transcripts of 911 calls), lists the type of call (e.g., assault/shooting), when reported, address, directions, occurred between (time and date estimates), complainant contact (name/anonymous), call ID# (c+seven digits), comments with times, dates, and names (e.g., "Mary Stevens: comp. would not answer any questions stated someone was shot across the street"), and radio logs from police agencies along with brief updates (e.g., "en route to call"; "arrived on scene") as the dispatcher creates a real-time log of events in progress. Section Thirty-Two lists the disks containing all the documents described here, and Section Thirty-Three, finally, contains various other information pertinent to the case, such as maps of the crime scene hand-drawn by the investigator to show a witness, or a Google maps printout of the crime scene location.

Taken together, the documents comprising the felony report are just one example of the rituals of documentation that render the justice assemblage real through its institutional structures and practices. They map out the actors, planes, and bonds formed and set into motion by the criminal event. In his brilliant book *Pictures from a Drawer: Prison and the Art of Portraiture*, folklorist Bruce Jackson observes that the process by which collections of documents—in his case, the prison dossier, or "jacket"—render particular events real is inherent to how institutions interpret and categorize individuals. After all, Jackson writes, such institutional interpretive processes are

> the function of a bureaucratic dossier of whatever kind—military, medical, academic, corporate, police, prison: turning the infinitude of

facts and emotions and connections that make each of us the ever-changing unique creatures we are into manageable things. Manageable things of this order are not alive; they are useful abstractions or constructs (Jackson 2009, 21).

Legal and administrative actions made possible through these rituals of documentation transform individual actions into crimes and mundane objects and human bodies alike into state's evidence. The process through which the state achieves these transformations is simultaneously a testament to its power and illustrative of the numerous steps justice assemblage actors must follow to attain their goal.

Consider, for example, how easy it is to make a mistake that voids the otherwise careful work in these rituals of documentation: failure to utter a certain set of words at the crime scene, a witness who refuses to provide a statement for any number of complex reasons, or touching an object the wrong way before it goes into evidence. The list goes on, and all these realities take place in an environment saturated with numerous similar criminal cases and enormous time pressures to move each case closer to resolution. Having focused intensively on the felony report, a central aspect of the administrative processes by which an action becomes a crime prosecuted by the state, we now turn our attention to how prosecutors experience the temporal dynamics that inform case disposition.

THE TEMPORAL DYNAMICS OF CASE DISPOSITION

Prosecutors use a set of institutional logics to navigate the institutional structures and practices shaping their work and do so in ways that will result in a finite range of outcomes in cases involving guns. A prosecutor finds sufficient evidence in the felony report to move forward with an investigator's case or explains to the investigator why the case lacks sufficient evidence for prosecution, a defendant accepts or rejects a prosecutor's plea offer, a jury reaches a guilty or not guilty verdict. All of these are finite options that occur within what we have termed the conceptual abacus at work in the justice assemblage and in an extremely time pressurized environment.

"If it's not a murder or a rape," Shadrian Gayles says, "anything less than that, you're probably going to get a week's notice" from the judge that a case is going to trial. This short notice means that Shadrian needs to remain in contact with victims and witnesses in cases he believes are likely to go to trial so that they will be prepared to testify in court with limited notice. He knows, for example, that fatal shooting cases from several years prior are likely to go to trial in the coming year, and in those instances, the judge will "let us know this case has gray hair on it" so that Shadrian can begin trial preparation for that case. While this means that the pressure to settle cases is tremendous, especially when judges call cases for trial within such a short amount of time, it does not mean that prosecutors modify their offers to speed up case processing.

"Regardless of how many cases I have," Kymberly explains, "I can physically only work on so many at a time." While she is currently working on ten different cases, all of which involve guns, she can never forget that after those ten cases settle or the jury reaches a verdict at trial, another five hundred and fifty cases assigned to her still lurk in the background. Susan, who was routinely amazed at the almost abstractly large number of cases assigned to each prosecutor, asked Kymberly how the job would feel different if the number of prosecutors in the office doubled. "It feels like I'm climbing Mount Everest," she says. "Whereas if I only had a hundred more, it probably wouldn't feel as bad. I would imagine it would feel like, 'Okay, this is manageable. Once I finish these cases, I only have this many left.' Even though, like I said, it's cyclical. It's cyclical. They'll keep coming."

The fact that the cases just "keep coming" often prompted comparisons to other prosecutors' offices, with federal prosecutors' perceived much lighter workload a frequent source of consternation. Lyndsie, whose caseload was at 516 active felony cases when we spoke at length about her work, echoes many of her peers in wishing she had the kind of time federal prosecutors do to work on a case. "I've got a friend who works in a federal prosecutor's office," she explains, "and I swear to you, he's been working on the same freaking case for a year. And I'm just like, 'Man, you have time to spend with your victims and your witnesses and your officers, prepping them, to look at every single area of the law, to think about everything that could possibly come up in evidence. You can play this out fully, know every single little thing about that case.' There is no way a state prosecutor can do that . . . it's not a realistic expectation."

Corey, who is from a small town located an hour south of Tuscaloosa, closely monitored the contested race for District Attorney in her home jurisdiction. While she was watching the debate between contenders, the incumbent proudly stated that her home jurisdiction's District Attorney's Office had reduced the number of county-wide pending cases from 800 to 120. "And I was just thinking," Corey says incredulously, "I'm at eight hundred cases on a Tuesday." Prosecutors take a range of approaches to managing the workload associated with such a massive number of cases, many of which involve guns. For Paula, who has practiced law for thirty years, managing this workload means recognizing that nonstop work is the expectation. "Being an attorney is never an eight-to-five job," she explains. "Some days you can cut out early, but all that's going to do is mean that you're here Saturdays and Sundays and late and early. And so, if that's not for you, then this is not the place. And that's just the reality. That's not being harsh. There are not enough minutes in an eight-to-five day to have time to do everything that has to be done. So, recognize that about yourself coming in. If you're not comfortable, if your lifestyle does not work that way, then you're just going to be frustrated and we'll get frustrated and it's never going to be a good fit."

"People will always keep committing crimes," Kymberly smiles as she explains her philosophy of work-life balance as the only means to avoid the potential for the kind of burnout Paula describes. "You'll always have things to do. There will always be something that you can do. So, you have to prioritize and work on as much as you can get done in that eight to five as possible. And so, I think it's important to have that balance. Otherwise, you burn out. You don't get to enjoy your family. You don't get to enjoy what is actually your life. Because the truth is, regardless of how called you are to this profession, it is your profession and not your life. Your life is outside of here. And so, I advise people to stick to their work schedule unless it's something important."

Lyndsie often considers the difference between, as she puts it, "doing an adequate job and doing a good job and doing a really, really good job." For her, the difference between a good attorney and an excellent attorney is the amount of time the excellent attorney spends combing through evidence, statements, and other elements associated with the case. The significant time pressures associated with a large caseload and extremely limited number of hours in which to work on them forces her to prioritize cases with victims. "I don't want to say that the other cases aren't important," she says. "They still are. But if you can't dig into everything for forty hours the way you want to, I think we have to prioritize those." This is particularly true when the victim has been threatened or injured with a firearm.

Corey remembers her early days as a prosecutor as a time when she sat at her desk in a constant panic, thinking "I wish I were just six months ahead" or "I wish I was just a year ahead." As time passed, she became more comfortable with the reality that being ahead of schedule means being prepared for next week and let go of the hope that she would ever feel prepared for next month or next year given the sheer volume of cases assigned to her and her colleagues. This gradual process of accepting the reality that the work of prosecution means being constantly overwhelmed by a barrage of cases was a common theme in discussions about workload, which most prosecutors handled through the shifting prioritization of cases, with those cases scheduled for trial given the top priority.

This shifting prioritization of cases involved both a shift of energy and attention to trial preparation and a literal physical shift in case materials. Prosecutors preparing for trial frequently posted elements of the upcoming case, such as evidence photographs and other documents from the felony report, on their office walls to help them visualize the theory of the case and subsequent arguments they would make in court. Meanwhile, documents pertaining to cases they regarded as more likely to settle might be tucked into an organizer perched in a desk corner to make way for documents necessary for trial preparation. Kymberly's desk has this look about it as she prepares for trial, gesturing to the documents spread across her desk and those nestled in a file folder where, as she explains, "I still have access to the case, but I'm not delving through it as deeply as I might if I were going to trial. I'm really just getting enough information to make an informed offer. And being that you do consider what you would have to prove at trial in making that offer, then, yeah, you have to dig a little deep, but it's not nearly the same as when you're actually preparing for trial."

The temporal shift in prioritization that accompanies trial preparation stems from the dual realities that trial preparation is both extremely time intensive and tends to occur solely in violent cases, most of which involve guns and criminal charges resulting in lengthy prison sentences. When Corey makes the temporal shift to prioritizing trial preparation, she reminds herself that while she may only have seven days or fewer to prepare for trial, she has previously reviewed the case to evaluate the suitable plea offer. She has already met with witnesses in the case and has worked on aspects of the case in the midst of her other responsibilities. "We get a sense that cases are getting ripe for trial," she explains of how she begins to amplify the intensity with which she focuses on a case. "It's really when it's called for trial that's when everything else shuts down, everything else can wait. My inbox can pile up. Everything else can wait because I have this murder case that's going to trial and that's going to be what I'm doing for the next seven days until we start."

Prosecutors' relationships with other assemblage actors dramatically impact the temporal dynamics of case disposition, which by definition cannot occur in a vacuum unique to the prosecutor. Thomas cites his fiduciary relationship to the state as paramount in making plea offers, observing that "it takes a lot of our time, but we don't want to sacrifice what we think the punishment should be just to avoid a trial." Trial is likewise extremely anxiety-producing, given the dramatically increased number of assemblage actors much more closely involved with one another at trial relative to a plea offer and subsequent sentencing. The office feels physically different when trials are actively in progress due to their anxiety-producing nature. The energy feels palpable, especially in murder trials where victims' and defendants' family members are in attendance, their grief and suffering adding palpably to the already high levels of tense energy.

Prosecutors feel tremendous pressure during this time as they memorize extremely complex case details so they can spontaneously recall the minutiae of these cases in court. For example, one day Susan was working at a computer when she saw Ben pass by and asked how he was doing. "I'm gonna run through these names with you so I can make sure I have them straight in my mind," he said as he began to weave an extraordinarily complex account of a case with multiple codefendants and witnesses in a very complex shooting case. These key details are central to establishing credibility in the courtroom, in addition to the enormous amount of time prosecutors have already devoted to preparing the case. A prosecutor who slips up with a name during trial may spark doubt in a juror's mind that leads to a spiral of other doubts that result in a mistrial or losing the case.

Considering the temporal realities likely to accompany a case raises several questions for Thomas. Sometimes these questions begin to occupy his mind at the first signs of a case failing to settle, such as when a defense attorney calls him to say, "We don't like the offer." Or when he empathizes with the reasons why a defendant's victim and sister are too scared to testify against a defendant who has shot someone close to them. "What can we do at trial?" he asks himself in such circumstances. "And not just short term 'Can we make an offer?' but long term, are we going to have the people, the evidence, the testimony, the videos, the witnesses, the physical evidence, the shell casings, the gun? Can we make it to trial? And if we can make a trial, can we win a trial?"

These temporal realities encompass relationships with witnesses, judges, and other assemblage actors. Grace appreciates that, by law, prosecutors have input on docketing and cases set for trial, and in the courtroom where she prosecutes cases, that scheduling runs smoothly. As she plans ahead for a trial in two months, she imagines how different her approach to the case would be if she only had two weeks' notice when the case appeared on the call docket before trial. The sheer number of witnesses she needs to prepare in a complex multicount case, in which a woman orchestrated minors who committed at least nine armed robberies of businesses in a two-week span, would simply be impossible to coordinate with just a few weeks before trial.

For Maegan in District Court, which hears misdemeanor cases, communicating with victims and witnesses is a major struggle despite her best efforts. "Sometimes I go to trial in cases involving victims and I've never met the victim," she says. "We don't have a working number. They've moved. Can't get them hand served [with a subpoena to call them to court]. And then they'll just show up at trial. So, we're like, 'Okay, well we'll just see where it goes.' Try to talk to them for five minutes or so. But it is hard to manage. You just roll with the punches. You have to know that sometimes everything's not going to be perfect, which I think is hard for most attorneys, because we're all very type A people."

These temporal dynamics also include the relationship between the prosecutor and the defendant. One prosecutor described working with a judge, for instance, who will say, "I want this case gone. . . . He will throw up a case and say, 'This is going for trial, and you have eighteen hours to get it ready.' And it's because he wants me to settle it." This prosecutor isn't willing to settle in cases with a living victim or fatal shooting cases that have devastated surviving family members. "And then there's some that I just come across and they piss me off more than other cases," he says. "And I'm like 'No, we're not letting this go.'" Ultimately, this prosecutor makes a determination that balances the public safety ramifications of a defendant remaining in the free world with consideration of the devastation the defendant has caused for the victim and their family members.

These temporal dynamics include relationships with defense attorneys as well. Ashley shares responsibility for prosecuting an extremely large number of criminal cases with her trial partner, Ben, who is assigned to the same courtroom. With this many cases, it would be impossible for anyone to remember every defendant's name or the details of cases that are not currently the focus of plea offer development or trial preparation. This impossibility can create awkward moments with defense attorneys who have much smaller caseloads and may arrive at her office unannounced ready to have an impassioned discussion about a case. "They'll come in and they'll say, 'Hey, can I get an offer on this case?,' or 'Can I get an offer on that case?'" Ashley says. "And I don't even recognize the name, so I sometimes I feel bad saying, 'Hey, I'm not sure what that case is. I have to get back to you,' or 'Hey, can I take a minute to—.' Sometimes I'll fake it 'til I make it and just say, 'Hey, I need some more time to look at that. Let me get back to you this afternoon.' But it's hard when they come in and they're expecting you to know everything that they know, but you can't do that with the four hundred or five hundred cases that you have. So, I feel like I don't really get to know a case until maybe a day or two before it's set for a hearing, or maybe the morning of, or for trial. So, if it's just out there floating around then it's just something I haven't probably looked at until something calls it to my attention."

3. Relationships and Roles

"Lawyers are perceived as poker players," says Assistant District Attorney Grace Prince. "You don't share your cards. When a case is called for a trial, sure, I'm not playing all my cards. Before that, I think that the public doesn't understand the value of playing your cards. I'm not scared to play my cards in the beginning. I want you to know what I have, and I want to know what you have because that makes the system better and that makes us more likely to get to the right result. The public doesn't know the value of that. We're not poker players when we are dealing with the rest of someone's life." For Grace, who grew up in Tuscaloosa, attended law school just a few miles from the county courthouse at the University of Alabama, and knows most of the lawyers who practice in town, her relationships to other justice assemblage actors are core aspects of her everyday work.

The best lawyers, in Grace's experience, will meet with her before trial to discuss elements of a case that she might not otherwise know. They do this because they trust her to do the right thing, which means not taking advantage of knowing information the defense shared and not trying to win for the sake of winning. Information from any source, including defense attorneys, will be used properly, including if it supports the defendant's innocence. This trust is precious, because sharing information might lead to a defense attorney trying to take advantage of that rather than using it properly. In this way, doing the right thing requires developing a sense of people.

This trust is essential to the everyday administration of justice, which is why Grace believes that the best defense attorneys are also the most reasonable, meaning that they take a collaborative approach to a case. The process is adversarial, but it doesn't have to be a collision. Respecting this adversarial process means realizing that prosecutors are on the side of the state, to get the right result. Prosecutors and defense attorneys are professional opponents who start from a point of inherent disagreement, with inherently clashing roles, but this clash can also have trust in it. This trust does not mean a prosecutor makes a plea offer to a defense attorney just because he or she believes the defense attorney's client will accept it, but because the offer reflects the intersection of facts and law. A defense attorney's analysis of the evidence may give them a different take on the case. "We're not asking anyone to be lackeys for the state," Hays explains of information shared between prosecutors and defense attorneys. "It's us being trustworthy and taking it in good faith, not bad faith of using it further against the defendant."

"Here's what I think this should be," a defense attorney Grace trusts might say to her about a plea offer, and she will respond with "I'll give it credit, I'll go check" because what defense attorneys she regards as trustworthy say to her matters. They approach her with "I've looked at this case and here's what I believe," rather than defense attorneys who bluntly state some version of "You should just dismiss this."

When a defense attorney whom Grace trusts tells her that she has a problem with her case, she knows she has a problem that warrants further investigation on her part. Grace will not entertain someone trying to unduly influence her in a case, and so, while she will be polite to defense attorneys whom she does not trust and who tell her she has problems with her case, her underlying message will still be "Get out of my office, please. I don't have anything else to say. Thank you for your time, but please leave."

Earning Grace's trust takes time, and even defense attorneys she trusts still expect her to question everything, rather than be offended by the way that some of the less trustworthy defense attorneys she has dealt with have behaved at times. Working with defense lawyers she trusts produces the best results in a case, meaning that, as Grace puts it, "The right thing is happening, which sometimes means a dismissal, which sometimes means I can't prove it. Which sometimes means it did not happen." The right thing means that the administration of justice followed the law.

Grace prosecuted a murder case with two of the most skilled defense attorneys she knows, one of whom she studied with in law school and the other of whom she worked with when she was a defense attorney. They went to lunch together to discuss potential plea offers and Grace offered thirty years as the lowest potential recommended sentence, which the defendant rejected. The defense attorneys visited Grace at the courthouse to review every single exhibit she and her trial partners would present in court, and they determined pretrial which exhibits would be admitted into evidence and then were able to have a hearing before trial on all exhibits the defense objected to, instead of having to pause the trial to handle multiple objections in front of the jury.

Grace knew that her defense attorney colleagues would not take a case if they did not believe the defendant was telling the truth about his involvement in the murder. Yet Grace also knew that evidence in the case overwhelmingly proved the defendant committed the murder. "He believed him," Grace says of the defense attorney. "It was so hard for me to hear it, not only because I'm like, 'He's doing really well and I don't know what I'm going to say,' but also it was like, 'How can we look at the same facts and come to such different places?' I knew in my heart he [the defendant] did this. [The defendant] was involved, and he [the defense attorney] knew in his heart that he [the defendant] just stumbled upon it. That was hard to see because I respect him." That evening, one of the defense attorneys called Grace to congratulate her on the jury's verdict of guilty. "It was probably the best tried case I've ever been a part of," Grace says, "because they were correct on the law, I was correct on the law. We just argued the facts."

SITUATING PROSECUTORS' ROLES AND RELATIONSHIPS WITHIN THE JUSTICE ASSEMBLAGE

Chapter 3 argues that the human interactions comprising the everyday administration of justice are situated within relationships and roles that, in turn, directly shape the investigation, prosecution, and disposition of criminal cases involving guns. We explore three distinct aspects of how relationships and roles manifest within the justice assemblage for prosecutors. First, we examine how prosecutors understand their relationship to political will in their role as fiduciaries tasked with acting in the state's best interests, using the specific examples of the gun present policy itself, prospective jurors' attitudes and beliefs about guns, and prosecutors' perspectives on their fiduciary relationship to the people of the state as client. Second, we explore how prosecutors navigate their relationships with police, defense attorneys, judges, and jurors. Third, we analyze the relational context in which guns are featured in murder cases prosecuted at the Tuscaloosa County Courthouse.

We situate our analysis within two primary bodies of scholarly literature: law and society and legal cynicism. Drawing on law and society scholarship that examines relationships between assemblage actors and the cultural context in which they live and work, we focus particular attention on research pertaining to how justice assemblage relationships coalesce around evidence and courtroom workgroups, including juries. We also engage with the legal cynicism literature that (wrongly, in our view) depicts prosecutors and justice assemblage actors more generally as omnipotent actors on behalf of an all-powerful state.

Law and Society

Law and society research directs its energies toward understanding the dialogical relationship between statutory or customary codes and the cultural context where they are produced and enacted. One of the most interesting areas of law and society research as it pertains to our research is the relationship that forensic science establishes between assemblage actors and material evidence. As an important nonhuman actor in the justice assemblage, evidence develops its own social life and biography through forensic analyses, statements elicited by police investigators, and prosecutors' and defense attorneys' respective interpretations, and in turn, evidence also generates social relationships as cases progress from the crime scene to adjudication (Kruse 2016).

Law and society research emphasizes the embedded nature of forensic sciences and technologies within social relationships. For example, researchers note how evidence and case narrative have a reciprocal relationship such that while evidence plays a central role in how investigators construct their narrative of a case, that case narrative may also shift to accommodate ambiguous or contradictory forensic findings regarding evidence (Brookman et al. 2020b). Hence case narrative and case evidence work in a synchronous manner even when forensic findings contradict what investigators initially believed to be the nature of the relationship between case narrative and evidence. The role of evidence may also vary by type of crime. For instance, law and society research has found that forensic evidence, in sharp contrast with victim willingness to testify and documentation of victim injury, is not a strong predictor of outcome in sexual assault cases (Sommers and Baskin 2011).

Law and society researchers have also explored relationships between individuals in courtroom workgroups by attending to the socio-legal norms and dynamics that surround decision-making in criminal trial courts (Young 2013). This body of research has found that familiarity among prosecutors and judges reduces the number of days until case disposition and increases the odds of plea dispositions, while familiarity between defense attorneys and other members of the courtroom workgroup means that cases are more likely to proceed to trial (Metcalfe 2016). Relationships, and the nature of those relationships, clearly matter a great deal in courtroom workgroups.

Relationships between courtroom actors are especially significant when considered in conjunction with research findings that suggest cognition is a communicative process. Courtroom workgroups accordingly interpret knowledge produced outside the legal world in terms of its relevance to the law (Teubner 2017), and in so doing jointly construct a unique reality undergirded by legal discourse but situated within a particular courtroom workgroup's socio-legal norms. Collaboration within the courtroom workgroup is also evident in problem-solving courts, where judges engage with court participants in a supportive—rather than authoritarian—role alongside case workers and other members of the courtroom workgroup (Portillo et al. 2013). Courtroom workgroups in problem-solving courts share power among judges, prosecutors, defense attorneys, probation officers, and treatment providers as part of a case management approach to decision-making in each case (Rudes and Portillo 2012).

Relationships between jurors and other members of the justice assemblage are a focus of study among some law and society researchers due to what legal scholar Robert Burns calls "the death of the American trial" (Burns 2009). The decline in the number of trials relative to plea offers is significant, with the number of federal criminal jury trials declining by nearly half in the decade between 2006 and 2016 alone, making the sentencing hearing the primary public proceeding in most criminal cases (Conrad and Clements 2017). A national survey of attorneys and judges found that those who handle criminal cases attribute declining numbers of trials to the implementation of mandatory minimum sentences, and defense attorneys regarded sentencing guidelines and the bail system as additional contributing factors (Diamond and Salerno 2020).

Despite the declining prevalence of trials, jurors nevertheless loom large in prosecutors' minds as they craft case narratives by continually referencing how potential jurors might interpret these narratives, which emphasizes prosecutors' dependence on jurors' positive assessments of their case narrative during trial (Offit 2021). Jurors, as ordinary members of the public, bring their own lived experiences, expectations, and definitions of community to the courtroom, where they face the difficult task of applying the law (and its limits) to the defendant's actions and, in so doing, to their own lives as ordinary citizens (Carroll 2014). In this respect, optimistic law and society scholars argue that serving on a jury can guide citizens to become forward thinkers who actively participate in one of the most fundamentally democratic institutions (Chakravarti 2020).

Legal Cynicism

Legal cynicism research engages with the reasons why individuals view the law and its agents as illegitimate, ineffective, and focused on assembly-line justice practices designed to funnel poor black people into prison (Soller, Jackson, and Browning 2014). Legal cynicism helps explain why residents of high-crime neighborhoods are skeptical about whether criminal cases will resolve in ways that make their everyday lives safer yet nonetheless call police to resolve immediate threats of danger (Hagan, McCarthy, and Herda 2020). Accordingly, a legal cynic who hears shots fired in their neighborhood will see no contradiction in calling police to the scene and then subsequently refusing to provide a statement to officers or prosecutors.

Legal cynicism encompasses a belief system that creates a toxic feedback loop whereby violent crime occurs much more frequently in neighborhoods where residents who view criminal justice actors as illegitimate are less likely to comply with the law, provide information to police and prosecutors about crimes, or support one another in neighborhood efforts to reduce crime (Kirk and Matsuda 2011). As a result, legal cynicism creates a cycle of reduced cooperation with police and prosecutors and associated lower rates of case resolution. Inundated with "anti-snitching edicts, fear of retaliation, legal cynicism, and high-risk victims' normative views toward self-help" (Brunson and Wade 2019, 623), residents in high-crime neighborhoods interpret lower rates of case resolution as further evidence that police and prosecutors care little about them or their neighborhoods (Campeau, Levi, and Foglesong 2021).

High-crime neighborhoods, particularly in major metropolitan areas, are also home to higher-than-average numbers of people who have served time in prison. When such individuals return to community with negative accounts of their experiences with incarceration and criminal justice more generally, legal cynicism proliferates as their family members, loved ones, and other members of their social networks accept these experiences as further evidence in support of their belief in the illegitimate and ineffective nature of the law in practice (Kirk 2016). Yet just as legal cynics reject police legitimacy, a national sample found that individuals with higher levels of belief in police legitimacy are also most likely to support police acquisition of military-grade tactical gear and training (Moule, Fox, and Parry 2019) rather than traditional community-based policing that relied on police patrol officers' deep relationships of trust with the people on their beat. As Susan's father, a retired New York State police officer who spent most of his career working narcotics, put it, "When cops started sitting in their patrol cars drinking coffee instead of being out there on the streets talking to people, everything went downhill."

Residents of poor black neighborhoods call police more frequently than residents of middle-class neighborhoods and white people more generally, yet people who are poor and black are also more likely to reside in areas where legal cynicism is pervasive (Bell 2016). Researchers explain this paradox as the product of situational trust, whereby neighborhood residents trust police to resolve immediate crises in the short term but lack the trust in criminal justice actors required for longer-term cooperation. For example, Bell (2016) found that poor black mothers use calls to police to assert social control over their partners and children in specific situations where they trust an officer, believe the police encounter will result in therapeutic goals, such as drug treatment, and/or believe that they can navigate the institutional consequences of calling police. Yet this situational trust unfortunately does not override the all-encompassing negativity of legal cynicism. Some prosecutors might interpret what Bell (2016) terms situational trust as an effort to manipulate the justice processes by accessing their collective benefits in terms of police response without being willing to participate meaningfully, as part of the collective, in the administration of justice.

POLITICAL WILL

Political will, defined as the development and implementation of shared goals in relationships between individuals and the state in the everyday administration of justice, is central to prosecutors' everyday work. As fiduciaries obligated to act in the best interests of the people of the state, prosecutors are part of the ontological formations of political will that coalesce around gun ownership and use. Prosecutors must formulate and conceptualize their decision-making in terms of the state's best interests, which means engaging with both the everyday administration of justice and their own relational understandings of popular beliefs about guns. These beliefs, after all, will guide jurors' decision-making as they interpret and evaluate the divergent case narratives presented to them by prosecutors and defense attorneys.

This section explores how prosecutors engage with political will at three levels. First, we explore prosecutors' accounts of how the gun present policy impacts their decision-making in cases. Second, we analyze how prosecutors make assessments about prospective jurors' attitudes and beliefs about guns. Third, we examine how prosecutors interpret their fiduciary relationship to the people of the state as client.

The Gun Present Policy

Prosecutor John Halcomb is well aware that everything he and his colleagues do is dictated by statute, meaning that prosecutors' authority only exists within the confines of what statutes authorize them to do. John notes how the gun present policy is a unique approach to cases involving guns "that fall outside the statutes, where guns just are silent as to when they're not an offense or an element of a crime where they're there [at the crime scene] and they create that elevated element of risk just because of their presence." As we explored at length in chapter 1, guns often appear at crime scenes irrespective of whether they are involved in the commission of the crime itself. The ubiquity of the semiautomatic handgun tucked under the driver's seat, or the shotgun wrapped in an old bath towel under the bed, is such that—prior to the implementation of the gun present policy—officers did not always report a gun's presence at a crime scene unless the defendant fired the gun, assaulted the victim by using the gun as a blunt instrument, or brandished the gun to threaten the victim.

Officers did not report the presence of unused guns at crime scenes due to the sheer ubiquity of guns in Alabama, where it is entirely normal to see a person engaging in mundane activities such as pumping gas while wearing a holstered firearm. That guns would be present as inert objects at crime scenes was as obvious to officers as the fact that a crime had been committed at the scene. The gun present policy was accordingly conceived of as the office using its authority and good name to benefit the community as broadly as possible using all tools available to maximize positive results. There is nuance to this approach, as the office implemented gun present simultaneous to the Second Chance diversion program's offering hourly salaries much higher than most regional jobs through a local workforce services agency to defendants who are unemployed when they enroll in the program. Diversion court maximizes opportunity for drug and property crime defendants, while the gun present policy minimizes further harm violent and dangerous criminals can cause to the community.

Yet prosecutors in the Second Chance diversion court program and in misdemeanor-level district court still receive felony reports that erroneously fail to note when a gun was present at, but not used in, a crime. Given the ubiquity of guns in Alabama, why impose mandatory jail time in criminal cases where guns were present but not used in the commission of the crime? As prosecutor Ashley Ross explains of defendants who were already involved in criminal activity and are now armed with a gun, "When there's a gun present, even if it's not used, there's a potential for violence. We hear all these cases where people are driving around with guns and then they just get into an argument on the street, and they shoot each other because they have a gun. Because they have it, they can use it."

Requiring jail time because of a gun's inert presence at a crime scene is a completely unique approach, as noted by prosecutors with more than a decade of experience in other jurisdictions. Shannon Lynch, who has prosecuted violent crimes involving guns for most of her career, never considered whether a gun was present as she prepared her cases. "Of course a gun was present," Shannon says of violent crime cases she prosecuted earlier in her career. "Nobody had stamped it anywhere [on the felony report]. If your person is shot, there's a gun involved. . . . I wouldn't prosecute a gun present case, I would prosecute a robbery where a gun was present, but it wasn't where I hyperfocused on it." Ben McGough, who, like Shannon, prosecuted violent crimes in another Alabama jurisdiction prior to working in Tuscaloosa, echoes Shannon's assertions. For Ben, the uniqueness of imposing mandatory jail time in all criminal cases involving guns requires a tremendous amount of political will to support such a policy. "All of my former district attorneys have certainly taken violent crime seriously," Ben says, "but we didn't have a set policy of mandatory jail for gun present cases. So, I'm having to train myself to take notes on my docket to make sure I get the mandatory jail time."

As Ben makes notes on his docket to include mandatory jail time, he does so in a context where the political will exists to enforce a policy that requires using county resources to incarcerate more people for more time. "It seems like here," Ben says, "these judges are more willing to impose more strict sentencing. And it's got the defense attorneys and the defendants to where they're willing to accept one, two, three, four, however many days in jail, rather than roll the dice on the judge sending them [to a correctional facility] for some amount of time, months, or years." Ben acknowledges that a short stay in jail is most likely to impact first-time defendants, rather than those with lengthy criminal histories. "Now, for some people, it doesn't matter," Ben says of the gun present policy. "You're going to get people who've spent half their life in prison, so three days in jail doesn't matter. But the person that I think Hays is trying to affect, the first- or second-time defendant, who was riding around with a gun, smoking some weed, I think it'll get their attention. It would certainly get my attention. If you had to go spend a weekend in jail, and it was your first time ever, and you hear the bar slam, and you've got to sit in there for the weekend or seven days or whatever."

Beth explains that, despite initial resistance from the defense bar and from defendants, the gun present policy is now the accepted norm in the county. "And things like that really do seem to spread throughout different communities in our area," Beth says. "And once the word gets around, people understand the risk that they're taking by having a gun with them." The culture surrounding guns in our region is such that, as Thomas puts it,

"There's a good percentage of the population that owns guns, has guns, knows people that has guns." In a place where so many people are gun owners, the question of whom the state should allow to be in possession of a firearm and under what circumstances they may use it is particularly heated.

"Guns are amoral," John explains matter-of-factly. "It's who is with the gun and what they're doing with it that determines the narrative. That's the truest version of the story. What they do [at a crime scene] is bad, more times than not. What they're capable of doing [at a crime scene] is never good, but a gun in and of itself is otherwise inert, for the most part." A gun sitting on a table or dropped by the person carrying it rarely fires on its own, John notes, and such malfunctions are easily preventable through measures such as proper storage and handling. Yet a gun present at a crime scene has a different meaning altogether, especially in a context where, as was the case in most of the United States at the time of writing, shootings are at an all-time high.

"With the rising gun violence," another prosecutor explains, "it's more necessary than ever that we do take it as seriously as we do here. If people looked at it and thought, 'Oh, you're way too rough on gun charges,' they obviously don't see what's going on with the rising violence. . . . The work we're doing here is necessary and immensely valuable." This prosecutor provides an example of a defendant who pled guilty at the end of February to a misdemeanor pistol without a permit charge and received a 360-day suspended sentence, served his mandatory five days in jail for the gun charge, and then, two weeks after his release on probation, committed multiple auto burglaries while attempting to steal guns from vehicles and received another six months in jail on the original charge.

"I've been a prosecutor for a little over ten years," Ben says, "and the presence of a gun can turn a traffic stop into a cop either being murdered or the cop having to kill a person, very quickly." Ben spent the majority of his time prosecuting capital murder and murder cases in the last jurisdiction where he worked, which means he has seen hundreds of cases involving guns used to harm others. Drug deals gone wrong. Juveniles with guns executing drive-by shootings at the residence of another juvenile who disrespected their rap. Domestic violence cases. And then there are the cases that defy this norm. For example, Ben vividly recalls prosecuting a road rage case where the defendant had never even received a speeding ticket prior to the day that he became enraged after another driver cut him off in traffic, he chased the other driver for three miles, and when the other driver pulled into a neighborhood, the defendant got out of his own vehicle, walked up to the other driver's (the victim's) vehicle, and shot him dead.

Ben, who owns numerous firearms and is typically carrying one unless he is at the office or at the gym, observes how "the presence of a gun changes road rage and middle fingers into this dude sitting in jail and somebody being dead. . . . If the goal of the program is to have less guns in the hands of people who make bad decisions, then I'm all for it. I'm against any program that keeps law-abiding citizens, who are good decision makers, from having guns."

Ascertaining Prospective Jurors' Attitudes and Beliefs about Guns

Ashley has a lot on her mind as she considers how the prospective jurors seated before her during voir dire think about guns. Every time she asks prospective jurors to identify themselves as gun owners, "ninety percent of the hands go up because we're in Alabama." Once Ashley has this information about her prospective jurors, she needs to decide what else she needs to learn about them in the brief time she has during voir dire to question them. She may ask if they have a bumper sticker on their car with an image of a gun or an NRA logo. If prospective jurors feel strongly enough about their legal rights to own firearms that they want to publicly advertise their feelings with a bumper sticker clearly visible to all passersby, they may be more likely to support prosecutors' arguments in a shooting case with a defendant whose felony criminal record prohibits him from owning a gun. Yet the same prospective juror with the bumper sticker advocating gun ownership could also disagree with prosecutors' arguments in a case where the defendant claims he shot the victim in self-defense. After all, that prospective juror may believe very strongly that everyone has a right to defend themselves irrespective of the circumstances or the legality of a self-defense claim.

To understand how her prospective jurors might interpret the facts of a case involving a gun, Ashley begins by asking questions of those assembled in the room. Depending upon the facts of the case, the circumstances of the crime, and the defense attorney's claims, the questions might include the following: Who belongs to a gun rights organization? Of those individuals, who attends rallies or annual meetings held by the organization? In what circumstances is it right to carry a gun? Is it fine to carry a holstered gun through Walmart? What about leaving a gun in a car? Within easy reach by the bedside? Ashley will also ask her prospective jurors about their motivations for owning guns. Did someone break into their home, prompting them to purchase a gun for protection? Did they buy a gun because they wanted to hold one, because it looks cool? Answers to these questions will help her understand how prospective jurors may conceptualize the facts of a case involving a gun.

"You voir dire to your audience," Shannon explains of her approach to questioning prospective jurors, and in Tuscaloosa that means a group who are "incredibly red. They're all about the open carry, and they want to carry a gun into the Kentucky Fried Chicken." With jurors like these, Shannon would want to know their views on the gun's potential for violence and their feelings about their constitutional right to own a deadly weapon. The approach Shannon uses in Tuscaloosa County is different from when Shannon prosecuted cases in Selma with majority black juries who, she explains, "are going to feel differently about a gun. They're also going to be affected by guns differently ... [in] a place like Selma that is so high in crime." With jurors in Selma, Shannon wanted to understand the impact guns have had on their lives. Had anyone in their family or their past been hurt by a gun? Have they been a victim of a violent crime involving a gun? These questions are critical to understanding how prospective jurors' views will impact their interpretation of prosecutors' arguments in a case, Shannon notes, because "a gun in your hand is not going to hurt you or anybody else. The reason that they are inherently dangerous is what happens later."

Paula emphasizes how, despite the importance of determining which prospective jurors are most likely to side with the prosecutor's argument, the ultimate goal of voir dire is to determine which prospective jurors "can set their own personal beliefs to the side and listen to the facts and apply the law to the evidence." She acknowledges how challenging it is to stand in front of an audience of prospective jurors while fully aware that "there's no way to know the dynamic of how many people are on one end of the spectrum of having tons and tons of guns and love guns and want everybody to have a gun versus the person on the other end who thinks that no one should have a gun." The prosecutor's task is to cut through the broad views about gun ownership to get the prospective jurors talking, so that the prosecutor can ascertain who might, as Paula warns, "take those strong feelings into the jury room and impose their will on other people."

Paula tried something new during her last voir dire to encourage prospective jurors to speak up. She opened with the office's belief in responsible gun ownership and shared how she safely stores her firearm, emphasizing the words *legal, ownership, responsible,* and *safe* to build an ideological bridge between prospective jurors who believe strongly in gun ownership, while also using key terms that even those prospective jurors who may virulently oppose gun ownership can recognize as lawful. She then contrasted how she responsibly handles her own gun with someone who uses a gun under the influence of drugs and alcohol, which presumably no prospective juror would regard as responsible.

Ben, who was observing Paula during voir dire, noticed how well her approach elicited clear and specific responses regarding prospective jurors' beliefs about guns. "I got a bunch of guns, but I don't think it's any of the government's business what they are," one man said when Paula asked everyone to share the type of gun they own, "and I'm not going to say what they are in front of all these peoples, because I don't want anybody to break in my house and steal them. But I've got guns, and that's all I'm going to say." Ben worries about the potential for this approach to unduly shift prospective jurors' views of the prosecutor. "I don't want to telegraph my thoughts," Ben explains. "If I've got people on the jury who love guns, we're probably going to get along. But if I end up with somebody on the jury who abhors violent crime and abhors criminality, but thinks we need to take all the guns off the streets and I tell them, 'I've got six AR-15s in a gun safe at my mom's house,' we're going to have a problem."

"Look, ladies and gentlemen," John tells prospective jurors in a gun case, "you are going to probably see me at Walmart after I'm leaving here, and I just want you all to know that if you see me out there, there's probably a ninety-nine percent chance that there is a gun on me someplace, because I carry. And I believe in the right to bear arms. I believe in protecting myself, I believe in having a permit to do so. And I believe in doing all those things lawfully." Once he establishes himself as someone who regularly carries a gun, he carefully observes changes in prospective jurors' demeanor to distinguish between those more likely to align with prosecutors' arguments in the case and those who may disagree. Who is quiet, or shifting in their seat in response to certain questions?

John prosecuted a manslaughter case in which the defendant had a history of brandishing his .45 pistol with elaborate Latin phrases engraved on the handle and, after years of threatening others with his firearm, used it to shoot the victim during a fight they had over a woman. This case forced John to parse out prospective jurors who are "maybe potential militia types, your sovereign citizen types, or people with those kinds of leanings" from the more desirable prospective gun-owning jurors. This task posed a dilemma because, as John observes, there is "a fine, fine line between that person and probably most of your everyday folks in a place like Tuscaloosa, especially when you get out into the county areas." John's point speaks to significant differences in the meanings associated with guns in rural areas of the county, where violent crime is almost nonexistent despite the ubiquity of guns.

For example, it is unremarkable for Susan to see a shotgun balanced on the seat of a pickup truck whose driver pulls over to ask her a question as she is walking on the dirt road where she lives. Susan's neighbor farmers sometimes talk about Tuscaloosa as if it were a war zone, just as people in Tuscaloosa sometimes talk about the country area where Susan lives in ways that resemble representations of country life offered in the movie *Deliverance*. Yet, as is almost always the case, these stereotypes are rooted in realities about what guns mean in context. Guns are a core aspect of self-sufficiency for rural people who depend on wild game and livestock for protein rather than purchasing meat raised in abysmal factory farming conditions. When Susan is reading in bed late at night and hears gunshots echo in the woods surrounding her farm, she wonders if a coyote is threatening a neighbor farmer's livestock, a dangerous pack of feral hogs is rampaging through crops, or an opossum got into a compost bin. If Brittany or Hays hears gunshots at their homes in town, they would be wise to call the police because the only reason to fire a gun in town is to harm another person. While Susan may also hear shots fired where she lives because a poacher is illegally hunting for food, and thus breaking the law, gunshots have a very different meaning in the country.

The ability to make informed assessments about prospective jurors' attitudes and beliefs about guns requires what Grace calls "becoming a master of information about guns" to speak knowledgably to an audience of gun owners in court. Grace clearly remembers confusing the words *projectile* and *shell casing* during her first trial. She later joined a shared initiative with all other assistant district attorneys in the office to visit the police shooting range and learned everything she could about firearms. She juxtaposes her own knowledge with that of prospective jurors who are highly skilled at shooting, including those with military experience, to bolster the knowledge of gun owners with less training. For example, defense attorneys in attempted murder cases often argue that the defendant did not intend to kill the victim, an argument easily rendered hollow by those with significant knowledge about guns. "And what was your training with guns in the military?" Grace asks a prospective juror, who curtly responds with "Shoot to kill, ma'am," quickly establishing that any reasonable person holding a gun should be aware of its tremendous power. "If somebody slows their car down, comes to a complete stop, reaches their arm out and points, but they get the guy in the leg, they still intended to kill him," Grace says. "They just were a bad shot."

Shadrian prosecuted an attempted murder case with a victim who was shot twice and two witnesses who did not want to participate in the prosecution. The lack of meaningful victim and witness participation meant that Shadrian approached voir dire worried that the defense attorney might convince prospective jurors that the defendant did not intend to kill the victim because the bullets lodged in the victim's lower body. Shadrian accordingly wanted gun owners with experience around new shooters who, unaccustomed to the firearm's recoil, may shoot lower than their intended target. "Being a gun owner myself," Shadrian says, "gun owners like responsible gun owners and so . . . if you have a defendant who's obviously not a responsible gun owner, they are extra upset at them, which helps my case."

Prosecutors' Fiduciary Relationship to the People of the State as Client

Prosecutors represent the people of the state as their client as part of their fiduciary relationship to the state. This means respecting the rights of all parties involved in a case. "We still respect your role in the system," Hays says of a hypothetical defendant, "but when we're convinced you're guilty of this crime we're going to prosecute you." "Your guy did this to himself and to my community and the community is my client," Shadrian recalls telling a defense attorney who accused him of making a defendant, one of four charged with nine counts of first-degree robbery and one first-degree burglary, an unreasonable plea offer. Shadrian is in a protective bubble when he is in his office on the fourth floor of the courthouse reviewing felony reports and determining plea offers to make to defendants. Yet this bubble can rapidly burst, as it did when two of the four defense attorneys in this case accosted him with some version of "I can't believe this!" in response to his plea offers to the four defendants who together committed ten Class A felonies in just a few weeks.

Shadrian gestures to the neatly written notes about the case posted on his office wall. "They needed the offer they got, and that's why," he explains by describing elements of the case: the fact that the defendants traveled to Tuscaloosa County on multiple occasions specifically to commit the robberies, that they stole thousands of dollars from their victims, and, of course, that they used a gun to threaten their victims. "These are some of the most serious crimes in Alabama," he says. "I've managed a way to make myself comfortable with saying, 'No, your guy's got to go.'" In this example, we see Shadrian in his role as community defender through his work as a prosecutor.

Grace likewise carefully considers the risks a defendant poses to the community very early in her review of a case through a public safety analysis. As she asks herself what she needs to do to best serve the public by upholding public safety, Grace carefully examines the defendant's role in the community and the nature of their crime. "Violent [defendants], then I need to protect the public from them," she says. "Nonviolent [defendants], I need to help them serve the public because if they're not necessarily a danger, thefts, drugs, things like that, I think that it best serves a community to give them the resources that they need to succeed and then be a good member of society who gives back to society, has a job, provides for their family, and can give back."

Protecting the community, rather than specific individuals, is a key aspect of the ethos prosecutors embrace in their fiduciary role. Yet herein lies a paradox that prosecutors find themselves reconciling on a daily basis: how to protect the public when victims and witnesses refuse to participate in the case against the defendant. "We don't represent the victims," Thomas notes. "We're the state. We try to protect the public's health, safety, best interests, along with the victims and everyone else. Because I mean, if every victim, if every case got dismissed because a victim didn't want to prosecute it, we would not have a job." Grace makes a similar observation, describing this paradox as her primary source of stress at work. "I don't serve the victim," she states. "I serve every single citizen in Tuscaloosa County. How do I protect the public if I can't proceed? If the victim who's been shot won't come up here?"

For most prosecutors, the knowledge that their work upholds public safety on behalf of the state mitigates their considerable stress. This moral stance is in itself a powerful motivator. "You're doing a civic good to protect the public," a prosecutor explained, "and that's rewarding in itself, even though you understand that you're going to be sacrificing a little bit of sanity sometimes to be doing things that other people might not want to do. Because there is a burden. You feel a weight with your actions . . . you're affecting these people's lives. And so, with that work/life balance, you kind of understand like, 'Okay, I'm giving up this, but I'm getting to help the public in a way that others might not want to.'"

CRIMINAL JUSTICE ACTORS

Analyzing the roles prosecutors play in their relationships with other actors in the justice assemblage helps illuminate the distinctly human qualities of the justice assemblage. Prevailing conceptions of a *criminal justice system* interpret actions taken within it as machinelike and resulting in an assembly line that moves from arrest to adjudication with a fixed set of processes and outcomes. Yet the individuals charged with interpreting individual actions according to the law understand their work as fundamentally comprised of the individuals who carry out the justice assemblage's every-day administration. The justice assemblage relies on individuals—rather than an abstract system—to carry out its work, and points of individual connection and disconnection in the roles and relationships fundamentally inform how it functions. Simply put, how individual justice assemblage actors perceive one another as individuals has a fundamental impact on how they do their work. To understand how prosecutors perceive their role in relation to other justice assemblage actors, we now turn to a discussion of how individual prosecutors interpret their professional relationships to individual police investigators, defense attorneys, judges, and jurors.

"It's hard to keep fighting when everybody's against you," Ben sighs as he reflects on his decade-long career as a prosecutor. "The judges are against you. A lot of times the juries are against you. Defense attorneys are certainly against you. The defendant's against you." Ben's sense of besiege-ment at the beating heart of the justice assemblage is common among prosecutors, whose role requires them to view themselves as fighting a case on behalf of the state—and often despite victims and witnesses who do not want to participate—in sharp contrast to judges tasked with impartial adju-dication, juries saturated by inaccurate media portrayals of criminal justice, defense attorneys representing an individual client, and, of course, defend-ants accused of violating the law.

Police Investigators

"Our job is so hard as it is, and the relationships make things so easy, much easier," Grace says of her cooperative relationships with police investigators. This cooperation between police and prosecutors is not guaranteed by virtue of their roles, and instead depends on close relationships of trust between individuals. "Law enforcement, even the best of them, they have a different view than us," Grace notes of the short- and long-term perspectives respec-tively taken by police and prosecutors, with police more concerned with eliminating immediate threats to public safety through arrest and prosecu-tors more concerned with upholding public safety in the longer term through the adjudication of cases. These temporally divergent approaches can be a source of conflict between police and prosecutors. For example, 911 call records and police body cam footage are destroyed after a period of time, making it essential for police and prosecutors to coordinate early in a case to ensure preservation of these important pieces of evidence. Yet these different perspectives can also be a strength as police and prosecutors work together.

"The officers are on the street. They know it better than we do," Thomas says. "So they do have a different perspective from what we have, and they might have different feelings on someone than what we have." For officers who see firsthand the fear and suffering people experience while living near a residence they know contains illegal firearms and controlled substances, it can be extremely frustrating when insufficient evidence exists to stop that suffering by arresting those causing it. Officers have far greater familiarity than prosecutors with individuals involved in cases, and since many officers grew up in Tuscaloosa, they accordingly have greater familiarity with neighborhood dynamics than do prosecutors. While Thomas, who is not from Tuscaloosa, may use the statewide Alacourt system to search a defendant's criminal history, that system does not document the fact that a defendant has been a suspect in fifteen different crimes. "It is difficult when an officer comes up [to my office] and they want to really hammer someone on the charge," Thomas explains, "but I want proof, I'm bound by the guidelines. I can only do what I can do."

Consider the significant differences between what police officers and prosecutors see in a shooting case that results in a murder. Police who respond to the scene see the angry tears left by a bullet hole in the wall in front of them, hear distraught family members and bystanders traumatized by their victimization, smell the body in the summer heat at the crime scene, and, if they arrive soon enough after the shooting has occurred, detect the metallic odor hanging in the humid air following a gunshot. These sensory experiences surround policing day after day and stay with them even when they do not have sufficient evidence to build a case. Prosecutors, in contrast, review the felony report from a climate-controlled office—albeit one where they work extremely long hours—and visit the scene long after the crime has occurred. Hence Thomas's characterization of police who want to "hammer someone" captures their unique perspective as people who experience the crime almost in tandem with the victim and defendant and so understandably envision justice as encompassing the totality of circumstances surrounding the case, rather than just what is written in the felony report.

Prosecutors rapidly hit the limitations on their abilities to move forward with a case when faced with insufficient evidence recognized by the law, such as seized guns and drugs or victim and witness statements. Multiple confidential reports and neighbor complaints to police are sufficient grounds for a judge to issue a search warrant on a residence neighbors know contains illegal guns and controlled substances, but police cannot make an arrest without evidence of a crime. The case may go nowhere, leaving neighbors angered by what they sometimes perceive as police inaction, police frustrated with their insufficient evidence to make an arrest, and prosecutors dismayed with the knowledge that the residence may become another shooting or murder scene in the wake of a drug deal gone wrong.

John sees three ways to get perspective in conversations with police investigators, as he has yet to read a felony report containing all the information police have about a case. So, he reads the felony report, speaks with the officer who wrote the report for a second perspective, and then accompanies the officer to the scene where the crime took place to more fully understand its context. On scene, John wants to be able to visualize how a case unfolded by examining the scene's depth, range, and dimensions.

For Ashley, working with police is a collaborative decision-making process that bridges the gap between their respective areas of expertise. "They sometimes don't know a lot of our world, we sometimes don't know a lot of their world," she says, "and it's bridging that gap because they've got the facts, I've got the law, how do we piece them together in a nice puzzle?" Piecing this puzzle together requires asking a lot of questions, particularly for new prosecutors. What does that police acronym mean? How did police get a confidential informant's tip in this case? How did the officer carry out the knock and talk, a police procedure in which officers visit an individual to inform them of mounting evidence that they are breaking the law?

Prosecutors effectively function as state-appointed translators tasked with interpreting events, as relayed by police, according to the law. For Kymberly, this act of translation requires detailed information that she will potentially present to a jury, which means asking many questions of police who worked a case. What did the officer do on a case? Was he or she the lead investigator? What did all the other police do? What was done with the evidence? Was the evidence tested? What are the results? If the evidence wasn't sent for testing, why not? Was everyone who might have seen something interviewed? If not, why? Where are their statements? These are the questions Kymberly will have to answer in court to convince a jury.

"Each time our office talks to the jury after the trial, whether it's a guilty or a not guilty," Kymberly says, "one of the things they say is 'Oh, I wish I had heard from such-and-such' or 'Why didn't they do this?'" She prosecuted a murder case with a defendant and victim who both used flip phones that police placed in evidence but had not sent for forensic testing because flip phones only record calls made and received, rather than other potentially helpful data such as location, text messages, and a record of internet searches for information by the defendant. Yet posttrial, jurors still wanted to know why no one forensically examined the flip phones, even though prosecutors explained that such examination would not have yielded any further relevant information. As a result, Kymberly always asks investigators detailed questions about the investigation. "And, of course," she says of newer investigators who lack extensive experience testifying in court, "he looks at me like I'm crazy, and then I'll explain to him why we're going through all of the things that didn't happen in the investigation, whether they were needed or not."

Lyndsie takes a similar approach in preparing investigators to testify in court. She finds that this approach works best when she presents it to the investigator as "Okay, so when you're on the stand, if I'm questioning you, here's what I'm going to be asking. Tell me your answer. You need to have an answer for this question, because it's going to be asked of you." By establishing rapport with the officer as they jointly prepare for trial, Lyndsie is able to effectively address any potential issues in the investigation that may emerge in court. "I'm not attacking you right now," she wants the investigator to know. "I'm just trying to get you ready for the person who's going to later."

This can create challenges for police investigators who may interpret this questioning of the evidence as questioning their professionalism. Lyndsie's goal in questioning police is to find the truth, not get to a particular result, because the truth should be able to withstand any scrutiny, which requires asking a lot of questions. Even seemingly minute details of a case can take on extreme importance, which means that prosecutors who do not challenge all aspects of a case from multiple angles are unlikely to succeed.

Defense Attorneys

As prosecutors prepare police investigators to testify in court, they simultaneously craft their case narratives in silent dialogue with how they anticipate defense attorneys might respond. For Corey, this involves a balance between developing a case narrative based on the facts she knows she can prove while remaining mindful of the defense's argument. "You can get so deep into a case whenever you're preparing for trial," Corey warns, "that you are so on defense for what the defense is going to say, that you end up playing ball on their field. . . . You end up, 'Okay, I know this is what they're going to do. I know this is what they're going to say. So let me frame my case on that field' and that I don't ever think is helpful. . . . You play on your field, don't ever veer off to theirs because then I think the impact of what you're saying loses force and effectiveness."

Allowing a defense attorney to distract from the facts of the case also creates a potentially winning argument for the defense with something that is irrelevant, ending in jury nullification or otherwise when prosecutors pander to interests outside facts and law. "We might have a hundred facts and use seven most relevant to the case," Hays explains. "Defense attorneys want to draw you out to fight on their field. If there's any potential doubt about evidence that can be the nail on which jurors hang their hats to find the defendant not guilty. We lose force and effectiveness if we fight/play on their field. We've done all the explaining and should have the evidence to win without distraction."

Defense attorneys who regard prosecutors as a powerful enemy and their relationship as inherently adversarial are making a major mistake, Corey believes. "I think a lot of defense attorneys don't trust that we're actually trying to get it right," she says as she describes observing numerous flaws in cases defense attorneys present for trial. "I just think, 'Why is that case going to trial?'" she says of those instances. "You don't have enough. What are you doing? I just think that if we are truly trying to get it right, then it should work out," meaning that the facts of the case intersect with the law to produce a fair and just result.

"Defense attorneys all the time will tell me, 'Hey, this person—the victim—doesn't want to prosecute,'" Thomas shares, regarding defense attorneys who attempt to persuade him to dismiss a case before making a plea offer. "I don't give a damn. I don't think he should get away with that. I don't care if that person, the victim, does not want to prosecute. I'm going to do what I can. And at the end of the day if my hands are tied, that case gets called for trial. My victim's the only witness. I don't have anything else to prove it and I've got to dismiss it. All right. Well, that's it."

Persevering until reaching a case's procedural limits is a key aspect of a prosecutor's job, and one made considerably more difficult when defense attorneys envision themselves as social justice crusaders. "I was born in Alabama. I've lived in Alabama my whole life. I've only been outside of Alabama maybe five times. I'm all Alabama," Ben prefaces his discussion of the ease with which defense attorneys are able to step into the crusader role. "Of course, Alabama has a horrible reputation for everything except football. And everybody thinks we're down here just locking people up." These stereotypes make it even more important for prosecutors to conduct themselves in a collegial manner by always acting professionally in the face of mudslinging.

Ben recalls prosecuting cases in an Alabama jurisdiction that participates in a program that pays graduates from prestigious northeastern law schools to work in underserved public defenders' offices. After trying a case with a defense attorney paid through this program, Ben came away with the sense that the defense attorney's attitude was "we're just a bunch of backwoods hillbillies that are just locking up everybody. . . . 'Oh, there's a poor black man. We'll just throw him in prison.'" Such experiences intensify the sense of besiegement prosecutors experience within the justice assemblage, particularly given the reality that, like most defendants, most victims of violent crimes in our jurisdiction are black.

Judges and Juries

"Sometimes it feels like defense attorneys and the judge are just like, 'Well, nothing we can do,'" Grace says, acknowledging how this sense of hopelessness can vary tremendously depending on the case and the individuals involved. The judge in the courtroom where she prosecutes cases, for example, is unrelenting in cases involving guns. Yet this is not the case for all judges and all cases. For example, domestic violence cases—particularly when the victim does not want to prosecute—may quickly be dismissed. The shifting nature of approaches to these cases depends entirely on the individuals involved.

"In a murder case, I often ask for life," says Ben, because of the severity of the charge and its surrounding circumstances. Ben used to experience intense stress around judges' decision-making when he prosecuted cases for ten years in Montgomery prior to coming to Tuscaloosa. "If the judge gives ten years, that's on the judge. You've done your job. You've gotten your conviction, once we either hear a jury say 'Guilty' or we hear a defendant say 'Guilty.'" Judges no longer dictate Ben's level of stress, although this is challenging given what Ben describes as the "judge-centric" nature of prosecutors' work. "They dictate all the outcomes of our decisions," he explains. "They decide if your evidence comes in or not. They decide your objections. . . . I got to rely on this judge to know the law and care about the law. . . . I can do everything right, and this judge can just totally tank it and go, 'No, I'm not letting you get into that,' and it's extremely frustrating, and juries are the same way."

Prosecutors are not freelancers. They work collectively, and much is indeed out of prosecutors' hands and up to the judge. Judges make determinations as individuals and are elected officials, which means judges may also be ideologues, although that does not happen in our jurisdiction. Yet judges also make these determinations within the boundaries of the law, as they do when they rule on admissibility of evidence, while also exercising discretion while acting as community representatives in, for example, determining bond amounts and sentencing length.

Like judges, juries wield tremendous power in cases as part of their roles within, and relationships to, the justice assemblage. Prosecutors' relationship to jurors begins with the grand jury, which makes determinations regarding whether sufficient evidence exists for a case to proceed.

Prospective grand jurors, like their counterparts on a petit jury for trial, receive notice by mail and then arrive at court to be sworn in by a judge, who asks them questions regarding whether they have been convicted of a felony and any reasons they cannot serve on the grand jury. Responses to these questions eliminate those disqualified to serve on the grand jury, after which the judge randomly selects eighteen people to serve on the grand jury, including a foreperson and assistant foreperson. A bookkeeper and assistant bookkeeper volunteer to keep records of the cases they decide, as they deliberate each case and vote whether or not to indict in each case based on their determination of whether probable cause exists.

Ashley Ratliff, the grand jury law clerk, envisions herself as the office ambassador on the grand jury. She makes it her mission to educate grand jurors, who typically have five hundred cases per grand jury session, about their central role in the justice process because she knows that personal testimonies are powerful and that grand jurors will share their experiences with their spouses and community. "This is an office on behalf of the people," she explains, "teaching the law and sharing hospitality. We have the same standards for all cases, all people. Grand jury is everyone and they make the decisions. I wish more people knew it's community that makes the decision and everything goes through them. . . . What our community doesn't see is how hard these prosecutors work. People have no idea about the grand jury process, that there's no picking which prosecutor is assigned to each case, no manipulating this system. I didn't even know that was a thing until I worked here! In school we learn about Alabama government, but we don't learn about it at the county level, so people don't know."

Typically, each grand jury handles five hundred cases, and despite this high caseload, the office is the fastest in the state because cases are presented to the grand jury within thirty days of arrest. "Everything that happens here is a secret," John explains to the eighteen grand jurors who will review the facts of five hundred cases to determine whether the state has sufficient grounds to proceed with criminal charges. He emphasizes to the grand jurors that "they're the boss" because they decide what questions and facts are important and the truth of the matter based on the facts of the case. His goal is to put the grand jurors in the mindset of "they're the boss, they control, they dictate what questions they want to ask, what witnesses they want to call."

Grand jurors should remember one thing, John says, and that is "government has no business deciding whether or not we should prosecute people. The community just needs to decide that. . . . If you say there's no case, there's no case. The government can't touch this person. So, I want you to understand and appreciate how important your role is. Not just how important, that it's vital. And I sleep well at night knowing the government does not have the authority to decide what you think needs to happen with a member of your own community."

John reassures the grand jurors because he knows that, for some of them, the decisions they make in the grand jury room are some of the most momentous they will make in their lives given their impact on the potential defendants. "And you're not deciding ultimately what's going to happen to him," he reminds the grand jurors. "It's going to take another group of jurors to figure that out only if you indicted him or her, but I love this system better than any other because of that reason. And I believe in limited government for that reason. I would be scared to death if it were left up to us to decide all those things."

John's efforts to build a professional relationship with grand jurors as decision-makers on behalf of the community are a version of those same efforts prosecutors and defense attorneys undertake with prospective jurors during voir dire, the first step in a jury trial. Understanding the beliefs and values prospective jurors bring to that relationship is key to determining how jurors will interpret the facts of the case. Thomas recently prosecuted an attempted murder case where his only evidence was a 911 call. "Why would someone not want to testify against someone else?" was the first question he asked the prospective jurors, who immediately cited fear or not wanting a family member to go to prison. For Thomas, this implants his theory of the case in the jury's collective mind so that the jury, when he returns to a victim's or witness's fear of testifying during closing arguments, "they're connected to me and my story."

Building a relationship with the jury is also critical to establishing a prosecutor's credibility, Thomas notes, "Because if I get up there at opening and say, 'I'm going to prove one, two, three,' and seven, eight, nine comes out, and nothing I said has been proven, how can they believe anything I say?" Prosecutors have a strong belief that jurors must trust, and even like, them for the verdict to go in the state's favor. "You could do this job and you could glance at the file before you go up there and you could do an open and say, 'You know what? I wasn't there, but they're going to tell you, and this is what I think they're going to tell you happened,'" Corey acknowledges, "and you could just ask them general questions about what happened and get them to say, 'Yeah, that person shot that person' and be done, but that's not effective. We just want to do so much more. We want to get the facts right. We want to tell those facts in a compelling storylike way that really makes jurors interested and care about getting it right. That takes a ton of work, a ton of work."

This work involves mastery over minute case details to avoid losing credibility that, as Corey says, "is the worst thing I think you can do in a trial." When she is presenting facts to a jury about events she did not witness, Corey relies on her witnesses who are willing to testify to help her tell the story. Every detail must be correct, or she risks losing the jurors' trust. "Even if it's a small detail," she says, "if you're wrong in the small things, a juror could say, 'Well, what else are you wrong about?'"

Successfully building a relationship with jurors also requires consideration of the relationships that jurors have in their own lives and how those relationships will influence their evaluation of the facts of the case. Kymberly prosecuted a discharging a firearm into an occupied vehicle case involving extremely fraught family dynamics in a tightly knit rural community. Parents of a teenage girl grew increasingly frustrated with her sneaking out at night to drink and use drugs with older men until one night her father parked his pickup truck on an isolated dirt logging road near their home to await her arrival. When the man driving the teenager pulled into a nearby parking lot because they needed to clean up the beer she spilled all over the inside of his truck, her father jumped on the man and began assaulting him. The man freed himself, and while he was driving away, the father started shooting into the air and then lowered his gun and shot into the truck.

"Well, Dad never denied doing any of this," Kymberly explains as she reflects on her considerations during voir dire of the prospective jurors' own family relationships. To win her case, she needed prospective jurors to understand that "it doesn't matter that you thought that this guy was sneaking your kid out. Doesn't matter that you thought that he was helping her to drinks and drugs, et cetera. The fact of the matter is you shot into a vehicle while someone was in it." She did not want people on the jury who had difficult children, and accordingly might identify with the defendant, or who had themselves been difficult as a child and might not be able to impartially apply the law. "What really mattered is what he did, not why he did it," she explains. "Because it's not a legal defense. And so that's how I went into that jury selection, just trying to see who would agree with that behavior and making sure they're not on my jury."

"It's extraordinarily stressful to try to craft questioning that leads random people into a place that you would like for them to go," Shadrian acknowledges, and so he uses the jury selection process as a time to begin presenting his theory of the case to prospective jurors. He observes how keenly some prosecutors observe prospective jurors' reactions during voir dire and later, during trial, but notes that there is no real way to know what they are actually thinking. "Even if six people aren't paying attention or they're really apathetic towards the whole thing," he says of his attempts to engage the jury, "hopefully there's six people who are like, 'Actually, the state's point made sense.'"

While we can never know what jurors were truly thinking during a case, surveys of jurors can help provide some insights into how they arrive at their decisions. The Tuscaloosa County District Attorney's Office sends all jurors a detailed survey posttrial that asks a range of questions about their experiences serving on the jury. We randomly selected surveys from jury trials in cases where a gun was present and at least two jurors completed the survey. We focused our analysis on two survey questions pertinent to the relationships prosecutors build with jurors in the course of a jury trial. The first question asked, "Was there any particular event during the trial that helped you make your decision?" The second asked, "In your opinion, did the State need to strengthen its case or the presentation of its case?"

The eight jurors who completed the survey after the trial of a defendant in an attempted murder case noted they were variously persuaded by video evidence pinpointing the victim's position in the vehicle at the time he was shot in relation to the defendant's position at the time he fired, the victim and three witnesses providing testimony to the facts of the case, and the identification of forty-five spent shell casings in both the defendant's and the victim's vehicle at the same time. The jurors wished prosecutors had presented character witnesses, better quality video that conclusively showed the defendant aiming at the victim and firing (rather than randomly firing in fear), fingerprints on the shell casings, the option to convict on lesser charges of assault, "a clear declaration of motive," witness testimony from a man witnesses stated attempted to break up a fight between the defendant and victim, and witness testimony from the police chief who was on scene.

We see evidence of the CSI effect in these and many other juror surveys through high—and even unrealistic—expectations of forensic evidence that then affects jurors' trial decisions without their even being aware of how media has influenced their decision-making (Hayes and Levett 2013). In a mock juror experiment, frequent crime drama viewers returned more confident not guilty verdicts compared to those who infrequently watched crime media (Hawkins and Scherr 2017). Differences in personality or political orientation did not explain these differences among mock jurors, as when researchers exposed mock jurors to crime dramas more frequently they began to offer more confident not guilty verdicts at the same rate as mock jurors who were frequent watchers prior to the study (Hawkins and Scherr 2017). Such results have led some criminologists to conclude that juror bias from the CSI effect "has resulted in increasing the burden of proof laid upon the state at trial from beyond a reasonable doubt to beyond any doubt. This raised standard of proof has allowed guilty defendants to go free because of this bias" (Eatley, Hueston, and Price 2016, 1).

In a capital murder and kidnapping case, the five jurors who completed the survey were persuaded by codefendants' testimony, the defendant's apology to the witness for shooting him, and physical evidence on one of the weapons. The jurors wished prosecutors had presented witnesses who were not under subpoena and law enforcement witnesses who were more familiar with the details of the crime scene. In a first-degree (armed) robbery case, the two jurors who completed the survey were persuaded by an expert witness's identification of the defendant's DNA on a mask and testimony from the defendant's sister, although the jurors wished they had phone records, video footage of a car chase involving the defendant, and further explanation of DNA analysis in layperson's terms to help understand their results, definitions of analysis terms, and meaning. The CSI effect again emerges in these cases given jurors' frequent references to DNA evidence in police and forensic dramas (Rhineberger-Dunn, Briggs, and Rader 2016). Likewise, a study of mock jurors found they regarded DNA evidence, followed by video confession evidence, eyewitness testimony, and fingerprint evidence, as most important at trial (Schweitzer and Nunez 2018).

Some jurors reported being wholly convinced of the defendant's guilt and found no faults in the prosecutors' presentation of the case. In another first-degree (armed) robbery case, the three jurors who completed the survey were convinced by a video of the defendant holding a gun and saw no faults in prosecutors' presentation of the case. Likewise, the two jurors who completed the survey in a kidnapping, burglary, and attempted murder case were convinced solely by watching a video of police questioning the defendant. Two jurors who completed surveys in an attempted murder and shooting a firearm into an unoccupied residence case were convinced by the testimony of a witness who saw the defendant with the gun and tried to stop him from shooting, and regarded the fact that the codefendants fled the scene as incriminating in itself.

In a shooting into an occupied building case, the two jurors who completed the survey were persuaded by a recording of the defendant talking about the night in question but felt that prosecutors should have presented additional witnesses. Two jurors who completed the survey in a murder case were convinced by the accuracy of the shots fired and the fact that the defendant made no attempt to leave the scene before shooting, although they felt the case lacked context in terms of the relationship between defendant and victim. Five jurors who completed the survey in an attempted murder and shooting into an occupied building case were convinced by witness testimony, the confidence with which one of the witnesses testified, and the 911 recording featuring the defendant's sister naming him as the shooter. These jurors noted the case would have benefited from more witnesses, video of the investigator questioning the defendant, and DNA evidence.

These juror surveys raise questions about the role of video and eyewitness testimony at trial. Yet even video evidence is susceptible to interpretation, as is evident in a law review article aptly titled "Do You See What I See?" (Birck 2019). Its author notes "how implicit biases and the myth of video objectivity can create problems in viewing body-camera footage" and that lawyers and judges should emphasize the limited nature of police body camera footage given its subjective nature (Birck 2019, 153). Video evidence is hardly objective at trial because jurors are watching it in a context that asks them to draw broad conclusions about what they are seeing and, in turn, brings jurors' own unconscious biases to the fore of their decision-making (Granot et al. 2018). The same set of problems arise around eyewitness testimony, with a national survey using mock trial video evidence of eyewitness testimony indicating that mock jurors gave the most weight to eyewitness confidence expressed in the courtroom irrespective of their confidence levels during the police lineup, crime type, expert testimony, or judicial instructions, or race of the defendant or eyewitness (Garrett et al. 2020).

Six jurors who completed surveys in an attempted murder and first-degree assault case were convinced by photos of the victim's entry and exit wounds, the state's physician witness testimony, a video of the defendant lying to the detectives, the defendant's guilty plea, and the defendant's lack of emotion throughout the trial. These jurors wanted additional evidence in the form of witness testimony from the victim's friend who spent time with him earlier that night, a diagram of the scene to show the bullet's trajectory, and evidence demonstrating the number of shots fired.

Images and other visual impressions are inherently visceral because most people understand images at an emotional level before they begin to process them intellectually, which poses problems for justice when jurors lack the knowledge and skills necessary to interpret images (Silbey 2012). The tremendous popularity of crime media among the general public—of which jurors are a part—may stem in part from the reassurance its neatly organized narratives provide about why people commit crimes and how criminal justice practitioners investigate and prosecute those crimes, which, in the process, conveys to the viewer that the world is a safe place where justice prevails (Murley 2019). Yet the reality, as we have seen, is that many real-world cases involving guns lack both this neatly organized narrative and the extraordinary amount of evidence and dramatic testimony often depicted in crime media.

These randomly selected survey results are representative of the surveys as a whole, in which the jurors who responded found prosecutors' cases generally convincing yet still longed for more physical evidence and additional witness testimony. This demonstrates why prosecutors must engage in such extensive preparation for trial in order to make a convincing case, especially given the frequency with which victims and witnesses are reluctant or unwilling to participate in prosecution and the limited amount of physical evidence available relative to what jurors "educated" by mass media understand to be the expectation at trial. The justice assemblage clearly relies on relationships between individuals tasked with fulfilling specific roles within its institutional structures and practices. Yet, as we will see, relationships are also central to the dynamics at work in murder cases, a majority of which result from shootings.

THE RELATIONAL CONTEXT OF VIOLENT CRIMES COMMITTED WITH A GUN IN MURDER CASES

Murder is often a crime of a relational nature, with victims and defendants likely to share demographic, residential, and behavioral characteristics, as well as social connections to one another. Relative to other crimes, murder victims and defendants are much more likely to know one another, be involved in other forms of lawbreaking together, and have other important demographic characteristics in common, such as age, race, and neighborhood of residence (Pizarro, Zgoba, and Jennings 2011). Murder also captures more of the justice assemblage's time and attention through very detailed investigations, as is evident in the much lengthier felony reports for these cases. Murder cases also involve a greater number of assemblage actors, such as the Violent Crimes Unit rather than individual police investigators. These cases are additionally more likely to go to trial because of the lengthy sentence facing the defendant, which requires the involvement of a jury and more interaction with the defense attorney than in cases where a defendant accepts a plea offer.

Here we review four primary dynamics at work in Tuscaloosa County murder cases to explore the significant reciprocal relationship between these extreme forms of violence and the demographic, relational, temporal, and environmental contexts in which that violence occurs. Taken together, examination of each of these four different contexts illuminates general trends in murder cases in terms of *who* is involved in these cases and *how* they convey information to police (demographic), *who* is involved as defendant and victim (relational), *when* the events escalate from interpersonal conflict to murder (temporal), and *where* the murder occurs (environmental).

Demographic dynamics include victim and defendant age, gender, race, neighborhood of residence, criminal history, and law enforcement caller type. Patricia Southerland, a postdoctoral researcher funded by the National Collaborative on Gun Violence at The University of Alabama, performed a statistical analysis of all Tuscaloosa County murder cases. She found that the mean defendant age is 30.86 years, with the youngest 18 and the oldest 66. Mean victim age is 35.59, with the youngest 18 and the oldest 82. Defendants are 86.25% male, 12.5% female, and 1.25% transgender, and victims are 79.49% male and 20.51% female. Defendants are 78.75% black, 20% white, and 1.25% other, and victims are 77.5% black and 22.5% white.

In terms of neighborhood of residence, 22.5% of defendants live outside Tuscaloosa city limits but still within jurisdiction, 21.25% live in west Tuscaloosa, and 16.25% live in southwest Tuscaloosa. Victims similarly reside in west Tuscaloosa (29.49%), outside Tuscaloosa city limits but within jurisdiction (25.64%), and southwest Tuscaloosa (12.82%). With regard to charges, 72.5% of defendants were charged with murder and 27.5% with capital murder, and a gun was present in 71.25% of these murder cases, with 75.32% of victims shot, 16.88% wounded with blunt force, and 7.79% stabbed. A majority (92.41%) did not receive additional charges postincident, and most (76.25%) cases had only a single victim.

Police calls to murder scenes typically come from neighbors or bystanders, hospital staff, or an anonymous 911 tip. For example, neighbors called police to report hearing gunshots and the victim's girlfriend screaming for help, and upon arrival, deputies found the victim's body sprawled in a driveway with multiple gunshot wounds. The victim's girlfriend told police how the shooter fired from a white Mercedes SUV before speeding away and earlier in the evening she heard the victim arguing on the phone with someone who claimed the victim owed him money. Due to the description provided by the victim's girlfriend, police were able to quickly identify the vehicle's owner as the defendant, and when questioned by police, the defendant claimed he shot the victim because he was "acting strange" when they were discussing the money owed to him by the victim.

Bystanders who report shootings to police may have no connection to the shooter or the victim. For instance, police received a call from a discount tobacco store worker who witnessed a shooting in the parking lot. Officers arrived, observed the defendant running from the scene, and took the defendant's statement in which he claimed to have shot the victim in self-defense. Surveillance footage from the discount tobacco store showed the victim walking into the store and confronting the defendant by pushing him into a clothing display, then shoving him against a car and holding a gun to his head before lowering the weapon and firing at the victim's hip, which led to the victim's death at the hospital later that night. The defendant told police that he recently found the gun and made social media posts about his new firearm, which the victim saw and then contacted the defendant and accused him of stealing the gun from him. After an argument over the phone about ownership of the gun, the defendant told the victim he would sell him the gun and then the confrontation ensued.

Alabama law requires hospital staff to call police in cases involving gunshot wounds. Police may receive multiple reports of a shooting from both the hospital and bystanders who witnessed the shooting and provide police with information. For example, hospital staff called police to report their treatment of an unidentified black male whom a driver dropped off with a bullet wound in his back that led to his death. The driver also called police to identify the victim and explain how he had been socializing at a house with the victim and the codefendants, and when he and the victim were leaving, the codefendants began arguing about a woman. One of the codefendants began shooting at the other codefendant, who returned fire. The driver fled in his car and the victim flagged him down after he realized he had been shot in the exchange of gunfire between the codefendants.

In some cases, the hospital makes the sole call to police about a shooting. Police responded to the hospital following a report of a gunshot victim dropped off at the emergency room, although a witness in the waiting room identified the driver, whom police located as he was cleaning the blood from his vehicle. The driver told police he did not know the shooter's identity and found the victim lying on the ground and took him to the hospital but did not stay because he had marijuana in his vehicle and feared being arrested. The victim's mother informed police that others told her who shot her son, and four days after the shooting the defendant came to the Violent Crimes Unit to tell police he did not know the victim and was not at the location when the shooting occurred. Yet the victim, after multiple surgeries, ultimately identified the defendant as the shooter in a police photo lineup he viewed from his hospital bed before he died.

Anonymous 911 calls to police about shootings vary in the amount of information relayed, ranging from callers who remain anonymous but provide the shooter's name to callers who simply report that a fatal shooting has occurred. For example, police received an anonymous call reporting the address of a shooting, followed by a second anonymous call an hour later in which the caller identified the shooter. Officers responded to the scene, where they found the victim unresponsive in the backyard. An ambulance transported the victim to the hospital, where he died several hours later. When police questioned the person identified by the second 911 caller at his residence next door to where the shooting occurred, he was uncooperative and released. Several other witnesses named the defendant in interviews with police, and days after the shooting, a witness told police he was in the backyard working on a truck with the victim when the defendant came over and shot the victim in the back. Although this witness could have been one of the anonymous 911 callers, he told police he did not make a report because he feared for his family's safety. Police located a firearm matching the witness's description at the defendant's residence.

Other anonymous 911 calls provide police with limited information beyond the fact that a shooting occurred. Police responded to a shooting call at a gas station, where they found the victim, who later died at the hospital, shot in the head and leg. Surveillance footage from the gas station identified the vehicle's owner, who told police he barely knew the defendant and was giving him a ride home. The driver told police that when he and the defendant stopped for gas, the defendant saw the victim pumping gas and began arguing with him about a gun the defendant claimed the victim stole from him. The driver attempted to stop the defendant before he shot the victim but, the driver told police, the defendant said he had to "get him before he gets me." The defendant told police he did not see the victim with a gun, but he believed the victim was armed because mutual acquaintances told him this was the case.

Relational dynamics surrounding fatal shootings include relationships between victim and defendant as well as between defendant and 911 caller; 76.25% of defendants and 73.42% of victims have a criminal history, and defendant is known to victim in 91.89% of cases. Defendants' relationships to victims most commonly include domestic partnership or family member (33.82%), acquaintance or friend (29.41%), criminal conspirator (23.53%), undetermined other (7.35%), or neighbor (5.88%). Most (73.75%) cases did not have a codefendant, and the defendant had a history of threatening the victim in just over half (53.66%) of the cases. Only a quarter (25%) of victims refused to cooperate with police during the initial investigation. Minors were present at crime scenes in 23.75% of cases.

Law enforcement callers included bystanders (38.75%), victim's domestic partner or relative (22.5%), unidentified other (16.25%), defendant

(7.5%), medical personnel or other first responder (7.5%), victim (6.25%), and law enforcement on patrol (1.25%). Law enforcement callers are majority black (63.16%), and almost evenly split between men (53.45%) and women (46.55%). Law enforcement callers who gave their name had a criminal history in 64.15% of cases.

Murders in our jurisdiction typically occur within one of three relational contexts between victim and defendant: an illicit drug sale dispute, a party gone awry, or domestic violence, although sometimes the nature of the relationship between defendant and victim remains unclear to police due to lack of information. Illicit drug sale disputes occur over debt, accusations of intentions to inform police, rivalries, and attempted robberies, and as is the case with other types of fatal shootings, may escalate into murder due to defendants' compromised abilities to make good decisions due to illicit drug use. For instance, police responded to a call about a decomposing body of a woman lying face down on the side of a dirt road with a gunshot wound in her back and multiple shell casings nearby. The victim's family and friends told police she left a party three days prior with three people, who confessed to police how they beat and then shot the victim because they believed she was setting them up to be robbed.

In another illicit drug sale dispute, police responded to a shooting call at an apartment complex to find the victim dead on scene. One of the codefendants, who admitted to police he was one of the shooters, told police that the victim and the victim's brother accused the codefendants of making a Snapchat post accusing the victim and his brother of acting as police informants. This codefendant told police he was at a friend's apartment when he heard the argument and told the victim that if he wanted to fight someone, he should come fight him. The victim's brother then told the victim to go get his gun, which he did, and then began shooting at the codefendants. The codefendant told police he returned fire, and when his gun jammed, he fled while the victim continued shooting at the other codefendant until the other codefendant shot and killed the victim.

People who sell illicit drugs are frequent robbery targets by their acquaintances because they often carry valuable items, such as cash, illicit drugs, and guns, and are unlikely to report the robbery to police. For instance, police responded to a shooting to find the victim's body beside his vehicle in his front yard. Two witnesses on scene described the shooter's vehicle and direction of travel to police, who were unable to locate him, and one of the witnesses told police that while she was spending time with the victim in his vehicle, he received a call from someone attempting to buy narcotics. The victim told the caller he would have to wait until the next day, which infuriated the caller and led the victim to hang up the phone. A few minutes later, the witness saw a vehicle drive toward them and two men forced the victim and witness out of the car by aiming an assault-style rifle and a handgun in their direction. One of the codefendants began removing the witness's clothing while the other codefendant restrained the victim. She heard gunshots as she fled naked into the victim's brother's residence, and when the victim's brother came outside, he saw one of the codefendants searching the victim's pockets before both codefendants fled the scene.

A fatal shooting at a party gone awry is likely to involve illicit drug and alcohol use and, like shootings related to illicit drug sales, may result from interpersonal disputes about impugned reputations. Police responded to a residence where two shooting victims were lying on the ground, one a child with multiple gunshot wounds and the other an adult male with a fatal gunshot wound to the head. A woman who heard gunshots while smoking a cigarette on her porch and observing the large crowd gathered at a party across the street told police she saw the defendant run through her front yard while shooting at her neighbor's house. As the defendant continued firing, bullets hit the woman's residence and struck one of her daughters. Another witness told police he saw the victim confront the defendant, who was brandishing a gun, at which point the defendant laughed and fatally shot the victim multiple times before running through the yard firing his gun.

At another party gone awry, police arrived to observe a large crowd gathered around the body of the victim, who was pronounced dead on scene. Police spoke with the defendant's mother, who was hosting a backyard party in honor of a recently dead friend when the heavily intoxicated victim began instigating fights with partygoers and accusing her of attempting to steal people's money under the guise of raising money for the friend's funeral. The victim punched the defendant's mother in the face, and when the crowd's attempts to restrain the victim failed, the defendant's sister called her brother to come to her and her mother's aid. The victim left the residence just as the defendant arrived at the residence and shot the victim multiple times. In a similar incident, witnesses told police a partygoer had spent the evening threatening other partygoers with a gun because he believed they were taunting him, and when other partygoers asked him to leave, he began shooting and struck two victims who were attempting to calm him down, one of whom later died from his injuries.

Domestic violence murders, like fatal shootings that occur at parties gone awry, may be facilitated in part by the compromised decision-making that accompanies illicit drug and/or alcohol use, especially when the defendant has a mental health issue. For example, police responded to a shooting to find two victims with life-threatening gunshot wounds lying on the ground. The victims, who later died at the hospital from their injuries, told police the defendant was still inside the residence. The defendant's daughter—who lost her mother and young son in the shooting—told police the defendant had struggled with serious mental health issues that caused uncontrollable anger for the past year. His erratic behavior prompted the family to remove all the guns from the residence and the defendant's daughter was unsure where the defendant obtained the gun he used in the shooting. A neighbor who witnessed the defendant shooting the victims with a shotgun told police he witnessed multiple previous arguments between the defendant and the victims. After the shooting, the defendant barricaded himself inside his residence and police negotiated with him for eight hours before deploying tear gas canisters into the house and forcibly extracting him from the residence.

In another domestic violence murder, officers found the victim dead on scene from multiple gunshot wounds to her face and hands, which she held up as she tried to defend herself from the shooter. Her three adult children found their mother dead in her bedroom after they heard gunshots and saw her visiting boyfriend leave the home. The victim wanted to end her relationship with the defendant because he was married, and they were arguing about her decision when he fatally shot her. In a similar case in which defendant and victim were in a heated argument about ending their relationship at the time of the murder, police responded to a mobile home park to find the victim, who was pronounced dead on scene, with a gunshot wound to the back of her head. The defendant traveled to the sheriff's office to surrender and told police that the victim and her two children moved in with him a month prior after being in a relationship with him for several years. He told police they had been arguing about her leaving for two weeks, and as she was moving out on the day of the murder, he shot her when he believed she was trying to grab a knife.

Fatal shootings can also feature unclear relational dynamics between victim and defendant due to police receiving either conflicting reports regarding the events or little to no information from witnesses. For example, police arrived at a shooting call at an apartment complex where the victim lay dead in the yard with multiple gunshot wounds. Witnesses told police the defendant started an argument and began to choke the victim because he objected to the victim and several other people setting off fireworks. The defendant then got into his vehicle with another person after telling the victim "we'll be back," and hours later the defendant and several others got out of the car and all began shooting at the victim. While it is possible that multiple codefendants decided to shoot the victim over something as trivial as fireworks, there are probably more complex dynamics at work in this deadly shooting than witnesses and the codefendants shared with police.

In another fatal shooting with unclear relational dynamics between victim and defendant, police arrived on scene to find a victim with a fatal gunshot wound in his chest. Two people on scene, the defendant and his wife, told police they were inside when they heard gunshots and saw a man they claimed to be the shooter run into the woods. Police spoke to the defendant and his wife, who offered conflicting reports, and their son told police he saw the victim and his father arguing before he went inside the house and heard shots fired. Despite the defendant telling police he had not fired a gun that day, his hands tested positive for gunshot residue. The man that the defendant and his wife claimed was the shooter had alibis to support his claim that he was at home and then at work the day of the shooting, and he informed police that the defendant sold illicit drugs and likely argued with the victim about an unpaid drug debt. In the absence of further information, relationships between the victim and defendant in this case are otherwise unclear.

Temporal dynamics at work in murder cases in our jurisdiction pertain to the time in which a case unfolded. Murder was committed in the process of committing another crime in 45.57% of cases, with the defendant self-surrendering to police at a separate location after the crime in a majority (81.25%) of cases. The defendant disposed of evidence in just 21.79% of cases. These temporal dynamics have two primary features in terms of the time frames surrounding escalating events and when police apprehended the suspect. An escalating interpersonal dispute ending in a murder can take temporal forms similar to the preceding examples, such as the unplanned shooting that occurs when a fight breaks out at a party and a defendant fires a gun at a victim. Fatal shootings can also be planned over a period of hours or longer, as in the preceding examples where the codefendants left a scene as a conflict escalated and returned with a gun to murder victims.

Yet the temporal dynamics of fatal shootings can also occur in instances where the defendant has a reasonable fear of the victim due to the dynamics of their relationship and that fear has prompted the defendant to carry a gun. For example, police responded to a shooting call at a victim's residence, where he suffered several gunshot wounds to his pelvic area before being transported to the hospital where he was pronounced dead. The defendant was at the victim's residence to exchange sex for money when they argued and began to wrestle. The defendant, who told police she carries a gun to "scare off little nasty men" she encounters while selling sex, pulled a gun from her cleavage and shot him. The defendant told police she did not intend to kill the victim and was so distraught she wanted to commit suicide.

In a similar case, police responded to a scene with the victim dead in his residence from a gunshot wound to the neck. Witnesses told police where to find the defendant, who admitted to shooting the victim, an acquaintance she made four years prior while working as a cashier when he initially purchased her EBT (electronic benefit transfer) card and later exchanged sex for money with him. On the day of the murder, the defendant brought her gun with her to the victim's residence after he called to ask her to bring him a sandwich. Once she arrived, he asked her for oral sex and when he insisted on vaginal sex and she refused, he became aggressive and grabbed her, at which point she shot him fatally.

Unplanned murders involving guns may also occur during home burglaries and robberies, which are a unique dimension of the temporal dynamics at work in murder cases. In one unusual yet significant case, police arrived at a murder victim's apartment after his friends searched the premises when they had not heard from the victim in several days. The victim's body lay in his bed, where he was sleeping when a bullet penetrated his skull after a defendant fired a gun outside while committing a robbery. The defendant had no idea he killed someone until after he was apprehended by police and held in jail for several days.

Police responding to a burglary-in-progress call found a victim's body lying in the grass outside an apartment building and clothed in black with a bandana covering his face, with a fatal gunshot wound to the neck. An apartment tenant advised police that the victim was one of two men he shot at after they broke into his apartment several hours after attending a party there. The burglary victim awoke and grabbed his gun from his closet and began shooting at the codefendants after they kicked down his apartment door and stood his living room. The codefendants then escaped through the balcony door and leapt to the grass outside, where one died from gunshot wounds and the other limped to his vehicle.

In another burglary-in-progress incident that ended in a murder, one of the victims returned from the grocery store to find one of the armed codefendants holding her husband on the ground with his knee lodged in the husband's lower back. As the wife begged the codefendant pinning her husband to the ground to stop because of his heart condition, the other codefendant entered the room carrying a long gun and threatened to hurt the victims if they did not give them guns and money. The defendants stole a gun, almost $1,000, and their vehicle, and the husband suffered a fatal heart attack while attempting to call 911, resulting in a murder charge after a medical examiner ruled the heart attack that killed the victim was triggered by the armed defendants' assault.

The second temporal dynamic in murder cases involves the elapsed time between the fatal shooting and when police apprehend the suspect, with defendants either arrested at the crime scene or apprehended at a later point. Defendants apprehended at a murder scene may be in a mental state so compromised they don't flee the scene, either because of the shock that, for most people, accompanies committing a terrible crime or because they are mentally incapacitated by illicit drug and/or alcohol abuse and/or a serious mental health issue. For example, police arrived at a victim's and defendant's shared residence, where they lived with the victim's mother, father, and sister, and a family friend. A long-simmering conflict between victim and defendant escalated to a fight the day of the murder after the defendant quit his job and returned to the residence to find the victim smoking marijuana. The defendant was taken into custody at the scene shortly after the shooting occurred.

In another fatal shooting case where the defendant lived with the victim and was apprehended on scene by police, the defendant told police he had been hallucinating and hearing voices for three weeks and had been denied treatment at the hospital because he was uninsured. He recalled speaking with his wife, to whom he had been married for fifteen years, on the drive home from the hospital about his sadness at not being able to visit their three children, who resided with her brother. When he became lucid again after losing consciousness upon their return home, he saw he was holding a knife and a gun as blood gushed from his wife's neck. He called 911 to report shooting his wife, whom he had previously physically abused and threatened to kill if she ever left him.

Just as defendants who remain on scene until apprehended by police may do so because of their shock at having taken another person's life, defendants may also initially flee the scene in fear only to later self-surrender to police at a separate location. Police responded to a report of shots fired and found a vehicle crashed into a light pole with the victim's body lying on the ground next to the passenger side door with a gunshot wound to his head. A witness told police he saw the victim's vehicle circling the area prior to the shooting and, after hearing multiple shots fired, saw the victim attempt to crawl out of the vehicle. The defendant turned himself in to police a few hours after the incident and admitted to shooting at the victim in what he claimed was self-defense after the victim tried to rob him during a meeting arranged for the victim to buy marijuana from the defendant and the defendant to purchase a gun from the victim.

Environmental dynamics in murder cases include the incident location, which, like the victim's and defendant's neighborhoods of residence, tends to be either in west Tuscaloosa (31.65%), outside Tuscaloosa but in jurisdiction (22.78%), or in southwest Tuscaloosa (16.46%). The type of location where murders most commonly occur include the victim's residence (27.85%), a business or public area (26.58%), the victim's and defendant's shared residence (12.66%), or the defendant's residence (10.13%). Police apprehend a majority (80%) of defendants away from the crime scene, with 18.75% of defendants self-surrendering to police.

Environmental contexts in murder cases in our jurisdiction are directly informed by the location where the shooting occurs, including the victim's home, outdoors, a place of business, or the defendant's home. Defendants who murder victims in the victim's home are often involved in a domestic violence relationship with the victim. For example, a victim going through a divorce awoke to gunshots in her bedroom as her estranged husband, who had persuaded one of their young children to let him into the house, fatally shot her new partner in the head and then shot her in the chest before she wrested the gun away from him before he fled the scene. While on the phone with the 911 dispatcher, she attempted to use CPR to revive her partner, who died before assistance arrived.

In another domestic violence murder committed in the victim's home, police found the victim dead from a gunshot wound in her bedroom. Multiple witnesses identified the victim's ex-boyfriend as the shooter to police. When police apprehended the defendant at a traffic stop in Mississippi, he said he entered the victim's home through the apartment's unlocked door to wait for her in the bedroom with the intention of committing suicide if she refused to take him back. He told police that when he pointed the gun at his head and was about to pull the trigger, the victim wrested the gun away from him as it fired into her face, a statement inconsistent with findings in the crime scene report that noted the victim's injuries as consistent with a shot fired from a greater distance.

These domestic violence dynamics in fatal shootings that occur in the victim's home may be exacerbated by disputes over money and/or illicit drugs. A victim fatally shot several times had been fighting with his girlfriend and brandished a gun as he told her and her friend to leave the premises, firing a shot in their direction and striking her vehicle as she left the scene. A witness told police he overheard the girlfriend tell the victim she planned to return with her brother, whom the victim's neighbor and grandfather told police shot the victim following an argument over $500 and marijuana.

Outdoor murders may occur when victim and defendant encounter one another in public and a long-simmering conflict rapidly escalates to a fatal shooting. Police responding to a fatal shooting in a parking lot learned that victim and defendant had an ongoing feud because of their involvement with the same woman, who left the defendant for the victim. The defendant told police he was getting into his car and giving the victim the middle finger when the victim turned his vehicle around, striking the defendant's vehicle and challenging him to a fight while throwing a rock at the defendant's vehicle and charging at the defendant, who called police immediately after the shooting and claimed he feared for his life when he shot the victim. The defendant's ex-girlfriend told police that the defendant previously had threatened the victim and told her that he could commit murder with impunity by making the crime look like self-defense, since Alabama is a stand-your-ground state.

In another outdoor murder where the defendant claimed to be defending himself by shooting, police responded to a shooting call outside a gas station and found the victim dead in the parking lot from multiple gunshot wounds. Police retrieved surveillance video footage from the gas station that showed the victim walking toward the defendant's car as the defendant shoots at the victim and his acquaintance, who identified the defendant as the shooter, before driving away. The defendant, who knew the victim because both were students at the alternative school for troubled youth, told police he shot the victim in fear for his life because the victim had previously livestreamed a statement on Facebook in which he threatened to shoot the defendant .

In some outdoor murders, the crime scene moves locations as the dispute escalates. Police responding to a shooting at a mobile home park where both the victims and defendants resided found two victims lying on the ground, one with fatal gunshot wounds and the other severely beaten. A witness identified the defendant and his girlfriend, whom police located at the mobile home park. The victims and defendants had their first encounter at a gas station, where, the defendant told police, one of the victims was rude to him. The codefendants then walked through the mobile home park after their gas station encounter and started to fight with the victims after a verbal altercation. As the codefendants beat the victim unconscious, his friend attempted to aid him and was shot in the back of the head and side by one of the codefendants.

Murders occur less frequently at places of business. In one example, the defendant and victim were coworkers at a construction company owned by the defendant's brother when they began to argue after the defendant returned to the site with the wrong type of screw and the victim began mocking him. Victim and defendant began shoving each other before the defendant pulled out a gun and fired three shots, fatally wounding the victim in the chest. In another instance, a woman working at a factory shot her coworker whom she believed to be bullying her and then told police she grossly overreacted because she was struggling with unresolved trauma as a victim of childhood sexual abuse.

Murders that take place at the defendant's home typically occur during a drug deal gone wrong or an interpersonal dispute among individuals who live together. For example, police responded to a shooting at a defendant's residence to find the victim, who later died at the hospital due to his gunshot wounds. The victim's sister and cousin told police they went with the victim to the defendant's apartment to buy marijuana when the defendant pointed a gun in their direction and attempted to rob them. Although one of the victims wrested the defendant's gun away, the defendant still shot the victim and then fled from the house. Officers who responded to a shooting at a residence shared by defendant and victim found the defendant's ex-girlfriend in front of the apartment with a gunshot wound to her left hand, and she advised that her current boyfriend, who lived with both her and her ex-boyfriend and was later pronounced dead at the hospital, had been shot inside the apartment. She told police her ex-boyfriend came into the bedroom and told her current boyfriend to leave the apartment, at which point the current boyfriend/victim told the ex-boyfriend/defendant to put the gun down and physically fight him. Standing between the two men as the defendant fired fatal shots at the victim, she was struck in the hand before running from the apartment to call police.

Despite these recurring demographic, relational, temporal, and environmental contexts, sometimes there is no clear-cut *why* to explain the dynamics surrounding shootings. Instead, we see a series of bad—and often sudden—decisions that change the lives of victims, defendants, and their loved ones forever. Crime media, by contrast, derives much of its power and its audience from clear-cut explanations of why a defendant committed a particular crime, yet, in real life, the *why* is a much murkier set of contextualized actions. These are the realities that surround the everyday administration of justice for prosecutors.

WHAT DOING JUSTICE MEANS

"A prosecutor is in a position to provide their community a blanket of protection," Ashley's mentor told her, "whether they want it or not." This blanket of protection can encompass a wide range of actions. It might mean prosecuting a domestic violence case with a victim who does not want to appear in court because the defendant is the father of her child. The woman is the domestic violence victim, but the community also becomes a victim in a society that allows violence to go unpunished. Justice also means punishing those who jeopardize the rights of others by using guns to threaten or harm others, as Paula notes, because their actions endanger the rights of others to own a gun.

"I know nothing I ever do will ever bring your person back. I get that," Thomas tells murder victim's loved ones and family members. "But I'm going to do everything I can to help and to bring justice to that person for the community." Kymberly likewise recognizes that while some wrongs can never be righted, she can offer someone who has been hurt or traumatized the opportunity to feel heard and know that what happened to them matters, especially in cases that take years to move from arrest to adjudication. "Most of my victims, when I meet with them, they go, 'Oh, well, I just figured y'all had forgotten. I just figured it got dropped. I figured nobody really cared,'" she says. "And, so, for me, justice is providing what I can to the person that was wronged."

"Gun cases are a specific subset where there is a real risk to the community and that has to be taken into account," Corey says. "There are people who are not safe if they're out on the streets, their communities aren't safe, our city's not safe." For John, justice accordingly involves "looking very, very closely at all the circumstances in the particulars of a case to see if there's a method within the rules for someone who's a particularly dangerous type of criminal, for that person to be removed" from society. Yet justice also means recognizing the tremendous responsibility that comes with being a prosecutor. "You do have a lot of control," Corey acknowledges. "You have a close working relationship with law enforcement. You have a close working relationship with judges. You're in the driver's seat of what happens with that case. You decide what type of offer you're going to make. You decide if you're going to move to dismiss it. You make the calls up to a certain point. And I just think if we are doing our job correctly, then justice should be happening."

Justice means different things depending on circumstance and must accordingly be tempered with mercy. Is the defendant who is charged with second-degree marijuana possession while carrying a pistol living in a rough neighborhood where they feel they need to be armed at all times for their safety? Or are they carrying a pistol with them to intimidate others? Doing justice means understanding that there are always multiple factors involved.

The defendant charged while carrying for their safety, for instance, should probably not receive the standard 365 days for a Class A misdemeanor.

Justice also means different things according to the defendant's stage in life. "Justice to me as a juvenile prosecutor is going to be different than justice to me as an adult prosecutor," Shannon explains, having prosecuted both juvenile and adult defendants. "These kids are walking around with guns in their pants," she says. "They've taken the thing in their hand, and they have unlocked its potential. To me, justice in a certain person [prohibited to possess a firearm] case with a kid is for there to be consequence enough to where no one up here ever meets him."

Throughout her law career, Lyndsie has always questioned whether justice means treating everyone equally or treating everyone according to their abilities. She was a defense attorney in Bessemer, a Birmingham suburb with high crime rates where, as she says of the juvenile defendants she knew, "that's just life for them. They felt like they had to. That was normal." This reality creates a stark calculus in her mind whereby she has to consider how incarceration might positively intervene in an otherwise bleak life trajectory.

For prosecutors, doing justice first and foremost means following the law to represent the people of the state as client. "We represent the state," Hays emphasizes, "we don't have any clients. I understood that when I came here but over time my understanding became refined. Community is not our client because that means someone could tell us what to do. We are completely unfettered, and our only job is to find where facts and law intersect and prosecute those cases in a way that honors our laws."

The fact that prosecutors have the people of the state as their client means that elections are the chief means by which they are bound to the state. "We are free from being directed by people within the boundaries of our system as long as we act with propriety," Hays explains. "A defense attorney's fealty is to a client whose interests may be at odds with the community's interests and that's great because they're challenging us, so they hold the state accountable. Our goal, through proper use of tools in the system, is to actually get violent defendants to a place where they can't hurt other people. We serve and are responsible to all the people in the community, including criminal defendants and that includes respecting them in the system. How can we have anyone's confidence if we don't respect the defendant's role in the system? We're not respecting their bad act. If we don't believe there is proper evidence, we won't prosecute."

Doing justice also necessitates that prosecutors follow the convictions of conscience. This means consistently accompanying assertions of advocating for a safe community with severe penalties for people who commit crimes using guns. "We want to protect everybody," Hays says. "But we will not excuse misconduct. We'll consistently apply the law to the facts and, for anyone who has committed misdeeds, we want you in jail or prison. If you get out, we want you to get a job and we'll help you." Doing justice also means remaining highly cognizant of guns' potentially deadly power and the need to take crimes committed with guns very seriously. Hays moves his curled index finger slightly and says, "That's all it takes to kill someone. The media should be reinforcing to people what it means when you point a gun at someone and pull the trigger."

4. Moral and Emotional Worlds

It's 8 a.m. on a Friday morning and the grand jury room is filled with ener-gized prosecutors, some already on their second or third cup of coffee, bus-ily chatting with one another and checking messages on their phone as they wait for everyone to assemble for the weekly lawyer meeting. Every week, all Assistant District Attorneys gather for an hour or two to listen to Hays and Paula discuss pressing matters and receive mentoring about important issues. This weekly meeting is a key part of the socialization new prosecu-tors receive into the everyday work of prosecution.

Today Paula is leading the group by talking about the importance of not personalizing cases. She uses her own examples to advise against sharing personal phone numbers with victims and witnesses, and other strategies prosecutors can use to set boundaries with their cases. As Paula talks from the position of her many years of experience, setting these boundaries seems like a simple task because to her, at this point in her career, they are second nature. The situation is very different for new prosecutors who are balancing enormous caseloads with the sometimes extremely high levels of emotion that accompany cases.

As a new prosecutor, Ashley expected to leave the courtroom feeling victorious following a youthful offender status hearing for a defendant who stabbed his victim thirty-six times. Justice, after all, had been served and Ashley had succeeded in persuading the judge that the defendant should be tried as an adult. The judge's ruling meant that the defendant would likely spend the rest of his life in prison for committing a horrific crime. At trial, everyone present would watch crime scene photos projected at near-life-size onto the courtroom's screen, eyes lingering on wounds and the varie-gated shades of drying blood. They would listen to police investigators' accounts of what they saw when they arrived at the residence, what they

heard on scene. They would hear a forensic expert explain the medical consequences of repeated knife wounds for the body, how the viscera that ani-
mates life reacts to the blade's repeated intrusion. Testimony would center
on the number of wounds, on how much sheer rage propels the energy
required to plunge a knife into another human being. "Thirty-six times,"
everyone present would hear repeated again and again.

All this was to follow that initial youthful offender status hearing, which
was to be only the initial victory in the case. As a hearing, there were only
a minimal number of people in the courtroom, versus the much larger
number who would be present for a trial. A nearly empty courtroom has a
ghostly feel that amplifies sound and makes those who are present especially conspicuous. "Oh, man, it feels like people hate me," Ashley vividly
remembers thinking as she sensed the rollercoaster of emotion among the
defendant's family members when the judge determined the defendant
would face trial as an adult. "I'm hated because I did the right thing."

The defendant, who was seventeen years old when he murdered his
mother's boyfriend, did not receive youthful defendant status from the
judge due to the brutal nature of the crime. Ashley remembers the defendant's mother and family members watching her from the gallery. "You
don't get the victory of like, 'Yes, it's right!'" she says of the feeling at the
end of the hearing. "[Instead] you get the walking out of the courtroom,
people staring at you with the evil eye."

Courtrooms often have this kind of conflicted energy in the room after
the jury foreperson reads the verdict. The sense of uncertainty as the judge
announces that a separate hearing will be set for sentencing. Family members of defendants and victims seated on long benches fixed to opposite
sides of the gallery, as if at a gruesome wedding, eyes darting among, or
avoiding, each other. The solemn atmosphere as everyone stands until the
jury files out and the courtroom begins to empty, the energy transfer
almost palpable as the space itself transitions from an emotionally charged
stage to a drab institutional space as all present exit the swinging doors. The
deputy leads the defendant found guilty back to county jail to await the
sentencing hearing. The prosecutors take the elevator upstairs to regroup
on the fourth floor. Those seated in the gallery shuffle onto the sidewalk
outside before scattering along the grid of streets to the parking garage or
the waiting car driven by a sympathetic friend. Everyone disperses to their
respective home site in the justice assemblage.

For Ashley, real-life experience at this hearing sharply diverged from her
initial expectations. "I just thought," she says, "if you do the right thing,
then everybody's happy. It's a win-win and that's not the case, so it was

eye-opening, for sure. And it's hard to walk out and be like, 'I know that was right, but that mother hates me for putting her child away for the rest of his life.'" She reconciled this divergence between expectation and reality by recognizing that her job requires her to match the facts of a case with the law to determine how the administration of justice should proceed. "It's hard," she says, "but you just have to remind yourself: it's right. It's right, I wouldn't treat him any differently from a fifty-seven-year-old, from a ninety-nine-year-old, if it was the same offense, and so I have to ignore that he's young, I have to ignore that his mom is glaring at me from the back of the courtroom, and that his entire family came and they're sitting there."

This initial sense of shock Ashley experienced in the courtroom taught her the importance of separating the facts of the case from her own emotional investment in its outcome. "You can lose with emotion," she says, "but not with facts. So, if you're very factual in your case rather than being emotional with it, then it makes it a little bit easier. But the more emotion you put into a case, especially a murder case with a gun, then you become more sympathetic, you become more attached to the case, it makes it harder for you to prosecute, and that in itself makes it stressful. So, the more factual and just neutral you can be with it, the better."

The kind of neutrality Ashley describes can only come with practice, and as we will see, even then the ability to be impartial is never completely separate from an individual prosecutor's moral and emotional worlds. "It doesn't give you that reward feeling sometimes," Ashley sighs, her sentiment a window into how prosecutors become habituated into their relations to others as they manage the moral weight of the work.

SITUATING PROSECUTORS' MORAL AND EMOTIONAL WORLDS WITHIN THE JUSTICE ASSEMBLAGE

Chapter 4 argues that individual prosecutors each have their own inner moral and emotional worlds that intersect with, and are simultaneously constituted by, the institutional structures and practices as well as the relationships and roles that comprise the justice assemblage. We explore three distinct aspects of how these moral and emotional worlds manifest within the justice assemblage for prosecutors. First, we examine how prosecutors experience and manage the moral weight of their everyday work in the context of their own identities and pressures to obtain what the law and the facts of the case indicate is the right case outcome. Second, we explore prosecutors' moral and emotional worlds in a relational context, with a focus on how the moral weight of the work unfolds in the context of relationships with those most directly impacted by crime. Third, we analyze prosecutors' habituation into the moral weight of their work as they become more experienced.

We situate our analysis within three primary bodies of literature: critiques of prosecutors, prosecutorial discretion, and moral injury. We first explore critiques of prosecutors to illuminate the broader cultural context in which individual prosecutors navigate their own moral and emotional worlds. Drawing on scholarly work about prosecutorial discretion, we examine how researchers variously conceptualize the operations of discretion in prosecutors' everyday work. Research on moral injury helps us situate individual prosecutors' moral and emotional engagement within their inherently challenging work.

Critiques of Prosecutors

Early one morning, Hays was making his customary rounds to greet everyone on the fourth floor when he reached Susan, who was, as usual, perched on a swivel chair in front of a desktop surrounded by case files. "Here's one for you, Hays," Susan said, laughing and pointing to the front page of a law review article displayed on her phone screen, "another really good article to include in our book." Leaning forward earnestly toward the screen, Hays joined Susan in bursting into laughter as they read the article's title, which the author apparently intended as a rhetorical question, out loud together: "Can You Be a Good Person and a Good Prosecutor?" (Smith 2001). "Wait," a passing prosecutor asked as she looked at the article's title page on Susan's screen, shaking her head in dismay, "that's a real article, in a real law journal? People really hate us, don't they?"

Critical assessments are, of course, the norm in academic research, where the sheer extent and duration of intellectual disputes between individuals would put most lawyers to shame. Brittany and Susan were nonetheless shocked by the level of vitriol directed toward prosecutors by scholars who, with very few exceptions, had never prosecuted a case. These critical assessments often center on the misguided belief that prosecutors are omnipotent state agents whose discretion knows no limits. Researchers have suggested that prosecutors' powers are so vast and far-reaching that their decisions extend beyond discretion into the realm of sovereignty. "The sovereign power of prosecutors is most vividly on display when they decline to bring charges where there is legally sufficient basis for doing so," Sarat and Clarke (2008, 387) argue, "By exercising what is, in most jurisdictions, an all but unreviewable power, they can and do exempt individuals from the reach of the law."

The notion that prosecutors hold, as Sarat and Clarke (2008) argue, "all but unreviewable power" echoes throughout the academic literature, which largely depicts prosecutors as accountable to no one. For example, Bar-Gill and Ben-Shahar (2009, 2) ask, "How can a prosecutor, who has only limited resources, credibly threaten so many defendants with costly and risky trials and extract plea bargains involving harsh sentences?" Angela Davis echoes this assessment in her 2007 book *Arbitrary Justice: The Power of the American Prosecutor,* in which she argues that prosecutors seek convictions rather than justice as a result of the increased politicization of the office and mandatory minimum sentences that consolidate prosecutorial control over case disposition.

In an article titled "The Problems with Prosecutors" (Sklansky 2018), the author observes that most scholarship on prosecutors either attempts to diagnose the source of these ostensible problems or prescribe a solution to them. Sklansky identifies seven commonly cited critiques in the academic literature: "the power of prosecutors, the discretion they exercise, the illegality in which they too often are found to have engaged, the punitive ideology that shapes many of their practices, their often-frustrating unaccountability, and organizational inertia within prosecutors' offices . . . [and] the ambiguity of the prosecutor's role" (2018, 452). Taken together, these critiques present a rather bleak portrait regarding the state of academic critiques of prosecutors.

Former federal prosecutor Bennett Capers, in his 2020 article titled "Against Prosecutors," offers an exception to critiques of prosecutors written by those who have never prosecuted a case or, in some instances, even practiced law. Capers writes at length about the profound regret he feels about the work he did as a federal prosecutor and takes critiques against prosecutors cited here even further by arguing for the abolition of prosecutors altogether. He contends that the only way to diminish "the enormous, monopolistic power public prosecutors wield" is to replace public prosecutors altogether with the early American practice of private prosecutions, which required a victim to file a complaint against a specific individual for a case to move forward (Capers 2020, 1564). Fortunately, a second body of literature—on prosecutorial discretion—offers a more nuanced approach to critiques of prosecutors by examining the operations of discretion in practice.

Prosecutorial Discretion

Critiques of prosecutors lack insight into how prosecutorial discretion operates in everyday practice, as such critiques center on the belief that prosecutors have unlimited time, resources, and energy to devote to their cases as well as unfettered powers to exert their will. Green (2018) argues that there are two reasons for limited public understanding regarding the scope of prosecutors' discretion to bring criminal charges in a case and, when they do, how they make decisions about the type of criminal charges. First, vague expectations regarding how prosecutors should use their powers tend to prevail at both the public and professional levels, and second, parsing out the decision-making processes prosecutors utilize in cases is challenging at best given the numerous considerations typically involved (Green 2018).

Levine and Wright (2013) note that one potential solution to the dilemma of limited public understanding of prosecutors' work is to explore the multidimensional nature of prosecutors' work in context, as we have attempted to do in this book. These coauthors observe that most contemporary legal scholarship examines the exercise of prosecutorial discretion in just two dimensions by exploring either outward, toward the institutions that impact case disposition, or inward, to prosecutors' individual consciences. Yet office structure and the associated professional identity encouraged by office culture is an important third dimension that profoundly "define[s] who a prosecutor is" in the workplace (Levine and Wright 2013, 1119).

Prosecutors' professional orientations may shift over the course of their careers as they gain experience and having prosecutors with a range of experience levels working together in an office, Levine and Wright (2013) suggest, helps provide less-experienced prosecutors with case studies of the consequences of using discretion inappropriately. Studies of prosecutorial discretion have examined how prosecutorial discretion operates in a range of contexts, including the construction of objectivity, the impact of charge bargaining on sentence length, the impact of race on plea offers, and the impact of the defendant's history and offense location on the decision to prosecute. For instance, a study examined seven ways that Swedish prosecutors accomplish objectivity in practice through appeals to "(1) regulation, (2) duty, and (3) professionalism; responses to violations by (4) incantations of objectivity, (5) corrections, (6) proclamation by contrast, and (7) human fallibility" (Jacobsson 2008, 46). This study emphasizes how prosecutors actively engage with concepts like objectivity as they go about their everyday work, and that this engagement is a fluid, dynamic process.

Prosecutorial discretion is significantly mitigated by a host of factors, many of which are beyond the prosecutor's control. A study in the District of Columbia Superior Court, for example, found that charge bargaining slightly increased sentence length, but the rate of charge bargaining did not change after the introduction of sentencing guidelines (Vance et al. 2019). Studies of prosecutorial discretion that consider race and gender emphasize how these identity markers may impact case outcomes, although they typically do so in extremely complex ways. For example, a study of how defendant race impacts prosecutors' decisions to make plea offers for a lesser charge or noncustodial punishment found that black and Latino defendants were more likely to receive custodial sentence offers (Andiloro, Johnson, and Kutateladze 2016). Yet these offers were largely explained for Latino defendants by legal factors, evidence, and arrest circumstances; black defendants, however, were still more likely to receive custodial sentence offers after including these controls (Andiloro, Johnson, and Kutateladze 2016). A study of prosecutors' decisions to prosecute stalking in comparison to other domestic violence charges produced similarly complex results, with the location of the offense and defendant's history of physical abuse toward the victim playing a determining role in the decision to prosecute (Brady and Reyns 2020).

As prosecutors exercise discretion—within the limits of the law and within considerable constraints on their ability to act—their decisions have widespread impact on defendants, victims, justice assemblage actors, and the community more generally. Yet these decisions also profoundly impact prosecutors themselves, as individual people with their own unique life experiences and sentiments. These impacts stem in large part from the reality that "prosecutors are both witnesses to and agents of the pain felt and costs imposed on criminal defendants when they are prosecuted, convicted, and ultimately sentenced" (Didwania 2018, 26).

MORAL INJURY

Prosecutors routinely confront morally complex scenarios replete with human suffering and, as part of their job, must make life-altering decisions within the constraints of the law and professional procedures. The job of a prosecutor is to ensure cases are handled properly, yet during that handling prosecutors actively participate in various aspects of the justice process that may give them internal pause for reflection. Learning that a grand jury has no-billed a case of vehicular homicide in which a defendant's actions killed a family's young children, meaning that the defendant will face no consequences for their actions. Listening to victims' and witnesses' family members frustrated by the time it takes for a murder case to go to trial, where testifying forces them to relive their suffering. Reading social media posts in which members of the public discuss defendants as beyond redemption.

The everyday nature of prosecutors' encounters with human suffering and sadness has a cumulative impact over time, resulting in their experiencing moral injury, a form of trauma that can result in a profound sense of existential crisis and guilt when the decisions they make conflict with their own moral compass (Jinkerson 2016). While most studies of moral injury relate to military service—where researchers typically refer to it as "perpetration-induced traumatic stress" (MacNair 2015, 313)—individuals in any profession who participate in events that violate their own moral values may experience the distress associated with moral injury (Griffin et al. 2019).

Morals are fundamentally relational constructs that engage with individuals' unique life experiences, including their lived experiences of both their own and others' suffering (Bernstein 2015). Frontline workers in the justice assemblage and adjacent institutions witness and experience such suffering as part of their everyday work, which takes a toll on their ability to function when experienced in extreme form or accrued over the course of numerous repeated instances. Many justice assemblage actors are initially drawn to their professions because of their desire to help others and hold those who cause suffering accountable for their actions. Yet the murky nature of human interactions means that, especially over time, prosecutors and their justice assemblage colleagues find themselves haunted by memories of cases that were particularly disturbing to their own moral sensibilities and sense of justice.

Consider, for example, the police officer who is professionally obligated to call for emergency assistance to save a person injured in the process of killing her patrol partner (Papazoglou and Chopko 2017). Or the frontline child welfare services provider who routinely experiences existential harm-induced moral suffering related to his work from multiple sources: abusive parents, adversarial agencies, and underresourced work environments that increase harms to extremely vulnerable children (Haight, Sugrue, and Calhoun 2017). Both examples—the first relating to a sudden, one-time traumatic event, and the second to the long-term, accrued impacts of witnessing trauma—result in these frontline professionals' "troubling, existential issues including their ability to function in an ethical and moral manner within a system they viewed as deeply flawed and in an unsupportive work environment steeped in human misery" (Haight, Sugrue, and Calhoun 2017, 27). Herein lies the worst-case scenario as prosecutors navigate the moral weight of their work.

THE MORAL WEIGHT OF THE WORK

Individual prosecutors experience the moral weight of the work through the lens of their own life experiences, which, in turn, means that aspects of their individual identities inform how they approach their work. Individual identities are the product of many years of lived experience in particular contexts, yet individuals also shape their understandings of their own identities and professional roles as they navigate their daily interactions with other people. These interactions, in turn, are informed by broader sociopolitical conversations about criminal justice in mass media, in the workplace, and in prosecutors' home communities.

Kymberly, like anyone else who engages with mass media, routinely sees inaccurate media representations of prosecutors as omnipotent figures whose ultimate goal is to send people to prison. She experienced this firsthand when her father told her how proud he is of her success as a prosecutor and expressed his pride by saying, "I really hope you keep your conviction rate up." "Well," Kymberly explained to her father, "we're not nearly as concerned with conviction rates as we are with doing what's supposed to be done." Kymberly attributes misperceptions of prosecutors' roles to media representations that are profoundly oppositional to what she poetically terms "the truth of my reality" in the office.

"If anything," Kymberly told Susan when asked how the media impacts her work, "the media impacts the way certain members of my community see me. Because it's, I guess, surprising to them or sometimes even seen as traitorous that I'm a black prosecutor, just because so many defendants are black, and they feel like, 'Well, you're just helping to lock up black people,' and I'm like, 'Well, no, I'm just trying to make sure that justice is done.'" Kymberly responds to these morally loaded accusations by explaining her role as a prosecutor. "I explain to them," she says, "'You know, all a defense attorney can do is jump up and down and yell as much as they possibly can, but they can't dismiss a single thing. I can.' And if there is a place in which you can help truly innocent people to not be railroaded and not be punished for something that they didn't do, this is the place to do it. And so that's what I explain to people as far as why I do what I do, and why I do my job." Kymberly, like her colleagues, is well aware that prosecutors are far from omnipotent as part of their role in the justice assemblage. She files a motion in court to dismiss a case and then the judge determines the appropriate result, meaning that she begins the process of dismissal but ultimately the court decides.

As is true for all her colleagues, Kymberly's life experiences impact her work as a prosecutor and her unique individual experiences provide her with equally unique strengths as a prosecutor. She uses these life experiences as she develops her theory of a case, which requires understanding the context in which a defendant made particular choices. "Lots of our defendants are black people, and they could have been my cousins, my uncles, my brother," she says. "They're just regular black people, and I'm a regular black person who happened to go to law school. I didn't grow up privileged or in a well-to-do household or sheltered from your everyday black community. I went to my Grandmama house in the summers. I hung out with my cousins. So I understand the mindset. I've had conversations with my cousins growing up. Even as a kid, 'don't snitch' was definitely a thing. So, I understand certain mindsets just because of my life experiences, just because I have seen and known people that are similar to these defendants." Understanding how the normalization of mistrust in the justice process percolates through a community certainly helps Kymberly as she engages with victims and witnesses who may be reluctant to cooperate.

Ben, who describes himself as "the first lawyer I ever knew," echoes Kymberly in observing how aspects of his identity impact his work as a prosecutor. "I come from a family of, two generations ago, dirt poor sharecroppers," Ben explains as he describes feeling underestimated by people who make assumptions about him based on his distinctive regional accent. "I'm very acutely aware of being a white male from South Alabama," Ben intones in his slow cadence, which impresses a careful listener with the deliberateness of his words. "I'm very aware of the way that I sound. And when I hear my voice on a recording, I hate it. I'm very aware that I sound like and look like your typical racist, white supremacist. Race does not factor in any decision that I make in prosecuting at all, ever."

For Ben, the simple act of speaking out loud means that some individuals will make unfavorable assumptions about him and his abilities. Yet, like Kymberly, these aspects of his identity also work to Ben's advantage as a prosecutor. Ben loves jury trials because "you can't be fake. If you try to fake anything in front of a jury, they're going to tear you to shreds. I do try a little bit to talk like somebody that's never been out of the woods before, but I also use it to my advantage. . . . I think when people hear me, they think, 'Oh, it's another dumbass hillbilly.'" "Really?" asked Susan, who thinks that all southern accents, but especially those like Ben's from South Alabama, sound like beautiful music. "Are you sure?" "I think so," Ben nodded. "I hope so. I hope that defense attorneys and judges, I hope that's what they think. . . . Everything is geared in my life to being a better prosecutor. And I spend my spare time getting ready to take advantage of people underestimating me."

"There's two things that I take pride in being here, especially as a black man," Shadrian conveys in his characteristically forthright tone as he discusses his work with victims and defendants, "because I think that you want the people who are prosecuting the crime in the county to represent people in the county. And there are plenty of black people in the county, so

I think that having a face that looks like them is a good thing. And then also if you're worried about bias, like I'm not seeing you as black, or whatever you're worried about. Looking like a villain, a supervillain or whatever. No. You look my cousin."

For Shadrian, his identity as a black prosecutor helps him navigate the moral weight of the work by ensuring fair representation for black defendants and justice for black victims. "You have black people murdering black people," he says, "and you want them to have good representation and representation that looks like them." Yet, despite this strong core moral belief about his professional role, Shadrian, like Kymberly and Ben, still encounters assumptions and stereotypes about how his identity intersects with his work, such as when acquaintances comment on how few prosecutors are black people. "Well, unless you just think crime's okay," Shadrian says as he dismisses such commentary, "you shouldn't care that there's a black prosecutor there."

Prosecutors manage the moral weight of their work in conjunction with their understandings of themselves, their own identities, and their professional roles. For Ben, this means a strong belief that prosecuting cases entails seeking justice. "I'm a prosecutor because at the end of the day," he says, "I just can't stand for wrong to go unpunished. If it's my upbringing or whatever, I just can't stand for somebody to do something wrong, and it go unpunished. And for somebody innocent to be victimized and them not feel like they got some satisfaction out of it."

Being a prosecutor is challenging in ways very difficult to convey to people in other professions because of prosecutors' unique position in the justice assemblage, where they review all aspects of the case as they pursue justice on behalf of the state. "The job changes you," Ben sighs. "A prosecutor's job is to answer the door when the devil knocks. If you stay in it long enough you sit across from the nastiest, meanest people. If you believe in the devil, you know the devil puts people up to this, and a prosecutor has to answer the door when the devil knocks. I'm focused on the devil, so my trial partner focuses on the victim." Consider the moral burden Ben carries as he describes his work as crossing into a metaphysical realm wherein his work brings him into regular and close proximity with evil.

This burden can take an emotional toll, even when couched in the language of spiritual imperative. For example, in the midst of a recent murder trial, Ben turned to his trial partner and said, "We are idiots. We are sitting here, there's a dead guy, his family is behind us counting on us to avenge their extinguished hopes and dreams. Then there's the defendant's family sitting there giving us the stink eye." Ben shook his head and joked, "This ought to be something you get sentenced to." Yet for Ben, being a prosecutor is a calling. "This is who I am at this point in my life," he explains. "I went to law school to become a prosecutor. I can't lay on my deathbed—if I have any loved ones left at that point—and tell them I spent my life suing Walmart. I can tell them I tried twenty-six murders."

Such a view of oneself as an administrator of justice involves a profound belief in the justice assemblage's institutional structures and practices and that all those tasked with being part of carrying out the administration of justice can do so fairly and impartially. "The state has a burden to prove beyond a reasonable doubt," Thomas says. "Rightfully so. I don't think it should be easy for us to convict someone because of the punishment that person should be facing. I get that and I don't want to send an innocent man to jail. That's one of my biggest fears of this job is that I could send an innocent man to jail."

Yet Thomas's belief is the system allows him to reconcile this fear with the realities he sees at work every day. "I have not come across a case myself personally, where it was someone jumping up and down screaming left and right, 'That was not me,'" he explains. "If someone said, 'That wasn't me,' and the defense attorney says, 'That wasn't him,' I'm like, 'Give me something that says it wasn't him.' I'll look at it. If it ain't him, ain't him and that person didn't do it. Then that person don't need to be charged. And then we either need to find the person that did or get rid of the case."

Thomas, who is white, alludes to the heavy weight that surrounds black people's historical experiences with criminal justice in the South as he describes his empathy for victims, the majority of whom are poor and black. He tells victims, "'I'll never understand. I'll try to, but I'll never fully understand what you went through, what you grew up with, what you dealt with as a kid, what you deal with now. I never will.' I can try and I'll take into account, but I mean, it's impossible for me to tell someone that I really understand what you went through because I didn't go through it so that it would be a lie for me to tell you, 'I understand.'"

Managing the moral weight of the work can also involve a prosecutor making a clear delineation between their personal and professional lives. Shadrian describes the shock he felt when he clerked at the District Attorney's Office in law school and first began to learn about the number of robberies and other violent crimes in the county because they were so far removed from the realities of his everyday life. "I live in a bubble," Shadrian says. "My neighborhood's not particularly bad, and so these [cases] aren't directly impacting my personal life and I'm here [at the courthouse] and at home and I don't really go around anywhere." This separation between work, home, and community enables Shadrian to view cases in a way that, as he puts it, "is never really personal for me."

"You did something, and the community wants justice for it," Shadrian envisions himself communicating to a defendant. "And so that is what it is. For me, it's just a practical experience of like, 'Hey, you did bad thing. And now the process starts from when someone's accused of a bad thing. And then we work our way down the line. I'm not mad at you personally. I'm not mad at your defense attorney personally. You did something bad and that means you need to be punished for it. . . . I'm just looking at this to prosecute you for this thing.' It's not like I carry it with me, like, 'I can't believe this person.' It's just part of the process that happens when you do some bad things. But outside of that in general, it doesn't really affect my job. . . . We're genuinely trying to keep the community safer. And that is our goal. That's our ultimate goal. That's it."

When Shadrian is sitting with the family members of a shooting victim, talking them through the case and its possible outcomes, he feels the heavy human realities of their loss alongside their sometimes impossible expectations of him as a prosecutor. "It's the only part of the job where you're not doing legal analysis," he says of meeting with victims' families, contrasting these emotional conversations with the routine work of reviewing files, making plea offers, and preparing for trial. The family members' presence changes the dynamic for Shadrian, particularly in a murder trial, by adding what he calls "an extra element of 'Man, I really don't want to mess this up because they're going to be there,' especially if they're invested. Because you do have some victims' families that they just aren't invested into the person."

Most murder trials include at least some members of victims' families assembled in the long benches to the judge's right in the courtroom gallery, alongside victim service officers who escort them from the District Attorney's Office to the courtroom. "They're going to be there sitting behind you every day at trial," Shadrian says of the further scrutiny the victims' families add to courtroom proceedings, "and they're going to be critiquing and they're going to be emotional with things." Yet the substance of victims' families' critiques can vary dramatically from accusations of prosecutors' insensitivity to frustration with what they may see as the low range of punishment possible for the defendant within the boundaries of the law.

Prosecutors actively work with their victim service officer colleagues to prepare victims' families for what they will experience at trial. For example, one murder trial Shadrian and Grace prosecuted was attended by nearly two dozen members of the victim's family, who arrived at and departed from the courthouse together and stayed close to the victim service officers throughout the trial. Shadrian attempted to be sensitive to the family's potential reactions by making sure to inform the victim service officer working with the family to prepare them to look away from evidence photos displayed in court featuring their loved one's corpse sprawled nude on the floor and close-ups of the bullet hole at the center of his forehead.

Some victims' family members envision the defendant's prosecution in a more vindictive manner than is possible under the law. "You have people who genuinely don't care about the fact that I want to prosecute crime, don't care about crime in the community," Shadrian says of these family members. "They're only invested in what I'm doing for their dead family member." These family members may frequently call the victim service officer assigned to their case to complain about case handling or be angry at prosecutors whom they perceive as making too weak an offer or failing to perform to their standards in court. Hence as prosecutors do the difficult work of preparing for trial, they also must manage the reality that everyone processes grief differently and that some family dynamics may be such that individuals lack the knowledge, or even the self-awareness, to recognize the limits of the justice process.

The moral weight of interacting with victims' family members is compounded by the tremendous pressure many prosecutors internally impose on themselves to do exemplary work in extremely tough circumstances. John notes that this pressure is particularly high for prosecutors who attended law schools highly respected in the region. "I think they put such heavy, heavy burdens on themselves with such high expectations to just come out and just be ready to do everything," he says of this unrealistic expectation. This being ready for everything, as we will see, includes preparing for the inevitable lack of victim and witness participation in the prosecution of cases.

PROSECUTORS' MORAL AND EMOTIONAL WORLDS IN RELATIONAL CONTEXT: VICTIMS AND WITNESSES

Prosecutors manage the moral weight of the work in relational context, with a great deal of this management occurring with and around those most directly impacted by crime rather than assemblage actors. After all, assemblage actors share a mission and vision for their work, whereas victims, witnesses, and defendants may not share prosecutors' sense of mission and vision. Victims and witnesses most directly impact what prosecutors can accomplish in a case through the decisions they make regarding participation. Victims' and witnesses' decision-making is, in turn, the product of the relational contexts that create and sustain their own moral and emotional worlds.

Victim and witness participation is vital to determining case outcomes. In many cases, the likelihood of participation is evident from victims' and witnesses' first encounters with police. Police investigators rely on victims and witnesses to relay information regarding what occurred at a crime scene because, in the vast majority of cases, police arrive at a crime scene after a shooting has occurred. After reviewing thousands of felony reports compiled by police investigators in gun present cases where it was difficult for her to determine the relationships between, and instigating events among, actors at a crime scene, Susan began to wonder if she was missing some critical analytical ability to read the reports. She accordingly began asking prosecutors how often they likewise struggled to determine these critical aspects of a case.

"Spoke to this person, uncooperative," Ashley says as she describes many police investigators' characterizations of their encounters with victims and witnesses following a shooting. "Spoke to that person, uncooperative." Such encounters leave her with more questions than answers, particularly when there is no recorded video evidence available from a surveillance camera to help determine the parties involved in the shooting. Who was upset with each other? Why were they upset? Why was there a gun? Why were they shooting at each other? To answer these questions, Ashley calls victims and witnesses to determine what occurred and attempts to locate security footage from a nearby location that may have captured the events on camera.

"We can't, as a prosecutors' office, make it stop until we have some help," Kymberly says of crimes committed with a gun, as she describes her frustration at reviewing comments posted on social media accounts managed by the Tuscaloosa County Sheriff's Office and Tuscaloosa Police Department. "Why is he out, anyway?" commentators note in response to alerts posted about defendants who have committed new crimes while out on bond. "We can't lock anyone up if you're not willing to actually say what you've seen," Kymberly says. "And everyone seems to be the type where they're like, 'Oh, I'm just going to mind my business, and if it wasn't me, and it didn't happen to me, I don't know anything about it.' And that's not okay. We can't keep the community safe if that is the prevailing thought."

Yet despite this frustration, prosecutors also understand that victims and witnesses have reasons for this mistrust, and these reasons are likely the result of their own life experiences. "Our witnesses don't want to participate," Lyndsie says emphatically. "They don't want to have anything to do with the system because they don't trust it. It's not a thing that they view as a useful tool in their life. Sometimes they do, but for the most part, they don't." While Lyndsie was prosecuting an attempted murder case, the victim—who was subsequently charged with capital murder himself in a separate case—refused to assist her despite her multiple requests.

"Why?" Lyndsie asked the attempted murder victim. "This guy shot at you. He tried to kill you. Your brother was right there. So even if you don't care about your life, your brother's right there. Why don't you want him to go to jail? Why did you kind of protect him? Why did you do that?" "I know it doesn't make sense to people," the defendant told Lyndsie. "I just don't believe in jail." For this victim, who later became a defendant himself in another shooting case, the solution to the problem as he saw it had nothing to do with the justice assemblage. "That's just not how he handled it. And I am quite sure that, had the defendant not gotten arrested, my victim would've just gone and shot him, because he shot someone else later. But I think for a lot of folks, they just have such little trust in the system that they're like, 'We're just going to handle it on our own in our own way.'"

For some victims and witnesses, the fear of retaliation impedes their willingness to participate. Ben experienced a significant decline in victim and witness participation when he prosecuted cases in Montgomery, Alabama's state capitol where a witness left the stand after testifying at a trial and was shot to death on the steps outside the courthouse. "It's easy for me to tell someone, 'You need to do this. This is the right thing to do. You need to speak up. If you don't speak up, then how can we help prevent this?'" Paula acknowledges. "But I don't have to go home to a neighborhood where snitching or being a witness can be a death sentence. I don't have to live with that. I have to be mindful that whether it's real or imagined fear, that is at the core of most of it. It is not always just, 'Oh, I don't want to be inconvenienced.' Most of the time, it is fear, either fear from their family because their families don't want them to participate or fear from other groups of people, enemies real or imagined. You just have to understand it."

This fear is common among victims, and people from all demographics may refuse to participate because they don't want a relationship with people they fear. John, for example, recounted a case in which the parents of children whose private school gym was burglarized advised their children not to give statements to police because the parents feared that the individuals who committed the burglary would retaliate by harming their children. Here we have an instance in which wealthy and predominantly white parents adopted a "no snitchin'" ethos commonly associated with inner-city black communities.

"The public's cooperation, that is what's missing in this job," Grace says as she recounts the mistrust of criminal justice processes evident among some of the victims and witnesses who refused to participate in prosecuting cases. "I think that has just become the norm because [of the belief that] police are bad. Prosecutors are bad," she explains, "and they can handle it amongst themselves. That's what they do. So many of our shootings now are retaliatory." In one case, a teenage girl shot in the back while fleeing gunfire refused to participate in the prosecution of a defendant who, after he made bond in a first-degree robbery case where he was accused of robbing another man over a stolen gun, lost a poker game and then drove to find the winners, shooting into their car, paralyzing one and shooting the other multiple times in the arm. After he was released on bond again, he received youthful offender status and was placed in community corrections, after which he traveled to an apartment complex where two teenage cousins he was dating resided and began shooting.

Grace acknowledges that it is reasonable for a shooting victim to feel afraid, yet "they do such a good job of convincing me that they're not scared and they just don't want to do it." Grace, like her colleagues, struggles with maintaining the energy to continue her work. "I struggle," she says, "and it comes in waves because sometimes I want to keep going and I'm like, 'I've got to protect the community.' Then sometimes I'm like, 'I can't do it. They're preventing me from doing it.' I get so down and like, 'Why am I doing this?' Then sometimes I'm like, 'Well, they don't care. I don't care. They don't care. I don't care. I'm not wasting my time.' Then I come back to 'Well, I've got to protect this community.' My balance is I have to be at peace with myself that I've done everything that I can to get this victim to cooperate. If they don't want to, despite my best efforts, that's all I can do."

In addition to fear of retaliation, there can also be temporal reasons at work in cases where victims and witnesses do not want to participate in prosecuting a defendant, especially when years have passed between the crime and trial. The emotional and relational changes that transpire in those intervening years may mean that the victim has resolved their own moral sense of hurt or injury while the state is still moving forward with the case. Prosecutors must tread carefully in this morally complex terrain as they attempt to convince reluctant victims and witnesses to participate, a reality made even more challenging by the fact that prosecutors represent the people of the state, rather than victims.

The first challenge in getting victims and witnesses to participate involves their initial trip to the courthouse, including locating victims and witnesses whose phone numbers or addresses may have changed. Ashley works through this by trying to understand their hesitancy to make the trip. Is it that they're afraid someone will see them? If so, an investigator can transport them in an unmarked car from their residence to the courthouse. Ashley tries to emphasize the clarity that can accompany closure, as well as the potentially empowering sense, for a victim or witness, that they have prevented future victimization. "So, if you don't come in and we can't do our job," Ashley explains to reluctant victims and witnesses, "then there's a potential the court will dismiss the case and the defendant will keep engaging in bad acts."

Once victims and witnesses have made the trip to the courthouse, there is the challenge of establishing rapport. In one of Ashley's cases with Thomas as a trial partner, a reluctant witness changed his mind after a police investigator he had developed a bond with drove to his home with Thomas and asked, "Is there anything we can do to talk to you? Is there anything we can do to make you more comfortable?" "Hey, he could be out again, he could be doing this," Thomas and the investigator explained to the reluctant witness. "We need your help to make sure that this doesn't happen again." On the day of the meeting, the reluctant witness changed his mind when the investigator took him to lunch and convinced him of the value of participating, which ultimately led to his testifying at trial.

Lyndsie, who previously worked in victim services and so brings a survivor-centered approach to persuading victims and witnesses to participate in prosecution, always starts preparing victims and witnesses to testify by emphasizing that she is on their side. "I one hundred percent believe what you're telling me," she says to victims. "I wouldn't be taking this case if I didn't. So, I believe you. And I'm not saying that you did anything wrong, and I understand you did exactly what you had to do to survive and there's nothing wrong with that." Recognizing that practicing cross-examination may be upsetting for a victim or witness in a way that might negatively impact their relationship, Lyndsie and her trial partner in a particular case, Shadrian, opted to have the prosecutor who engaged in the practice cross—when a prosecutor asks a victim or witness the types of questions a defense attorney might ask in court—be different from the prosecutor who would actually question the victim or witness in court. This is a personal choice, as some prosecutors will practice directly with a victim or witness to build a bond that they believe will strengthen their ability to withstand a defense attorney's scrutiny of the accuracy of their knowledge in court.

Lyndsie emphasizes to reluctant victims and witnesses that her responsibility to prosecute cases on behalf of the state ultimately absolves them of what can feel like an enormous responsibility. "I'm not asking you for permission," she will tell them. "I'm not putting that on you. We have to make this decision as the state. We have to think about the community as well as you, but we do care about what you want, and that's something that I'm going to give weight to in making those decisions." Lyndsie makes it a point to talk with the victim about their goals in a case and what they would like to see happen. Is it important to the victim that the defendant face punishment? What should that punishment look like? Is it prison, or something else? How do they feel about testifying? Is it something they want to do because it will give them a voice that makes them feel heard, or will it be just one more traumatizing incident?

Shannon likewise understands the importance of connecting with victims and witnesses and, quite literally, meeting them where they are at. When Shannon worked at the District Attorney's Office in Selma, there were no victim service officers or investigators. If someone needed to convince a victim to participate in prosecution, it was Shannon who parked her car outside the rundown apartment complex or the ramshackle house with the paint peeling to convince them. "I react viscerally to victims," she says. "They've always been the thing that motivates me." Traveling to meet with victims and witnesses in Selma changed the way Shannon saw her work as a prosecutor, and she continues to travel to meet with victims and witnesses as a result. "I saw different people because you would have different gang factions that would enter into a shootout," she explains. "One day, they would be your defendant, the next day they'll be your victim. And the only way that I had to get to them was to go to them. . . . So, I just talk to people like they're people. I'll go out and come to your house. It's incredibly intimidating to come to the DA's office or to police station or something like that."

Being an effective storyteller requires a real appreciation of the scene, and so going to the crime scene is vital to understanding what happened. The remoteness of the location. The way the traffic flows. The dynamics of the relationship in context. Maegan, who often prosecutes domestic violence cases with reluctant victims in District Court, attempts to establish common ground with the women. "I'm a mother," she says, "and a lot of these women are single mothers. And I was a single mother. And so, I just try to be relatable . . . reiterate to them I want them to feel safe. I want them and their children to feel safe and protected, but that I can't do that without their help. And so, I'm like, 'If you're tired of being abused or hurt, you don't have to stay hurt. And I know it's scary to confront your abuser. But if you want this to stop, this is what we have to do.'"

In her initial meeting with a victim, Maegan's primary focus is on building a relationship, "because they do have to trust me. I have to ask them very, very personal questions that they probably don't want to share with other people. And I wouldn't want to share personal information about myself with a stranger. So, I just try to elicit that trust, get on their level. 'Okay, he's done this, or she's done this, three or four times. The next time, you could be killed.' And once I say that, and those are hard words to come out of my mouth, it resonates with them. They're like, 'You know what? Yeah. I may not have another next time to come up here.'"

"So, you're okay with this?" Thomas is likely to eventually ask a reluctant witness in a shooting case as he employs his own style of establishing common ground. "Someone shooting at you, almost killing you, and they get away with it?" He'll point to a framed picture of a toddler on his desk. "That's my son. You got any kids?" Thomas takes off his tie and sits with the reluctant victim. What do they want to talk about? Do they have anything in common? Can he get them talking about something? "We don't have to do what you want to do. I got to protect the community," he will tell a reluctant victim or witness, "and the last thing I want is to dismiss a case because you don't want to prosecute and in two months, I see on the news that you are now dead." Thomas is not being melodramatic here, as prosecutors routinely see real-life cases in which today's reluctant victim is tomorrow's murder victim.

Prosecutors may also appeal to a reluctant victim's or witness's sense of obligation to their own familial and social networks. "If you were killed," Ben will tell a witness who does not want to testify in front of the defendant and his family members in court, "your mama would want me to get on the stand and say that I saw. And I would do that for you. Don't you think you owe this dead guy's mama that same courtesy?" He asks witnesses to bring their mothers with them to meet with him at the courthouse. Ben will ask a witness's mother, "Mama, if he were killed or she were killed, and I saw it, and I had something better to do that day, wouldn't you want me to come down?" For Ben, appealing to witness's kinship networks, particularly mothers, draws on deep connections disrupted by violent crimes committed with a gun, and so his goal is to "try to get mama on my side. Black mamas have a very strong influence over their sons and daughters, but most of our witnesses are sons." Mothers, in Ben's view, have a powerful relational and moral pull that the state lacks on its own.

Grace and Hays took a similar approach in a first-degree robbery case involving a defendant with numerous prior convictions. The victim, who was incarcerated in county jail, refused to talk with Grace, and the victim's mother, who was a witness in the case, also initially refused. "What you're doing not only affects you and your son, but it affects his community,"

Hays told the victim's mother. "What the right thing to do here is to testify and to assist and to keep the community safe by locking this guy up. It affects more than just you and it affects more than just your kid. You need to step up to do the right thing, not only for the community, but to be an example for your child."

Victims and witnesses are often under intense stress when they prepare to testify in court. Hays worked with a victim-witness who previously had lied to law enforcement and needed additional preparation to withstand the scrutiny of the defense attorney's questioning in court. "He was sobbing, hyperventilating into a paper bag, sobbing," Hays says of this victim-witness's state of mind as he worked with prosecutors to prepare for his testimony in court. "But within three weeks he was testifying, and he and his testimony withstood a particularly scathing cross-examination and we arrived at the truth. He was cloaked with the armor of truth and that can withstand any scrutiny. You don't get that on the front side." In this and many other instances, preparation for testimony is a time-intensive process for prosecutors, victims, and witnesses alike.

Ultimately, moral appeals to community and family responsibilities and to truth may still fail to convince some victims and witnesses to participate in the prosecution of a case. Victims and witnesses who are well versed in the everyday operations of criminal justice because of their own extensive experience as defendants may believe themselves to be familiar with legal strategies to avoid testifying, even when they are required by law to do so and served with a subpoena. For example, a witness in a shooting case served with a subpoena by the office investigator believed that the law required delivery of the subpoena into his hands. Rather than accepting the subpoena to appear in court, the witness slapped the subpoena out of the investigator's hand and then sped away in his car.

Prosecutors face a moral and professional dilemma in deciding whether they want to issue a subpoena that legally requires the victim or witness to appear in court or risk the possibility of the case being reduced to a lesser charge or even dismissed. The decision to subpoena varies by type of crime. For example, a domestic violence victim who no longer wishes to participate in the prosecution of her abuser will receive a subpoena as an incentive to testify in court, yet she will not be arrested if she fails to appear because prosecutors are mindful of a victim's emotional attachment to an abuser and the day-to-day complexities of domestic violence cases. In cases of shootings and other violent crimes involving a gun, however, prosecutors must take a different approach given the severity of the crime and their responsibility to protect the community. "You got two choices, really one choice, you got two options," Ben will tell a victim or witness who refuses to testify in a violent crime case. "You can testify in street clothes, without handcuffs, or you can testify in an orange jumpsuit with handcuffs. Either way you're going to testify."

Ben has prosecuted two cases that required him to send an investigator out to arrest victims of violent crime who did not want to testify and bring them to court in handcuffs, which required the judge to issue a writ of attachment. Once each victim was on the stand, Ben asked the same question: "Why are you in handcuffs?" "Because I didn't want to come down here," both victims replied from the stand. "So, you don't care anything about this case?" Ben asked and received the response of "No, I don't care." Both cases resulted in convictions in less-than-ideal conditions, particularly since they forced Ben to, as he put it, "find a way, as a prosecutor, to convince that jury to care, even though the victim doesn't care." For the prosecutor, these steps are both morally and legally necessary because, as Ben notes, "at the end of the day, it's not the victim's case. It's the state's case."

The state's relationship to reluctant victims and witnesses does not proceed with the same moral and legal urgency in misdemeanor District Court domestic violence cases, where prosecutors often encounter victims who do not want to proceed with charges. This process begins when a victim service officer sends a letter immediately after the file is created and then calls the victim if they do not respond. The victim service officer notes this information and shares it with the District Court prosecutor assigned to the case, who then needs to determine how to proceed in the context of a particular case with the knowledge that many domestic violence victims feel tremendous pressure not to participate to avoid further abuse from an intimate partner with whom they live and have children. Yet prosecutors also understand the extraordinary complexity of domestic violence relationships, including the emotional attachment victim and defendant have to one another in terms of their shared lives and familiarity.

If a domestic violence case goes to trial in District Court, a prosecutor calls the victim to the courthouse for a meeting to prepare them, with a victim service officer present, for testimony and cross-examination. It is at this point that District Court prosecutors often find that victims begin to ignore their calls, refuse to meet, and otherwise indicate that they do not want to proceed with the case. This creates a moral and legal dilemma for prosecutors, who have already dedicated the resources of the court to pursuing justice on behalf of the state, which they attempt to resolve by having a process server hand-serve a subpoena to the victim's last known address to notify them they are required to appear in court at a specific date and time. This approach does not always work, and the victim will sometimes call the District Court prosecutor assigned to the case and inform them that they do not want to come to court. All the prosecutor can do at this point is tell the victim, "We filed these charges and we're not dismissing it. So, you need to come on that court date."

In these District Court domestic violence cases, the subpoena serves as what a prosecutor referred to as a "strong encouragement" for the victim to come to court. Victims in these misdemeanor cases will not receive a failure to appear warrant for their arrest from the court. Instead, their case is dismissed in court, resulting in a tremendous waste of time and energy among all concerned. "Is the state ready to proceed?" the District Court judge will ask in court and the prosecutor, noting the absence of the victim, has to respond, "State cannot proceed at this time due to the absence of our primary witness or victim." The thinking here is that the state cannot make its case in the absence of the primary witness, whose testimony is key. "You do what you can to the full extent of the law," a District Court prosecutor explains of these misdemeanor domestic violence cases, "and once it gets past that boundary, then you can't do anything else."

The same fears that inform victims' unwillingness to testify in a shooting case are at work in misdemeanor domestic violence cases, yet with very different results. This reality presents prosecutors in District Court misdemeanor domestic violence cases with moral dilemmas as they face many of the same challenges with victims as their Circuit Court peers prosecuting shooting cases: victims who hang up the phone when they call, who ignore repeated pleas for cooperation, or who are even openly hostile to prosecutors' attempts to contact them.

However, in sharp contrast to shooting cases, a victim in a misdemeanor domestic violence case can compile a written motion to dismiss that, in most cases, ends the state's involvement in her case. "And it's difficult because you read the depositions of these cases," a District Court prosecutor explains, "and it's 'Victim was struck in the face with a closed fist and was bleeding' and all these things, and you want to pursue justice, but either the victim is still living with the defendant or they have children together and they don't want to punish, or they're afraid to punish or prosecute them because they think they may be abused further."

Shadrian leverages the state's power to compel victims and witnesses to testify in shooting cases by simplifying the situation as much as he can. "I'm not going to ask you to talk about how bad a person they are, or how they don't take care of their kids or anything like that," he tells victims, "or anything that's going to actually defame their character. I just want you to get on the stand and tell the truth. You tell the truth about what happened and that's it. You're not pushing anything. I ask you a couple questions, they ask you a couple questions and then you're done." He provides the reluctant victim or witness with the option to express their reluctance to testify on the stand. "I can even ask you if you want to be there on the stand," he says, giving a reluctant victim or witness the option to respond with "'Oh no, I don't want to be here. I don't want to be here testifying . . . I didn't want to do this, the state made me.'"

PROSECUTORS' MORAL AND EMOTIONAL WORLDS IN RELATIONAL CONTEXT: DEFENDANTS

Corey vividly remembers ending her workday late one Tuesday with a years-old apartment complex shooting case dismissed in court because no witnesses came forward, only to wake up on Wednesday morning to the news that five people had been shot at the same apartment complex. When the police arrived on scene, no one came forward to provide information about what occurred prior to the shooting or who was involved, yet security camera footage revealed approximately twenty people standing in close proximity to the shooting when it occurred. One victim had been shot nine times. Four of the five defendants were out on bond in separate criminal cases. The next weekend, a three-year-old boy swimming in a community pool was shot during a dispute between armed men. Then a thirteen-year-old boy sitting on his bed reading his encyclopedia was shot when an argument escalated outside his apartment complex.

"I wish people could understand how those people are the listed victims in the case, but the community is the victim," Corey explains. "Those bullets don't have names on them. It so easily could go through one of those homes and could kill someone . . . I don't think anyone likes bullets flying around in their neighborhood . . . 911 calls . . . maybe that takes care of what they see as the immediate problem . . . [but] two, three years later, when we go to court, I need you to testify so I can keep this person out of your community, out of your neighborhood, off the street."

As we have seen, prosecutors must engage with victims' and witnesses' moral and emotional worlds to convince them to participate and understand their goals in a case. Yet prosecutors also need to make sense of defendants' decision-making processes as they build their theory of the case and, in so doing, establish a relationship to defendants' emotional worlds. Many defendants in shooting cases have extensive criminal histories that make them familiar figures to the justice assemblage's cast of characters. "As the years go by," Corey says of the familiarity she gained with repeat defendants' names and histories in her early years as a prosecutor, "you can pretty much see names on the piece of paper, and you know why they're there. You know their criminal history."

Shannon, who has prosecuted both adults and juveniles in her career, is keenly attuned to the life trajectories many adult defendants follow and the cultural meanings—status, protection, aggression—they associate with gun possession. "The kids love guns," Shannon says. "They love to hold them. They love to show them. They think of it in terms of the same way that they're fanning some twenty-dollar bills because they don't really have any concept of what money is. To them, a thousand dollars is eleven billion or a career, that they can't even wrap their brain around it because it's an immediate gratification thing." For Shannon, these beliefs among juvenile defendants congeal with age into the hardened, mistrustful worldview held by many adult defendants.

"A lot of these kids," Shannon says of juvenile defendants, "I've known since they were twelve years old. And they'll come in and they'll cry, and they want their mom, and they want approval, and then around sixteen, they're hard because there's not a whole lot that we can do to soften the world that they're living in." For Shannon, the malleable moral and emotional world of juvenile defendants is evident in juvenile detention facilities, which focus much more on education and therapeutic approaches than adult prisons. "They'll have this epiphany where none of their motivations mattered at the time because they see things [clearly]," Shannon says. "Then they get out, and they go straight back to that life and then they come back, and each time their motivation changes. I can't nail it down to one particular thing until you become that person who enjoys hurting people."

The moral and emotional shift from juvenile defendant arrested after engaging in criminal behaviors valorized and modeled for them in their home communities to adult defendant who "enjoys hurting people," as Shannon puts it, is a familiar arc to prosecutors. Shannon understands how circumstances shape intent. Proving intent is different from understanding why a defendant did what they are accused of doing, which requires prosecutors to ask a series of questions. What are the facts? What is the person's history? What is the history between the actors? Prosecutors rarely, if ever, have a written statement of intent in which a defendant threatens to kill a victim. Attempted murder cases, which involve an illegal act seeking to cause death, are good examples of the challenges inherent to proving intent, which requires prosecutors to focus on the facts of the case rather than their assumptions of what jurors might find most convincing. In attempted murder cases, prosecutors must ask themselves, what was the mindset of the person pulling the trigger?

If a defendant shot from a mile away and the discharged bullet killed a victim, he likely did not intend to kill. Yet a defendant who pointed a gun directly at a victim and fired engaged in a singularly human action in which a quarter-inch movement of his finger resulted in the loss of life, something anyone who has ever held a gun understands. Yet proving intent poses challenges; as Hays puts it, "You can't push on the [defendant's] left ear and the right ear spits out paper with his intent. The mere fact of killing or not does not matter, it's the circumstances." When Hays was a defense attorney, he defended a client in a capital murder case where his client's brother was murdered weeks prior, and the common misbelief in the community was that the victim in this case killed the defendant's brother. The victim was known to carry a gun and laughed at the defendant when he saw him in public after his brother's murder. While laughing in public is not illegal, any reasonable person can certainly understand why the defendant became extremely upset at the victim.

"To some extent," Ben explains, "you've got a lot of criminal defendants who never had a chance to start with. Their mom and dad are criminals, they were raised in criminality, they never had a chance, and part of me feels bad for them for that. But that's not my job. My job is to prosecute what they did." Doing so requires proving intent. Ben remembers prosecuting cases in a Montgomery courtroom where the judge would wave his hand and say, "You can't crack open a man's head and look down inside and see what his intent was," a line Ben now frequently uses in voir dire. Ben tells prospective jurors that, in fact, the law "requires you to do the very next best thing. You determine the defendant's intent at the time he did what he did, by looking at what he did, and the manner in which he did it." Doing so implicitly requires that the jury attempt to journey into the defendant's moral and emotional world at the time of the crime.

Yet these realities present challenges for prosecutors, who know a great deal of background information and context regarding the case, or can even relate to what the defendant did, but at the end of the day prosecutors can only work with the facts and prosecute according to the law. Understanding the defendant's actions requires prosecutors to have what Corey terms "a general sense of human behavior" because prosecutors need to craft a theory that will resonate with a jury if the case goes to trial. Effectively, this need forces prosecutors to make sense of events that otherwise appear senseless. "You have to be able to find the relatable storyline or the relatable reason for actions," Corey explains. "People like a motive and sometimes you don't have those things and you have to find a way to explain that you don't have them. . . . Everyone likes to know why someone did something and sometimes you just can't tell them, sometimes there's no reason, but I think being somewhat self-aware and being able to see, or kind of just on a human level, look at 'How did we get here?' is helpful."

Prosecutors undertake a complex cognitive journey toward answering the question of *How did we get here?* in developing the theory of a case. "The skills that I've developed over time, [what] I use more than anything else is critical thinking about why, why, why, why, why, why did this happen?" Paula explains. This means challenging herself, every time she assumes something to be true in a case, to make herself stop and consider the alternative. What if the defendant is telling the truth? What if the defendant is lying about some aspects of the case but not others? Determining what happened in a case sometimes takes precedence over why it happened because spending too much time speculating on a defendant's thought process can detract from time needed for case preparation.

"I do try to put myself in their shoes," Grace says of defendants, "but sometimes I'm never going to be able to know what they were thinking or why, because these things don't make sense. It doesn't make sense that people respond this way. Their automatic response is to pull a gun. That makes no sense, that defies logic." Limited time, enormous caseloads, and the limits of the human capability to fully understand the actions of others all work against prosecutors' deep engagement with defendants' moral and emotional worlds, although speculation about their life realities certainly inform case preparation. "I could sit here for days on end trying to get in the heads of some of these defendants," Grace says. "At the end of the day, they did what they did, and it has lasting implications in our community. That's what I got to focus on, is properly preparing these cases and getting to the bottom of it, and figuring out what happened, instead of why."

Morality is a relational concept that individuals derive from those around them, and accordingly, the *why* surrounding shootings can change over time as the victim, the defendant, witnesses, and their families and communities reflect on the events. The *why* can also change depending on who the victim or the defendant is talking to and what the victim's or the defendant's goals are in those communications. A defendant with multiple felony convictions that prohibit him from owning a gun who tells a police investigator that he shot his victim in self-defense because the victim attempted to shoot him a month ago may be telling the truth, but he also may be attempting to build sympathy to receive a reduced charge. These realities are not mutually exclusive. Shadrian navigates these murky moral waters by focusing on the facts of the case. "You're a felon, you're not sup-posed to have a gun," Shadrian explains. "The gun's stolen. You're not sup-posed to have it. So, I don't know what mindset you could present that would change my thinking about you committing this crime."

Maegan, who prosecutes misdemeanor cases in District Court, focuses her exploration of the defendant's decision-making on how the defense attorney might render the defendant's actions sympathetic to a jury. One of her recent cases involved a defendant who accidentally fired a gun tucked into his sagging pants as he pulled them up in a crowded public place. Multiple people were hit with fragments and injured. Maegan formulated her response to the defense attorney's anticipated argument and reviewed the felony report with a critical eye, with a view to, as she notes, "okay, this is a red flag. This doesn't make sense. If I was the defense attorney, this is what I would hit."

In general, the prosecutor focuses on the facts of the case—what happened—to emphasize the crime's severity, while the defense attorney focuses on the circumstances of the case—why it happened—to generate sympathy and a potentially reduced charge or sentence for the defendant. "I wouldn't be in this job if I agreed with what people did," Thomas says, further noting how "it does matter why they do it. It helps me explain to the jury. If I know the why, because a lot of times the defense is going to talk about the why, not just the how, and if I can understand the why I can formulate my case to be stronger against a why argument because the defense sometimes will, they will pull up the why and use that as a defense against the charge. And I guess the better I understand their position, the better I can build my case."

The challenging work of attempting to understand the moral and emo-tional worlds that inform defendants' decision-making inevitably involves other justice assemblage actors. Police investigators, particularly those with years of experience with hundreds of violent criminal cases, provide pros-ecutors with particularly rich contextual insights as they consider case realities. Investigators' interpretations of the scene, which they formulate in the context of their experiences at similar, previous scenes, helps prose-cutors understand the mindset of the person who committed the crime.

"The blood is going this way, or the shell casings are going this way," Ashley might say to an investigator as they review crime scene photos together. "So does that mean he was walking towards him, and he was angry, or he was walking back in self-defense because he was scared?" She matches this reliance on investigators with knowledge of the weaknesses in her case, "because if you're really hell-bent on 'Well, this is what I think happened, he was very malicious and he wanted to do this,' being open or having your eyes open to the opposite of that, because the defense counsel going to kind of get up there and flip it any way they can."

These shared beliefs about the minutiae of the administration of justice develop among prosecutors over time. Individual socialization into the work of prosecution occurs within a work environment that requires particular behaviors, tasks, words, and perspectives. This process of habituation also requires that individual prosecutors find ways to cope with their consistent exposure to human suffering while maintaining a firm stance in cases irrespective of their complexity in order to administer justice on behalf of the state.

HABITUATION

Shannon has prosecuted criminal cases for eighteen years. When she goes home, she stops thinking about the violence and suffering that suffuse her everyday work. This was not always the case. Early in her career, she felt haunted by the details of what victims endured in child sexual abuse or domestic violence cases she prosecuted in Selma shortly after graduating from law school. Their fear followed her like a contagion, making her hesitant to venture into public places when she could avoid it. "I saw criminals everywhere," Shannon explains of this early stage in her career, when she lived and prosecuted cases in the same small Alabama city. "Mostly because I saw criminals everywhere."

Now when Shannon switches off her engine in the Walmart parking she knows that she will likely see a former defendant in a case she prosecuted or a defendant who is currently out on bond awaiting trial on a case she is currently prosecuting. This is just her everyday reality now, but earlier in her career as a prosecutor, she says, "the world just seem[ed] inherently like a terrifying place. But the longer that you go on, you find out—obviously nothing ever happened to me—and you calm it down a little bit." Shannon sees the world through the eyes of a long-term prosecutor, which means she can get frustrated with her friends and family members who are unaware of just how many violent crimes regularly occur in the community. "There are people dying," she says, "and how do you not see that? How did you not hear about that? Because that's not the world *they* live in, but that's the world *you* live in."

"It's not terrifying to me anymore," Shannon says of being called to spend her professional life in the realm of the horrible suffering human beings inflict on each other. "It's business, for the most part." This process happened gradually, as did her transition from initially being thrilled with winning a case to accepting the reality that sometimes the best possible case outcome means that a defendant will be convicted and spend the rest of his life in prison. Shannon remembers experiencing a new perspective as she left court one day after a sentencing hearing where, following her success in obtaining a guilty verdict, the judge sentenced the defendant to life without parole. "I was focused so much on the case," she says, "and there was just something about it. When I walked out, I would always be like, 'Well, I won!' and then one day I was like, 'Well, I don't think anybody won here.'" Following this recognition, Shannon was left with the visceral reality that the victim's mother lost her child to murder and the youthful defendant's mother lost her child to a life sentence in prison.

Winning a case does not always generate a sense of victory, particularly for prosecutors who are well aware that a felony conviction and prison time are just more negative events in an already lifelong series of personal hardships. Recognizing that cases are inherently complex occurs as part of prosecutors' habituation into the administration of justice. Before Maegan began her work as a prosecutor, her understanding of victimization was far less nuanced. "A lot of times I have victims that are just as guilty as the defendant," she says of her work prosecuting misdemeanor cases in District Court where, for some especially troubled families, "It's a race to the courthouse, who gets the warrant first ends up being the defendant or victim. . . . These victims aren't victims."

Habituation also entails more nuanced understandings of justice that account for the victim-offender overlap in practice. When Maegan says that she began to realize that "these victims aren't victims," she is referring to the complex realities of the victim-offender overlap whereby a victim may have a longer criminal history than a defendant and may act in ways—such as refusing to participate in prosecution—that do little to further the administration of justice. When Grace first began prosecuting cases, her understanding of justice was centered on the individual victim. "That's not always the case," she says after years of experience. "Sometimes justice is doing what you can the right way to keep our community safe. That is number one."

CONCLUSION Criminology's Place in the Future of the Justice Assemblage

"Y'all need to stop harassin' me!" a male voice shouts through Victim Service Officer Marilyn Anderson's speakerphone. "My blood pressure's goin' up!" Marilyn waits for a pause in his impassioned monologue, during which he explains how he wants nothing to do with prosecuting the man who shot him. His reasons for not cooperating with prosecutors spill out in rapid-fire speech that feels as if he is picking up a new justification to hurl toward Marilyn whenever the previous one falls flat in its efforts to persuade her. The shooting occurred over a year ago, he tells her, before continuing down the list of other reasons: his injuries have healed, he does not believe in prison, it was an accident, he was not the shooter's intended victim. When Marilyn interjects after patiently listening to the man, she uses a deliberately measured and calm voice to explain why it is important for him to come to the courthouse to speak with prosecutors about his case. "And your blood pressure isn't going up because someone shot you and may do so again, sir?" Marilyn asks. "You don't care that he may shoot someone else in the community?"

As the second-longest-serving staff member in the office, having worked for five separate Tuscaloosa County District Attorneys, Marilyn has seen firsthand how the components of the justice assemblage come together in unique ways depending on the individuals involved. "Hays leads by example and cares like any defense attorney," Marilyn says. "He always says, 'We work together seeking justice, you don't work for me. We follow the law and the evidence.'" This vision of a District Attorney's Office as a collaborative set of relationships demonstrates how what was previously understood as the criminal justice system is more accurately described as a justice assemblage comprised of institutional structures and practices, relationships and roles, and individual moral and emotional worlds. Simply put, the justice assemblage relies on relationships between individuals to help prosecutors achieve their goals of, as Paula put it, "punishment, community safety, and moving on to the next case."

For prosecutors, seeking justice requires navigating the institutional structures and practices, relationships and roles, and individual moral and emotional worlds that together create a whole that relies on all its constituent parts to function effectively as an assemblage. Conceptualizing criminal justice as a *system*—with its machine-like connotations of orderly processes and outcomes occurring independently of the individuals tasked with carrying them out—misses the everyday human realities comprising the law in practice. As an alternative, we have proposed the justice assemblage as a more nuanced way to understand criminal justice as an amalgamation of individual people and the interactions they have with one another as they navigate the institutional structures and practices central to the administration of justice.

The untold stories of how prosecutors, whose professional lives and struggles form the substance of the preceding chapters, experience the law in practice feature a very different set of dynamics from scholarly and popular portrayals of their work. These differences raise a central question that we will attempt to answer in this conclusion: what does a District Attorney's Office in Alabama offer to ongoing debates about prosecutorial discretion, violent crimes involving guns, and criminologists' role in the future of the justice assemblage? Our answer unfolds in three parts. First, we refute critiques of prosecutorial discretion by demonstrating the significant limitations prosecutors face in their professional roles. Second, we explore how our ethnography of a midsize southern city contributes to a more nuanced understanding of how local and regional cultures shape gun culture, violent crime involving guns, and the law in practice. Third, we draw on our experiences of designing and carrying out our collaborative work to offer practical guidance to criminologists who want to do meaningful, ethnographically embedded work in partnership with practitioners but lack knowledge about where to begin.

We appreciate how some readers may want us to make assessments of how the Tuscaloosa County District Attorney's Office is representative of prosecutorial practices or an outlier. Clearly, practices discussed throughout the book demonstrate the unfounded nature of the criticisms of prosecutors. Readers can juxtapose our discussion of these practices with the existing literature discussed here to draw their own conclusions.

MISPERCEPTIONS OF PROSECUTORIAL DISCRETION

Understanding criminal legal processes as a justice assemblage—rather than a Fordist, factory-like system that mechanically sorts and transforms suspects from defendants to probationers, prisoners, or free people determined not guilty of a crime—demonstrates the fallacy apparent in prevailing sentiments among many critical legal scholars' and criminologists' depictions of prosecutors as city- and county-level potentates who wield enormous discretionary powers. This misperception leads some critics to argue for greater public awareness of "how much responsibility prosecutors bear for profound systemic failures like mass incarceration, widespread racial disparities in the justice system, and the persistence of violent crime plaguing the same communities for whom the system is most punitive" (Gonzalez 2019, 9). Yet this misperception also informs the sentiment that the present moment is ripe for substantive prosecutorial reform, with some scholars positing "a continuum of reformers, from the 'disruptor' who wants to fundamentally change multiple structural components of the system to the 'pruner' whose reform intent is more circumscribed" (Balboni and Grometstein 2020, 261).

Recent research on de-prosecution paints a bleak portrait of the consequences of prosecutorial reform. In his 2022 article "De-prosecution and Death," criminologist Thomas Hogan notes how virulent critiques of prosecutors fail to recognize how prosecutors' power "is only absolute in the decision *not* to prosecute crimes" (Hogan 2022, 492). This reality has led some major metropolitan District Attorney's Offices to experiment with de-prosecution by opting not to prosecute certain crimes. The Philadelphia District Attorney's Office reduced the number of criminal sentencings by 70% as part of a de-carceration effort from 2015 to 2019 and simultaneously saw a statistically significant increase in the number of homicides for the same period. "The public in Philadelphia will have to make a normative choice," Hogan notes, "between a reduction in the number of prosecutions and an increase in homicides" (Hogan 2022, 490).

No reasonable person would agree that increased homicides are an acceptable collateral consequence of deliberately reducing the number of prosecutions. Yet de-prosecution efforts are themselves the product of widespread public misperceptions of prosecutorial discretion. Three popular critiques of prosecutorial discretion focus their arguments on how racism, state authority, and economic disparities negatively impact the administration of justice. Here we respond to these critiques—as well as to more general critiques of prosecutors—by arguing that the questions framing current debates about violent crimes involving guns are fundamentally misplaced. As Hogan (2022) found in his study of de-prosecution in Philadelphia, lower rates of prosecution significantly correlate with increases in homicide rates.

Rather than asking, per Gonzalez (2019), how and why prosecutors are responsible for mass incarceration, systemic racial injustice, and persistent violent crime in poor black communities, we urge future researchers who are interested in prosecutorial discretion to tackle much more pressing questions. Why are so many people using guns to commit crimes? Are the people who are endangering their communities by using guns to commit crimes being convicted? Are their plea offers consistent with other similar cases? In our view, the justice assemblage is working well if assemblage actors follow the law, analysis is consistent from person to person, and the community trusts the administration of justice. Three common misperceptions of the amount of discretion prosecutors can exercise in their everyday work in the justice assemblage center on racism, lack of accountability, and plea offers made to poor or indigent clients. Here we correct each of these misperceptions with real-world examples from our jurisdiction.

The most common misperception about prosecutorial discretion is that prosecutors disproportionately charge black men with more serious crimes than their white counterparts, resulting in longer, harsher prison sentences. This misperception regards racism as rampant in criminal justice processes and envisions racism as particularly egregious in Alabama due to the state's shameful history of slavery and postemancipation Jim Crow segregation. Physical reminders of segregation are never far away in Alabama. Susan's office windows look out onto Fosters Auditorium at The University of Alabama, where in 1963 Alabama governor George Wallace stood in the doorway to block two black students—Vivian Malone and James Hood—from entering the building to learn. President John F. Kennedy had to deploy National Guard troops and the US Attorney's Office to ensure that the students could safely enter the building. Every day, Susan and Brittany pass a tall stone memorial to Malone and Hood as they walk into their offices in Farrah Hall, which previously housed the University of Alabama's law school.

For most people who are not from Alabama, the names of Alabama cities like Selma, Montgomery, and Birmingham have no other frame of reference than the March on Selma, the Montgomery bus boycott, or Martin Luther King Jr.'s famous 1963 "Letter from a Birmingham Jail," in which he wrote, from his jail cell after being wrongfully incarcerated for leading peaceful anti-segregation protests, "Injustice anywhere is a threat to justice everywhere. We are caught in an inescapable network of mutuality, tied in a single garment of destiny" (King 1963, 1). While this short but powerful letter was required reading as part of the US history curriculum in Susan's New York State public elementary school, almost none of her students at The University of Alabama recall having read it in school. During a discussion about this in class, one of Susan's students shared that she had a history textbook at her private, tuition-paying Alabama middle school that asserted "most slaves led happy lives," a claim Susan found so shocking that she had trouble believing it until she read accounts of similarly historically inaccurate textbooks used in private and predominantly white schools across the South (Klein 2021; Merelli and Timsit 2018; Minton 2020).

Alabama prosecutors carry out their everyday work in the wake of these realities, both historical and contemporary. Facts indisputably demonstrate the overrepresentation of black people in Alabama jails and prisons relative to population size: black people are 28% of Alabama state residents, yet 43% of people in Alabama jails and 54% of people in Alabama prisons are black (Vera Institute of Justice 2022). The current criminological—and, to some extent, media—focus on racism in justice processes derives from the reality that young black men are disproportionately overrepresented among people incarcerated across the United States.

Yet this focus on racial overrepresentation, while factual, leaves a central question unanswered: what is the alternative for violent defendants, most of whom are black, whose actions terrorize communities that are also predominantly black? Previous chapters feature myriad examples, from our systematic review of all Tuscaloosa County felony criminal cases involving a gun, of violent crimes committed by defendants with guns, and in many cases, these defendants have previous criminal histories that legally prohibit them from possessing a firearm at the time that they committed a new crime. These violent defendants' disrespect for human life, the law, and community make them a threat to public safety so severe that many victims and witnesses refuse to cooperate with prosecutors because they fear retaliation. What feasible alternative to incarceration exists for individuals who, to use just a few examples from previous chapters, press the barrel of a gun so tightly against a sleeping victim's forehead that a ballistics expert can find very little trace of the powder or debris—known as stippling—that accompanies a gunshot? How should society treat someone who, while attempting to shoot a rival, fired his weapon so indiscriminately at a public pool that a toddler suffered gunshot wounds?

The reality is that the vast majority of defendants in our jurisdiction have very limited knowledge of firearms beyond their awareness of the power and authority carrying a gun conveys to them. They have never practiced firing a weapon at a shooting range, do not know about proper cleaning and maintenance, and most have even less knowledge about how to fire a gun to reach the intended target. Their knowledge of guns, like that of many Americans who do not own a gun, comes from inaccurate media representations. An actor who pretends to fire a gun in a movie often does so theatrically, by extending a single arm to discharge the weapon held in his or her hand. Yet any responsible gun owner knows that firing a gun in this way is both impractical and unsafe because of the recoil, or kickback, caused—per basic physics—by the bullet exerting equal force in both directions as it leaves the chamber. A new or inexperienced shooter who is unprepared for this recoil has little chance of hitting their intended target.

These realities frequently led Susan to wonder, as she reviewed hundreds and hundreds of felony criminal cases involving guns, if our jurisdiction might have much higher murder rates if all defendants actually knew how to handle a firearm. The relatively few murder cases involving rural defendants, who typically have experience hunting to provide food for their families, often feature far fewer shots fired in a murder case because the defendant is an experienced shooter. Contrast, for example, the rural domestic violence victim dead from a single gunshot wound to the back of her head versus the urban victim of a drug deal gone wrong who bleeds to death before the ambulance arrives after being shot multiple times outside the center mass of his body.

The rhetorical focus on the overrepresentation of black men in prison eclipses a singular reality: black people are equally dramatically overrepresented among crime victims and witnesses as they are among defendants. Arguments from the perspective of mass incarceration contend that poor black men are overrepresented in jails and prisons relative to overall population size because of poverty, lack of opportunity, and systemic racism. Yet this argument does not explain why a vast majority of any group of people who face these same circumstances do not commit violent crimes.

Legitimate complaints about District Attorneys are the same as complaints generally made about any other elected official and are rooted in problems with the human condition's fallibility. District Attorneys who honor their role, uphold the law, and ensure consistent analysis irrespective of race, class, gender, and other differences will succeed in their work. On the other hand, District Attorneys—and prosecutors more generally—who view their roles as political positions that render them beholden to political elites or powerful allies will be compromised time and again.

A second common misunderstanding of prosecutorial discretion regards prosecutors as omnipotent, boundless, discretion-wielding bullies backed by an all-powerful state with tremendous resources at their disposal. As anyone who has ever worked in a county, state, or federal government office knows, the all-powerful state simply does not exist in the way critics of ostensibly omnipotent prosecutors believe that it does. What we have instead is a justice assemblage comprised of individuals. Nonetheless, the dominant image of prosecutors in both academic scholarship and popular culture continues to represent them as all-powerful actors with unfettered discretion to exert their will. The reality, though, is that prosecutors cannot wish into existence the facts and evidence needed to obtain a conviction. Sometimes they struggle to have the tools necessary to do their work. Ironically enough, as Susan and Hays were editing this book and discussing this incorrect public perspective in light of a particular case we wanted to revisit as part of our analysis, the electronic system housing all case records froze. Hays was temporarily unable to access the case records, which was extremely frustrating in the moment because this system glitch prevented us from locating information we needed to edit the book.

"Oh, fuck!" Hays loudly exclaimed as he threw his hands up in the air in frustration. "You see this?" he asked Susan as he gestured toward the nonfunctional computer screen in front of them. "Here's the all-powerful fuckin' state in action!" Such challenges with limited resources, technology, and personnel are realities for prosecutors and public defenders alike, both of whom are governmental employees. Far greater public sympathy exists for public defenders, whom many people associate with low pay, high caseloads, and a pervasive sense of overwhelm. This perception contrasts sharply with public misunderstandings of prosecutors' relationship to the state as bestowing them with endless resources and authority.

Yet the reality is that public defenders and prosecutors are both governmental employees earning comparable salaries, and public defenders have a much lighter workload than prosecutors because public defenders in our jurisdiction handle 60%–70% of felony criminal cases. Prosecutors, in contrast, handle all the felony criminal cases in their jurisdiction. Prosecutors at the Tuscaloosa County District Attorney's Office routinely have 500 criminal cases each, whereas public defenders have 150 cases each. This simple office-to-office comparison in terms of numbers reveals how the DA's Office is dramatically under-lawyered relative to the Public Defenders' Office. So those who accept the premise that public defenders are overworked must also acknowledge that prosecutors are three times as overworked as public defenders. Nonetheless, Tuscaloosa County prosecutors obtain convictions in 80% of their cases because of their level of preparation.

Despite this public misperception of prosecutors as omnipotent, prosecutors often feel extremely overwhelmed as they consider the many ways a case can fail. This sense of overwhelm, again in sharp contrast to other types of lawyers, occurs in a context where their jobs require prosecutors, working together as an office, to handle every single felony criminal case in their jurisdiction. Susan frequently felt great empathy for prosecutors as she observed them struggling to manage their cases in ways that revealed their heavily circumscribed state power and authority. Victims and witnesses can destroy a prosecutor's case by refusing to cooperate with police or prosecutors. In the absence of at least one victim or witness willing to cooperate with prosecutors, obtaining a conviction is unlikely.

Problems with police investigations in terms of evidence, questioning, Mirandizing, or other issues can also result in a case being lost or dismissed. Police typically arrive at shooting scenes with some knowledge of what they are about to encounter, but this knowledge remains confined to what a caller conveys to the 911 dispatcher. Some callers give their name and contact information, and the name of the shooter, and describe in great detail what has occurred and why they believe it happened, all before police arrive on scene. Yet anonymous callers inform the 911 dispatcher only that a shooting occurred at a particular address, which means police have extremely limited information prior to their arrival.

Once at the scene of the shooting, police often find chaos that can lead to mistakes that subsequently compromise a case. Even a flawless police investigation in a case that goes to trial years later will suffer from the passage of time, with memories lost and victims and witnesses who, frustrated at the time the case has taken to go to trial or simply disinterested in its outcome, do not want to cooperate with prosecutors. Inherently a case begins with a police investigation, but prosecutors spend dozens of hours reviewing what police have done at the beginning of an investigation. In the course of doing so, prosecutors may discover that insufficient grounds exist to proceed with a criminal case.

Highly skilled defense attorneys can often win a case when they successfully lure a prosecutor to "play on their field," to use a common office expression, by focusing on minutiae that detracts from the prosecutor's argument. Judges ultimately decide sentencing, probation, and other important decisions beyond the prosecutor's control. Prosecutors can also lose a case when members of the jury believe prosecutors have lost credibility because of some minute detail in the case. Prosecutors often lamented that jurors seem to want every aspect of the crime video recorded, an audio-recorded confession from the defendant, and DNA evidence.

Absent some illegality or demonstrable nonperformance of core functions, the electorate chooses the District Attorney. This democratic process provides voters with an opportunity to elect those whose actions reflect voters' values. Prosecutors, in this way, exert the will of the people rather than the kind of omnipotent discretion many critics argue compromises the integrity of the justice process. Yet while prosecutors' powers are limited by these same justice processes, as well as the many ways a case can go wrong, they do have more authority than any other assemblage actor in terms of their abilities to make changes in the community.

Prosecutors' authority—as distinct from their circumscribed power—allows them to formulate policies, as Hays has done with the gun present policy, consistent with the law and with the understanding that judges make the ultimate decisions in cases. Unlike defense attorneys, whose job it is to do their client's bidding within the boundaries of the law, prosecutors act on behalf of the community. Unlike judges, who remain isolated from the community with respect to decisions in their legal capacities, prosecutors can directly engage with the community to enact policies that provide opportunity, as Hays has done with the Second Chance diversion program, for first-time nonviolent offenders.

A third common misperception about prosecutors revolves around the equity of plea offers for indigent defendants. The Sixth Amendment guarantees defendants the right to a public trial with a jury of their peers, yet the vast majority of criminal defendants accept a plea agreement and never appear before a jury. Critics argue that the discretion prosecutors wield in making these plea offers to defendants, most of whom cannot afford an attorney, undermines the democratic process by creating a two-tiered system of justice: one for defendants who can afford to hire an attorney with time to devote to their defense, and another for defendants who cannot afford an attorney and must depend on a public defender who does not have adequate time to construct the same quality of defense. The Sixth Amendment also guarantees defendants the right to a public trial without unnecessary delay, yet years often elapse between a crime and a trial. Critics argue that prosecutors attempt to expedite cases through the system by relying substantially on plea agreements rather than jury trials and, in so doing, compromise the integrity of the justice process.

Yet this misperception does not withstand scrutiny. Eighty-four percent of people incarcerated in Alabama prisons are serving a sentence for a violent crime. When prosecutors make a plea offer, they do so after detailed review of the facts of the case and within the boundaries of what sentencing guidelines, which ultimately do not recommend prison for most nonviolent cases, allow. The burden of proof is on the prosecutor, and to ensure the process is fair and just in each case, prosecutors in our jurisdiction share all the evidence they have in a case with the defense attorney as soon as they have it. Critics, including some public defenders, who regard plea offers as unjust and unfair do not withstand scrutiny because defendants, of course, can reject a plea offer and proceed to trial. Public defenders, who have access to the same evidence and any other relevant case materials as prosecutors, are able to review this information in a work environment where they have far fewer clients—and so theoretically more time with each case—than prosecutors. If a public defender is encouraging the defendant to consider a plea offer, logic holds that either the public defender believes their client is guilty or the public defender is forcing their client to plead guilty.

SITUATING THE JUSTICE ASSEMBLAGE IN CULTURAL CONTEXT

Culture shapes violent crime, gun ownership, and the law in practice just as much as culture shapes ways of speaking, culinary traditions, and ways of relating to other people. Our ethnography of a mid-size southern city contributes to a more nuanced understanding of how local and regional cultures shape gun culture, violent crime involving guns, and the law in practice. The justice assemblage we have described here, while unique in some aspects to the Deep South, resembles its counterparts nationwide because it is shaped by its cultural context, particularly the ubiquity of guns in Alabama, the meaning of carrying, and legal cynicism among law-abiding gun owners.

Guns are mundane, unremarkable objects in Alabama and the majority of people who carry them do so safely and legally. It is not uncommon in Alabama, particularly in rural areas, to see a person who is wearing street clothes, and not law enforcement, wearing a holstered firearm. Highway billboards in Alabama, and throughout the South, advertise discount gun stores, shooting classes, and shooting ranges that offer those who purchase a ticket the opportunity to shoot expensive weapons that they otherwise might not be able to afford to own themselves. It would not be an overstatement to argue that guns are part of the fabric of everyday life in the Deep South.

Many people in the Deep South have an intimately sentimental relationship with guns as tools that constitute a means of survival. Rural people almost anywhere in the United States are likely to regard a gun as a means of providing food by hunting, much as an ax is a tool for splitting firewood to heat a home. This is true as much in rural Wisconsin or Alaska as it is in rural Alabama. Yet poverty is such a pervasive reality for so many rural people in the Deep South that guns used for hunting take on a particularly intimate meaning and gun ownership is a particularly important rite of passage in family life in our region.

Susan's husband, who grew up impoverished in a rural South Louisiana trailer park, first learned to shoot at eight years old and got a .410 shotgun as a tenth birthday present so he could shoot squirrels for gumbo to feed his struggling family. His rural school offered a hunter safety course with live ammunition and shotguns so other young people could get the hunter safety card required for young hunters in Louisiana. Yet, as discussed in chapter 1, these tools can also dramatically shift in meaning depending on their context; that same .410 that was a child's prized birthday present was subsequently stolen during a break-in by a neighbor who later went to prison for paying two men to murder his wife so he could collect the insurance money and use it to repay his significant debt. As the gun travels from person to person and context to context, its legal and cultural meanings undergo a profound shift.

High rates of intergenerational poverty in the Deep South may also contribute to connections between violent crimes involving guns and widespread feelings of hopelessness or being stuck in a particular place. People rarely move very far away from home in the Deep South. The extremely high value our regional culture places on family ties combines with poverty and its associated lack of opportunity to firmly root many people in the place where their family members have been living for generations. It is not difficult to understand how, in these contexts, community and relationship tensions can bubble up to the surface in complex ways among people who feel stuck, with no hope for the future and associated lack of initiative. Consider how the stolen gun resold as part of the illicit drug trade for fifty dollars enters into this social equation, particularly in a neighborhood where drug sales and shootings are common.

For the young man holding it, this stolen and resold gun may be a symbol of power and authority because he believes carrying the gun will benefit him in some way. His feeling is part of a shared cultural ethos among many young men, which helps fuel an illegal market for guns that, in turn, prompts so many home and car break-ins by those searching for guns to sell. Some of the guns stolen will be from rural people who regard their guns as tools used to hunt or to kill wild hogs or coyotes who threaten livestock, or people in town who regard guns as essential tools for home defense in the event of a break-in.

In these and many other instances, the central question is not what guns can do, but what people choose to do with them. We recommend that future researchers in this area consider exploring how attitudes and beliefs about gun ownership and use vary across extreme disparities in communities by race, class, and gender. It would be fascinating to understand why poor rural whites living in decrepit trailers who have no job prospects in an area where methamphetamine and opioid misuse is widespread commit so few violent crimes involving guns. Hopelessness, even when it is intergenerational, does not in and of itself explain why people choose to use guns to commit violent crimes.

This point brings us to the broader cultural meaning of carrying a gun and how this meaning varies by context. The gun is an artifact infused with socially constructed meanings, but the action of "carrying" is a central component to that meaning-making process. For example, simply owning a gun kept at home has a very different cultural meaning from the meaning and power attached to the same gun when it is affixed to a person's body or traveling throughout the day in close proximity to a body, such as in the glove box of a pickup truck.

In many contexts, the activity or practice of carrying creates a psychological bond between the carrier and the gun, enabling the gun to play a bigger role in the production of the identity of the carrier. This is true of people who carry guns for practical purposes, such as hunters, and those who must be armed as part of their jobs, such as law enforcement. Yet it is also true for others who carry for extensive periods of time, including those who carry guns while breaking the law. We even see the cultural meanings of carrying evident in how assemblage actors handle guns seized at a crime scene depending on the geographical context. In some areas, as in the Deep South, seized guns are resold via federal firearms licensees as part of the belief that a gun is itself a morally inert object. In other geographical areas, seized guns are destroyed for political purposes to promote the belief that fewer guns means less violent crime, aligning with the belief systems that promote programs that ask people with unused prescription opioids to turn them in because of the belief that doing so will reduce opioid misuse and dependence.

Our unique regional context also features a potentially unique dynamic confronting justice assemblage actors, particularly prosecutors, in terms of legal cynicism among law-abiding gun owners. Legal cynicism literature tends to be couched in discussions of race and marginalized communities' distrust for the law. Yet in addition to the legal cynicism we see with uncooperative victims and witnesses, we also see a whole new angle of legal cynicism that may be unique to law-abiding gun owners. In our case, we see legal cynicism among otherwise law-abiding people who believe in the system because of dishonesty and disinformation revolving around political debates about guns.

Consider, for example, Corey's disarming approach to voir dire in which she asks prospective jurors, who often respond with laughter, "Now we're in Alabama, so who here does *not* own a gun?" It is difficult to imagine prosecutors in New York State going to the great lengths prosecutors in our jurisdiction do to discuss gun ownership with prospective jurors. To succeed in their cases, prosecutors in our jurisdiction need to understand, from a law-abiding gun owner's perspective, what prospective jurors may be thinking in a case involving a gun. The prospective juror who is silently thinking "everything becomes an excuse to take my gun—your rifle is too powerful, your handgun is too concealable—and talk of gun safety is really about gun control" may understandably be very concerned about a case in which a gun features prominently. Without engaging thoughtfully and thoroughly with prospective jurors' beliefs, prosecutors risk losing credibility if jurors dismiss them as another group of governmental or legal actors they believe are trying to take their guns away.

For prosecutors in our jurisdiction, these realities mean that it is important to focus on a fair criminal justice process that considers the processes by which people end up in prison. This involves asking difficult questions. What does fairness mean? Is the failure in the system, or is the failure in the community? Where can we locate the failure? What sounds good versus what is true? Eighty-four percent of men who are currently serving a prison sentence in Alabama are there after being convicted of a violent crime. This leads to some tough questions. What if the process is good and people are not law-abiding? Abolishing prison or decriminalizing bad actions does not solve that problem. The defendant's bad action is supposed to be worth something to the community, otherwise the justice process loses credibility. State financial constraints do not define right and wrong, as fairness comes from the justice process and not from the result. Fundamentally, we can only deconstruct this process so much before we are back at anarchy.

ENVISIONING AN END TO DRIVE-BY CRIMINOLOGY THROUGH ETHNOGRAPHIC AND PARTICIPATORY METHODS

Brittany, who is a geographer, and Susan, who is an anthropologist, came to work as criminologists because of their extensive research and practitioner experiences with victims, defendants, and criminal justice professionals. We were drawn to criminology because of what we saw as the discipline's tremendous potential to engage with practitioners to solve real world problems. From our earliest days of graduate school, we both learned to approach our work with the goal of using research to support meaningful, evidence-based change for the better. We knew that learning what "better" means in a criminal justice context requires long-term, intensive immersion in institutions tasked with carrying out the everyday administration of justice. In the introduction, we explored some of the reasons why so few criminologists engage in participatory research, including the discipline's historical reliance on quantitative (and predominantly administrative) data, difficulty gaining access to criminal justice practitioners' everyday work environments, and the time investment required by participatory work.

We have come to think of this disciplinary failure to engage in participatory research as a phenomenon we term *drive-by criminology*. Criminologists conduct drive-by research when they regard criminal justice agencies as little more than repositories of data, such as police investigative reports, court records, or, less frequently, personal experiences recorded in interviews. This data, of course, is a state record of individual choices and, often, individual suffering. Failing to spend any meaningful time with criminal justice practitioners as they produce and collect such material ultimately compromises the integrity of the work, as it results in limited trust between academics and practitioners, academics' limited understanding of the challenges practitioners face in their work, and, of course, little real momentum toward evidence-based change.

Many criminologists place a naïve and almost fetishistic trust in secondary data that is novel among the academic disciplines in its utter disconnection from the realities of how criminal justice practitioners actually use that data as a primary source. Prosecutors, police, and all other assemblage actors know that any criminal case only begins with that information, which is necessarily incomplete because it omits context. For example, a defendant whom law enforcement notes "had been drinking" prior to a shooting may or may not "count" in a national database as using substances at the time of incident, yet that data point noted by police will (or will not) be substantially rehashed and regurgitated in criminologists' claims to truth from these datasets.

Criminologists' fetishization of such secondary datasets loses the nuance of criminal cases because, as Ben sagely noted, "the case is out here," meaning that the important details are those gleaned from discussions with people at the crime scene, or those who know the victim and/or the defendant. In short, criminal justice practitioners themselves, by and large, do not rely on these repositories of human suffering that criminologists gloss as datasets. And yet, despite this lack of knowledge, it is still common to hear criminologists wonder why many practitioners do not take them seriously.

Consider the objectives of recordkeeping, and with these objectives in mind, how cases are coded (and by whom) and to what end. Criminologists must consider how such recordkeeping limits us and what it reveals as well as what it eliminates or obscures from view. We acknowledge that analysis of secondary data takes a tremendous amount of time—after all, Susan spent a significant amount of her time in the office reviewing felony reports in gun present cases—yet it is not enough to make the kinds of meaningful arguments most criminologists would like to make about the nature of crime and justice. Immersive methods, such as the ethnographic work that formed the basis of this study, are much more likely to illuminate the complexities of these realities.

Quite honestly, criminologists who complain that practitioners aren't listening to them are often not speaking in a way that makes sense to practitioners. We see this when criminologists engage in drive-by criminology in cases where the realities of their subject of study remains, at best, abstract to them because of their personal disconnection from it. Criminologists whose only real contact with crime comes from secondary data use this data to make claims to truth based solely on their analysis of this data. In so doing, they risk experiencing an even more insidiously insulating effect while interpreting data they have had no role in collecting, and while simultaneously remaining personally detached from the issues they purport to study. While listening to criminologists present the results of secondary data analysis at conferences, Susan could not help but picture their research personas as hazmat-suited figures carrying industrial vacuums designed to efficiently extract material from a site with the minimum possible contact.

From the safety of a university desk or home office in a gated community, it is all too easy to make grandiose arguments that malign prosecutors and other assemblage actors as ill-intentioned while simultaneously identifying people who break the law as victims of an oppressive system. These arguments are easy for academics to make, after all, because they have little real relevance to their own immediate safety, as is evident when academics make decisions about where to live, which school district their own children will attend, and where they will spend their social time. Academics rarely, if ever, live in neighborhoods where violent crime occurs on a regular basis. They do not send their children to failing city schools where students must pass through a metal detector before going to class. Given a choice, most people would do the same.

Fortunately, a small but robust body of legal ethnographies rejects this dominant criminological trend by providing deep and contextualized insight into law enforcement practices and highlighting the importance of studying criminal justice practices and how practitioners understand and shape these practices. For example, ethnographic work on policing is not uncommon among European criminologists, and these studies provide outstanding examples of how ethnography's immersion allows researchers to understand the nuances of policing in practice. Ethnography with English narcotic investigation units, for example, revealed how contemporary police officers tasked with investigating drug cases have a wide range of political beliefs and life experiences, including experiences with illicit drug use and skepticism about the efficacy of their work (Bacon 2016). Bacon found that officers who had personal experiences with drug use used their knowledge in their investigative work of drug networks, and his ethnographic work emphasizes how increased regulation of police powers combines with austerity measures within police departments to complicate how police investigate drug cases, particularly since drug users and dealers remain the most valuable sources of information in building cases. Understanding *how* police navigate clashing administrative rules and street realities while staying within the boundaries of the law requires the long-term immersion only ethnography can provide (Bacon 2016).

Another English policing study followed homicide investigations in real time as they moved from the crime scene to documentation to adjudication, effectively allowing the researchers an insider's view of police investigations, which illuminated the central role of both narrative and collaborative sensemaking in homicide cases (Brookman et al. 2020a; Jones et al. 2021). Anthropologist Didier Fassin's (2013) ethnographic study of French policing likewise relied on his immersion as part of a plainclothes police unit in high-crime Paris suburbs and accordingly demonstrated how French police—who are largely unfamiliar with the communities they police—are unaware of how the normalization of routinized aggressive, intrusive policing impacts the community in which they work. Instead, they find themselves trapped in a toxic cycle whereby residents passively accept stop and search practices as routine and suspicion reigns in the relationship between police and the policed (Fassin 2013).

Such ethnographic work is especially important for criminologists in small and mid-sized cities to undertake because studies of major metropolitan areas completely dominate both scholarly and mass media accounts of violent crime, leaving a huge vacuum with respect to small and mid-size cities, like Tuscaloosa and its southern peers, which have rates of violent crime on par with Chicago, Baltimore, and Washington, DC. Criminologists who want to make a real and meaningful difference in the everyday operations of justice should focus their energies on the communities where they live and work rather than on communities where they have limited meaningful engagement or connection.

Criminologists who want to start and sustain a long-term, community-engaged research partnership with a criminal justice partner might consider the following five-step road map that we successfully followed to establish a mutually respectful and mutually beneficial career-long partnership. We provide this road map because of our observation that most criminologists appear to use the term *community-engaged* very differently from their peers in social work, anthropology, or related social science disciplines in which career-long relationships with research partners and participants is not only normal, but sometimes expected. Yet most criminologists tend to understand *community-engaged* work as encompassing a few meetings with a community agency followed by data sharing and delivery of a report, or perhaps speaking with media about the importance of criminological research to solve real-world problems. These understandings are not necessarily incorrect, yet we argue for the value of deepening relationships between criminologists and practitioners through community-based work.

During the course of writing this book, our academic department made a bold choice for our graduate program: each of our graduate students would have the option to engage in real-world community-based work as part of their graduate degree. We made this shift because we recognize that most students learn by doing. Graduate students who are interested in understanding how police conduct interviews, for instance, are actively pursuing partnerships with local police departments. Graduate students who feel passionately about ending violence against women are preparing to review case resolution statistics in all misdemeanor and felony cases with women victims to ensure that no victims are missed irrespective of the charge. Graduate students concerned about mental health treatment in correctional facilities are working with the county jail to speak with people who are incarcerated about their needs.

We made these choices in a cultural and political context in which pervasive perceptions across the country regard universities as out of touch with reality. Consider the following recent headlines from news outlets across the political spectrum. While some may seem patently ridiculous and regretful rather than indicative, the fact that so many exist points to a significant public crisis of confidence in universities on par with the crisis in public confidence in prosecutors and criminal justice processes more generally. The *New York Times* ran a story titled "Elite Universities Are Out of Touch. Blame the Campus" (Burns 2022), while *Fox News* exclaimed, "Cornell Professor Warns Universities Are Eliminating the Meaning of 'Objective Truth' from Classrooms with CRT" (Colton 2022). *Vox* ran an op-ed titled "I'm a Liberal Professor and My Liberal Students Terrify Me"

(Schlosser 2015). Couple this with cautionary tales from *Times Higher Education*, such as the piece warning "If You Love Research, Academia May Not Be for You" (Matthews 2018), and, of course, a demoralizing Reddit thread called "Fox News Moderator Suggesting 'Professor' Is a Lazy Job" (Reddit 2021). Taken together, these headlines—even as they draw on regretful stereotypes—give us a sense of the real crisis of confidence in academia's ability to do meaningful work in community.

Our five-step process for community-engaged work emerged in a fraught sociopolitical context that foments mistrust between academics and practitioners. We accordingly relay what we believe works best for researchers in terms of establishing a long-term research partnership, including finding a community partner, identifying shared research goals and parameters, developing trust and loyalty, and being open to evolving possibilities as the project develops. Criminologists who truly want to be community engaged all share practitioners' goals of decreasing crime and increasing quality of life for the community. As we will see, the central question academic-practitioner partners must address is *How do we get there?*

The first step in the community-engaged research process is for the criminologist (henceforth known as "you") to find a community partner with whom to hold your first meeting. As you embark on this exciting journey, keep an open mind while remaining keenly attuned to your own moral compass as you consider the research path you want to follow. Are you, perhaps without even being conscious of doing so, approaching the work with beliefs or political views that may preclude you from analyzing evidence from multiple perspectives? What is the likelihood that your own unconscious biases might shape the project in ways that do not reflect the full complexity of the human experience within the justice assemblage?

You may have a gatekeeper with community connections who is able to introduce you, such as someone at your university who previously conducted a successful project in community, or you may have to establish those connections on your own. Susan has always made her own connections with her community partners, although she also found it helpful to immediately emphasize that she comes from a family of police officers. If possible, attend community meetings about issues either related or adjacent to your subject of study to observe interactions/relationships between agency actors, with a keen ethnographic eye to fractious encounters to ascertain not just who you might work with, but how that work might unfold in practice.

Remember that just as academics routinely feel overwhelmed with sometimes competing research, teaching, and service demands, practitioners have their own struggles and time pressures that may make it difficult for them to see the value of research or, once the analysis is complete, to actually put the findings into meaningful practice. Agencies with practitioners who repeatedly mention feeling overwhelmed may not have the bandwidth to meaningfully partner with a researcher. Agencies that experience overwhelm as standard operating procedure, due to poor leadership or lack of staff training and preparedness to deal with everyday crises, will likely have limited capacities to work with researchers even if they express interest in doing so.

There is also the reality that agency leaders need to prioritize issues as they see them and participatory research with an outsider may fall to the bottom of their list because they lack the time or energy to see research as a potentially transformative endeavor. At some point, the researcher may need to distinguish between "I'm really busy right now but want to work with you" and "You seem like a nice person, but please leave me alone." For Susan, becoming part of the office and seeing that exhaustion firsthand deepened her understanding of prosecutors' workload. Early one morning Susan stood in an ADA's office doorway surveying his uncharacteristically messy desk and bleary eyes, both signaling he had worked all night preparing for a particularly difficult trial beginning the next day. When he saw Susan, he immediately and sincerely apologized for forgetting about a meeting they had scheduled to discuss uncooperative victims and witnesses in the case. It went unspoken, of course, that trial preparation took priority over their meeting, yet this instance impressed on Susan the differences between the energy necessary for trial preparation and her own much more flexible summer research schedule. In sharp contrast with the exhausted prosecutor, Susan had an idyllic nine hours of sleep the night before, awoke to her rooster crowing, and then drove at a leisurely pace through the beautiful Alabama countryside to the courthouse, where she talked at length with the front entrance deputies about their respective gardens and fruit trees. Had Susan not had firsthand knowledge from her long-term observations of the time constraints facing the exhausted prosecutor, she might have mistaken his forgetting their meeting for lack of interest or even disorganization.

Just as time constraints can hinder or even prohibit participatory projects from the beginning, practitioners who seem especially eager to collaborate may not have fully thought through their own understandings of research and what it can realistically accomplish for them. They may, for instance, have an entirely different vision of research than you do. Many a novice community-engaged researcher has found themselves unhappily positioned as an unpaid grant writer or data analyst by practitioners who lack understanding of the time commitment involved or that many practitioner-oriented federal grants cannot be submitted through university research offices.

As a criminologist, you indisputably bring tremendous skills and resources to community-engaged work. A thoughtful practitioner with a commitment to using data analysis as a tool to improve the everyday operations of justice will immediately recognize the great potential of a collaboration. Criminologists, especially those in stable academic positions, conduct research as part of their jobs and so have time to spend with data that would be unthinkable for practitioners. Hays, for example, knew that the Filemaker system containing all the criminal case reports filed in our jurisdiction contained a wealth of information that could prove extremely useful in understanding the dynamics at work in violent crimes involving guns. Yet the tremendous workload everyone at the Tuscaloosa County District Attorney's Office shoulders would make it impossible for them to systematically analyze these dynamics without the help of a dedicated research team like ours.

While you should remain mindful of the strengths you bring to a potential collaboration, we suggest that you attend your first meeting with your potential community partner ready to listen and take copious notes, rather than to convince your potential community partner of the value of working with you. Susan remembers saying approximately two full sentences during her first meeting with Hays because he was speaking so enthusiastically and at such length about the possibility of working together and had so many ideas to share. During that first meeting, Susan chose to use her many years of community-based participatory research experience to listen very closely to everything Hays said, thank him for his time, and then see what happened next.

This first meeting could have ended very differently had Susan misinterpreted Hays's lengthy explanations of his priorities as inflexibility or lack of interest in her own research experience. Instead, she acknowledged how practitioners' communication styles tend to be more direct and hierarchical, in contrast with academics' more indirect styles of communication. Consider how academic conference attendees often take several minutes to ask a question because academic norms favor deep contextualization of questions asked, so that the questioner is sharing as much about themselves and their perspective as they are asking for information from the person being questioned. Practitioners work very differently because their priorities tend to focus on immediate problem-solving, which requires directness and delivering clear instructions about the options for solving a particular problem.

Likewise, this direct communication style is part of a professional culture among practitioners that is much more hierarchical than the professional culture pervading academia, where faculty have a great deal of flexibility regarding how they structure their time and respective research agendas. In a practitioner setting with a clear leader who makes binding decisions on behalf of the group, there is always the ethical risk of researchers sliding over into administrative criminology with a practitioner partner dictating terms and outcomes, but—as we argued in the introduction—the core tenets of participatory research guard against these realities. In fact, Susan and Brittany learned from prosecutors how to use spoken language much more effectively and concisely. Their communications with others at the university benefited in some instances, such as faculty meetings, as they asked direct, concise questions rather than contextualizing these questions within meandering accounts of past practices and institutional norms elsewhere.

From the first meeting forward, have a realistic understanding of your professional strengths, available time, and personal limitations. This is especially important in the context of the unfortunately widespread disdain many practitioners have for academics, whom they see as disconnected from their everyday realities. Respect the fact that "I am a world expert in X" or "my book on Y" probably has little meaning to a hard-working person who has never met you or read your work, and has just spent the last week working midnight shifts investigating cases, apprehending suspects, or poring over the minutiae of a murder case while preparing for trial. As you prepare for the first few meetings with your community partner, ask yourself, "Am I presenting myself as someone I would want to work with if I was working at this agency?" and be honest about your response. When collaborators genuinely like one another and consider each other to be like-minded people, their partnership is much more likely to be a success.

Some researchers might ask whether ethical issues arise if a researcher loses objectivity when wholly immersed in an ethnographic research project with practitioners she regards as friends. For us, spending more time together only built stronger relationships and better research because of our mutual trust. Being among the decision-makers for the long term changes the research dynamic because over time it is more difficult to maintain preconceived ideas. The ethnographic researcher does not see snapshots or glimpses but the whole picture by actually seeing participants in a research study act versus hearing them discuss their actions. Ethnographic researchers have the opportunity to challenge themselves and their community partners throughout the study by noting whether differences exist between what is espoused and what is done.

Extended periods of time together also produced more research ideas and new directions, as when Susan and Brittany proposed the systematic review of all domestic violence cases we are now undertaking together, or when Hays began mailing jurors surveys posttrial to assess their perceptions of their experiences and then asked us to review the results to better understand jurors' perspectives. It also meant increasing openness to grant writing together, which was initially a point of disagreement due to concerns about dependency on grant funds, and allowed us to hire a postdoctoral researcher to statistically analyze all of the gun present cases. Our team's goal is to work together rather than to be cronies under the guise of science, as some criticisms of administrative criminology might have it. Having unlimited access to the unvarnished realities of prosecuting cases meant we had complete freedom to explore. Such transparency should be a goal for all practitioners and academics, as it inspires community confidence in the work and in justice processes done correctly.

The next step involves identifying shared goals and research parameters by answering a series of questions with your agency partner, while being transparent about your own goals and planned approach to the research process. Be clear in your own mind about what you *want* to accomplish as well as what you *have to* accomplish as part of your own work responsibilities as an academic. How your collaboration might initially approach publishing, grant writing, and involving students in the project are all valuable points of discussion at this stage, although you will certainly revisit these topics as the project develops. It is also worthwhile to initially discuss (and continue revisiting) the political framing of questions asked in the analysis and, as well, the political ends to which results of the analysis may be put.

There are also practical questions to consider as your relationship with your community partner deepens, especially if you will be spending significant amounts of time together. How will you spend your time at the agency? How will your presence balance meaningful engagement without being obtrusive in a way that is mutually beneficial to the agency and to you as the researcher? For those working in a law enforcement context, are there any safety concerns that exist, and, if so, how should the partners handle them? Are there specific things you can do to establish mutual trust and respect with agency partners, such as completing trainings or certifications, or is building trust just a matter of time and experience (as is often the case)?

There are also questions regarding confidentiality and trust that go well beyond the traditional Institutional Review Board confidentiality protections that, after all, truly pertain to the kind of drive-by, time-limited projects with a finite set of methods we are critiquing here. What can you do to build trust with criminal justice actors you'll interact with on a regular basis at the agency? Agenda-driven academics and, perhaps especially, journalists unfortunately have set a negative precedent that may make practitioners hesitant to engage in collaboration, and so expect that the early stages of your work together will involve ascertaining and working through perspectival differences that may otherwise cloud the work. Designing the project together will ensure that the researcher and community partner speak in one voice: developing research questions, interview guides, and data collection instructions, and clearly establishing how all end products—such as data, reports, conference presentations, publications, and so on—will be shared is also valuable at this stage.

Building and maintaining trust requires having difficult conversations that require both practitioners and academics to push their professional boundaries. For example, after Hays implemented major changes to the Second Chance program, he asked if we could evaluate the new program's success. Susan suggested offering this project to colleagues, who proposed a quantitative approach to the evaluation and presented him with a literature review on diversion courts as a response to mass incarceration. For him, some of this literature represented an example of determining a result in advance—in this case, the conclusion that justice practices are broken and discriminatory—followed by proof found to support this politically driven conclusion. Hays was also puzzled by our colleagues' proposal to review recorded data rather than events as they unfolded in the court's new iteration, which they felt would be too time-consuming. "Is the goal to save time, or to do the work the right way?" Hays asked our colleagues, whose perspective was that Hays was proposing an unreasonable amount of work.

This experience taught us about how any party in participatory research can bring bias to the relationship in ways that could predict results. Learning to speak in a unified voice as a participatory research team requires having hard conversations about our respective views and experiences because doing so builds confidence that everyone is operating in good faith by being forthright and trustworthy, with a shared interest in the community. Good governance means transparency and having high expectations for elected officials, irrespective of political alignment. In our view, we can either be constrained by political walls and limited views or we can make sure we do everything we can to maximize the resources available to us.

Ultimately our challenging conversations about the Second Chance program evaluation shifted the project from a quantitative to an interview-based approach, which required every defendant to complete an interview with Susan about their experiences, with the goal of using their collective insights to improve the court's performance even further. Initially Susan and her colleagues were hesitant about Hays's proposal to require all defendants to participate in the assessment, because the Institutional Review Board (IRB) mandates that all research participants have the right to consent. Yet Hays felt strongly that only including defendants who volunteered to participate would result in a biased study featuring perspectives only from those who volunteered to participate. Ultimately, we obtained IRB approval to publish the results of interviews with defendants who consented to the use of their interview for this purpose. The report containing de-identified results of interviews Susan conducted with all defendants will remain internal to the District Attorney's Office, with Susan handling all data as confidentially as if it were intended for publication. While some academics may not be willing to risk working on a project with potentially unpublishable data, for our team the potential benefit to community in the form of a court informed by all defendants' input substantially outweighed this risk.

It is perfectly fine for you to have your own set of research questions as you approach and deepen your relationship with your community partner. Having those questions can help guide the process of establishing trust and rapport because it will allow you to answer many of the questions posed here with your community partner. The fact of the partnership in itself creates potential for other opportunities after the initial project begins. However, opportunities must always be created, even when you share a sense of purpose and direction with your community partner from the outset. Be open to these opportunities as your work together evolves.

The third step involves developing relationships of trust in the project's initial stages by practicing emotional and, when appropriate and thoughtfully given, material reciprocity. Once you and your community partner have established the relationship to the degree that you feel part of the agency, do not take this access for granted. Keep listening and watching closely for ways to show others that you are a trustworthy person who highly values practitioners' expertise. Susan's mantra when working with practitioners is "You're the expert because you do the work." This humility goes a long way to dispel the mistrust and stereotypes practitioners might have about academics as disconnected from reality. Such humility also encourages practitioners to confide in you, and although statements made in confidence should always be kept in confidence, these statements provide valuable context to the research by demonstrating how practitioners envision the work they do and their place within that work.

Acknowledging expertise takes many forms, and for Susan and sometimes Brittany, it involved attending almost all the Friday morning lawyer meetings over the course of two years to learn from everyone present. These meetings typically discussed challenging cases in progress and case disposition but also had a didactic nature that allowed Susan and Brittany to experience how prosecutors, many of whom are recent law school graduates, hone their craft. In one meeting, Hays led the group in an exercise designed to define facts beyond change, which are immutable realities central to constructing the theory of a case. He asked prosecutors to pass an insulated coffee mug around the room while each stated a fact beyond change about it. "It's black," the first prosecutor said with confidence before passing it along to others, who noted other indisputable details about it. By the tenth prosecutor, ascertaining facts beyond change became much more challenging, and by the time the cup was in Susan's hands she struggled to identify a new fact beyond change. "It holds a lot of liquid," Susan said, prompting Hays to exclaim, "Really? Did you measure it? What is a lot? How do we know what that means?" Learning together in this way helped Susan and Brittany understand the pressures prosecutors face to publicly perform and how seemingly minor details—such as assumptions about the amount of liquid a cup can hold—can potentially derail a case.

Such humility is also a form of emotional reciprocity by providing hardworking practitioners with a nonjudgmental outlet for the difficulties they face in their work. Emotional reciprocity also requires being trustworthy in fact, and because you are in a criminal justice setting, understanding and respecting the laws and practices that undergird it. If you consistently show others through your actions that you are a trustworthy person, the inevitably firm boundaries they maintain with you in the beginning will begin to soften or even dissolve with time, greatly enriching the research partnership in the process. Initially you may feel that practitioners seem guarded around you, but this will change over time. Susan vividly remembers reviewing trial transcripts at a desk outside Grace's office when a police investigator came to speak with her about a particularly difficult and notorious case. While Grace, who trusted Susan by that point, spoke in a normal voice, the investigator lowered his voice to a near-whisper inaudible to Susan because he did not know her. Hearing, effectively, a one-sided conversation about the case truly impressed on Susan the importance of mutual trust and respect in sensitive situations where the disclosure of information—whether unintentional or otherwise—could have serious negative impacts on an agency's credibility and on people's lives.

Doing work in our own community on gun cases requires unique ethical sensitivities because these cases often attract considerable media attention and, of course, dramatically impact all community members' sense of security. Susan accordingly remained mindful not to discuss cases outside of the office, even when they involved public proceedings. For example, Susan attended an evening holiday party after spending the day at a murder trial that received some amount of public attention, and well-meaning colleagues asked her how the trial was proceeding. Susan, who was exhausted at that point in the day, politely said she could not discuss the case since some sensitive aspects she observed during prosecutors' trial preparation might slip out in a discussion of public trial proceedings. Doing work in community also means potentially coming across sensitive information about neighbors. For example, it was hard for Susan to ignore what she heard from victims and witnesses seated in a conference room just feet away from where she sat reviewing cases, especially when they discussed crimes committed in areas she frequented. Resolving this dilemma means adopting the same strategies practitioners do by setting clear professional boundaries, specifically, by not separately forming relationships with defendants, victims, or witnesses and thereby not having the power to do them harm or change their case outcome.

Material reciprocity is a normative practice in anthropology, as well as among human geographers who work outside North America and Western Europe. When Susan conducted National Science Foundation–sponsored research on the Pacific island of Fiji, for example, her research partners routinely sent her long lists of items to purchase for them and transport to the island. On one lengthy prop plane flight to remote Koro Island, Susan and her research assistant carried enough fabric to sew highly coveted curtains for every thatch-roofed home in the village. Susan found herself laughing while boarding the plane back to Los Angeles on one research trip because she was carrying only her passport and her laptop, which of course contained hundreds of hours of audio files and other precious data that her research partners generously shared with her. While this might appear to be a crass exchange to those unfamiliar with the importance of reciprocity in most cultures worldwide, Susan's adherence to pan-Pacific cultural norms about reciprocity greatly enhanced her community-based research there.

To use another example of thoughtful material reciprocity's utility in community-based research, our team's location in the Deep South means that food is an exceptionally important part of everyday life for us. Our cuisine is famous throughout the United States for its delicious pairings of intoxicating sweetness with bright, salty flavors, as anyone knows who has ever eaten farm-raised fried chicken with fresh collard greens and a glass of sweet tea followed by a piece of Mississippi mud pie. For southerners who have lived in our region their entire lives, food is a powerful means of communicating care and friendship. No meeting of any real substance occurs without food, and lengthy conversations about food are often as much a way for the speakers to find points of commonality with one another as they are about recipes and eating.

With these cultural norms in mind, Susan routinely brought fresh eggs, herbs, honey, peach tree seedlings, and other plants from her small family farm to prosecutors, victim service officers, paralegals, and office staff who patiently and kindly explained their work to her. "You the egg lady?" a newly hired deputy asked early one morning as Susan entered the courthouse with a basket of eggs destined for a prosecutor's desk. Such expressions of friendship and goodwill considerably build trust because they are not straightforward financial incentives that may feel coercive or even dismissive if viewed as the researcher's perceived value of practitioners' knowledge. No matter how you might choose to engage in thoughtful material reciprocity, considering how you might offer everyone at the agency something of unique value to them helps all concerned feel equally included as important and rewarded participants in the work.

While incentives are universally accepted as a norm when they are not coercive, researchers must be careful to balance local cultural norms with their decisions. Here in Alabama the rural barter economy is normative, as is sharing food as an expression of kindness, care, and gratitude. Obviously no prosecutors or other office staff felt compelled to speak with Susan because she shared food with them. Becoming part of the office as an ethnographic researcher directly facilitates such deep relationships. Prosecutors might understandably be guarded in their responses with a researcher who drops in for an interview, yet will be much less so with a long-term ethnographer who shares her lunch with them when they've been in trial prep for days with no time to eat. Presence matters in building trust.

Fourth, we strongly encourage you to stay loyal to one agency for the duration of the project. It can be tempting, as you begin to meet other practitioners through your community-engaged work, to speak with them about other projects you could develop and even to initiate those projects. Make sure this is a good idea before moving forward by fully thinking it through and speaking to your original community partner about it. Keep this approach consistent throughout your work together by avoiding discussion of everyday office practices with other potential community partners, as some version of what you say may be misconstrued as it makes its way back to your partner agency. Your community partner will likely have less confidence and interest in you if you appear chaotic or unfocused in your interests or, worse still, act as though you consider them a rung on your own professional ladder. Your absolute commitment to the partnership will show over time and you will likely find that your community partner reciprocates with the same level of commitment.

Due to the reality of the assemblage's composition of institutional structures and practices, relationships and roles, and individual moral and emotional worlds, the way one agency—or one decision-making authority in an agency—sees an issue might be different from how another agency sees it. Splitting our research time between the District Attorney's Office and the Public Defender's Office, for example, would likely have diluted our ethnographic approach and even compromised the research because prosecutors (and public defenders) might reasonably wonder about the potential for us to accidentally divulge case details or other sensitive information. Attempting to simultaneously learn two office cultures, likewise, would have been extremely challenging. Over time, becoming part of a shared mission only makes the work stronger because your own thoughts and reactions will begin to resemble those of your community partners. By the time we wrote the book, Susan was able to predict Hays's reactions to aspects of our argument with remarkable frequency. This kind of deep knowledge about others can only come with time and long-term engagement with one another.

Doing work in multiple criminal justice agencies would have presented what we regarded as insurmountable ethical obstacles to building trust. In a physical example of this type of "choosing sides," during trial observations Susan initially preferred to sit on a courtroom bench directly behind the defendant's family members and other loved ones to get a sense of their perspectives on the proceedings. This was an unconscious holdover from her many years of work in jails, prisons, and a transitional housing facility. One day immediately before trial proceedings began, a friendly prosecutor slung a friendly arm around Susan's shoulders, leaned in close to her ear, and whispered, "I would just *hate* for the judge to think you were supporting this guy" and gently pulled her over to a bench on the other side of the room with the victim's family members.

Fifth, and finally, be open to evolving outcomes and flexible definitions of impact that consider multiple audiences. Academics typically have very narrow definitions of impact, and these definitions have narrowed even further in the past decade. Many R1 (highly research productive) universities now rely on algorithms such as the h-index to ascertain the impact of a researcher's work, which, of course, rely exclusively on the number of citations a publication receives, amount of grants obtained, and other measures that treat knowledge production as a factory-like enterprise with little regard for community impact.

One of the most powerful aspects of participatory research is its potential to reach and impact multiple audiences. Researchers receive clear rewards from publishing in journals with high impact factors, but the reality is that work is limited in its ability to reach a broader, nonacademic audience because the publication is obscured behind a paywall. Popular media such as traditional news stories and also podcasts, such as our team is currently developing, will reach much larger numbers of people with the potential to exercise greater influence. Agencies will vary widely in terms of their involvement in the analytical and publication process. Including agency actors in the analysis and writing process seems ideal, but limitations on time (or even interest) may compromise their ability to do so. Such partners may only want to review the researcher's final written report or draft publication to understand the results and accompanying recommendations. One potentially effective compromise might involve, as it did for our team, one or more researchers taking the lead with a strong first draft, followed by input from the agency partner in specific areas guided by questions noted by the researcher in areas where the researcher may be uncertain as to whether their representation is fair and accurate.

The time has come for criminologists to make the shift to real and meaningful community engagement with practitioners in community. At present, too many criminologists passively critique practitioners' work from the sidelines, which relegates our discipline to being an association of professional ivory tower critics offering opinions based on partial (and often highly politicized) perspectives. As coauthors, we collectively envision a brighter future in which criminologists and practitioners work together to make the shift from adversaries to real-world problem-solvers.

Works Cited

Abu-Orf, Hazem. 2013. "Fear of Difference: 'Space of Risk' and Anxiety in Violent Settings." *Planning Theory* 12, no. 2: 158–76.

Adelman, Clem. 1993. "Kurt Lewin and the Origins of Action Research." *Educational Action Research* 1, no. 1: 7–24.

Alabama Sentencing Commission. 2023. *Sentencing Standards.* https://sentencingcommission.alacourt.gov/sentencing-standards/.

Anderson, Ben, Matthew Kearnes, Colin McFarlane, and Dan Swanton. 2012. "On Assemblages and Geography." *Dialogues in Human Geography* 2, no. 2: 171–89.

Anderson, Ben, and Colin McFarlane. 2011. "Assemblage and Geography." *Area* 43, no. 2: 124–27.

Andiloro, Nancy, Brian Johnson, and Besiki Luka Kutateladze. 2016. "Opening Pandora's Box: How Does Defendant Race Influence Plea Bargaining?" *Justice Quarterly* 33, no. 3: 398–426.

Andreescu, Viviana, John Eagle Shutt, and Gennaro Vito. 2011. "The Violent South: Culture of Honor, Disorganization, and Murder in Appalachia." *Criminal Justice Review* 36, no. 1: 76–103.

Archibald, Ramsey. 2021. "Birmingham Has a Homicide Problem. Here's What the Mayor Says Needs to Be Done." AL.com, April 19, 2021. https://www.al.com/news/2021/04/birmingham-has-a-homicide-problem-heres-what-the-mayor-says-needs-to-be-done.html.

Arora, Ashna. 2018. "Too Tough on Crime? The Impact of Prosecutor Politics on Incarceration." American Economic Association, December 31, 2018. https://static1.squarespace.com/static/5c8e59f6e8ba44fdeb42f85f/t/64aoe4cfe7fbef49bc4a5b7a/1688265935733/Ashna+Arora.pdf.

Bacon, Matthew. 2016. *Taking Care of Business: Police Detectives, Drug Law Enforcement and Proactive Investigations.* Oxford: Oxford University Press.

Balboni, Jennifer, and Randall Grometstein. 2020. "Prosecutorial Reform from Within: District Attorney 'Disruptors' and Other Change Agents, 2016–2020." *Contemporary Justice Review* 23, no. 3: 261–90.

Bar-Gill, Oren, and Omri Ben-Shahar. 2009. "The Prisoners' (Plea Bargain) Dilemma." *Journal of Legal Analysis* 1, no. 2: 737–73.

Barrera, Leticia. 2013. "Performing the Court: Public Hearings and the Politics of Judicial Transparency in Argentina." *PoLAR: Political and Legal Anthropology Review* 36, no. 2: 326–40.

Bechky, Beth. 2021. *Blood, Powder, and Residue: How Crime Labs Translate Evidence into Proof.* Princeton, NJ: Princeton University Press.

Bell, Monica. 2016. "Situational Trust: How Disadvantaged Mothers Reconceive Legal Cynicism." *Law and Society Review* 50, no. 2: 314–47.

Bellin, Jeffrey. 2019. "The Power of Prosecutors." *New York University Law Review* 94, no. 2: 172–212.

Bellin, Jeffery, and Junichi P. Semitsu. 2011. "Widening Batson's Net to Ensnare More than the Unapologetically Bigoted or Painfully Unimaginative Attorney." *Cornell Law Review* 96, no. 5: 1075–1130.

Bennett, Luke, and Antonia Layard. 2015. "Legal Geography: Becoming Spatial Detectives." *Geography Compass* 9, no. 7: 406–22.

Bennett, W. Lance. 2010. "Unraveling the Gordian Knot of Implicit Bias in Jury Selection: The Problems of Judge-Dominated Voir Dire, the Failed Promise of Batson, and Proposed Solutions." *Harvard Law and Policy Review* 4, no. 1: 149–72.

Benns, Matthew, Matthew Ruther, Nicholas Nash, Matthew Bozeman, Brian Harbrecht, and Keith Miller. 2020. "The Impact of Historical Racism on Modern Violent Crimes Committed with a Gun: Redlining in the City of Louisville, Kentucky." *Injury* 51, no. 10: 2192–98.

Bernstein, J.M. 2015. *Torture and Dignity.* Chicago: University of Chicago Press.

Birck, Morgan. 2019. "Do You See What I See? Problems with Juror Bias in Viewing Body Camera Video Evidence." *Michigan Journal of Race and Law* 24: 153–76.

Boden, Deirdre. 1994. *The Business of Talk: Organizations in Action.* Cambridge, UK: Polity.

Boutwell, Brian, Erik Nelson, Zhengmin Qian, Michael Vaughn, John Wright, Kevin Beaver, J.C. Barnes et al. 2017. "Aggregate-Level Lead Exposure, Violent Crimes Committed with a Gun, Homicide, and Rape." *PloS One* 12, no. 11: 1–12.

Brady, Patrick, and Bradford Reyns. 2020. "A Focal Concerns Perspective on Prosecutorial Decision Making in Cases of Intimate Partner Stalking." *Criminal Justice and Behavior* 47, no. 6: 733–48.

Breetzke, Gregory, Amber Pearson, Shiqi Tao, and Rui Zhang. 2020. "Greenspace and Violent Crimes Committed with a Gun in Detroit, USA." *International Journal of Criminal Justice Sciences* 15, no. 2: 248–65.

Brookman, Fiona, Helen Jones, Robin Williams, and Jim Fraser. 2020a. "Crafting Credible Homicide Narratives: Forensic Technoscience in Contemporary Criminal Investigations." *Deviant Behavior* 43, no. 3: 340–66.

———. 2020b. "Dead Reckoning: Unraveling How 'Homicide' Cases Travel from Crime Scene to Court Using Qualitative Research Methods." *Homicide Studies* 24, no. 3: 283–306.

Brown, Andrew, Ian Colville, and Annie Pye. 2015. "Making Sense of Sensemaking in Organization Studies." *Organization Studies* 36, no. 2: 265–77.

Brown, E. 2014. "Expanding Carceral Geographies: Challenging Mass Incarceration and Creating a 'Community Orientation' towards Juvenile Delinquency." *Geographica Helvetica* 69, no. 5: 377–88.

Brunson, Rod, and Brian Wade. 2019. "'Oh Hell No, We Don't Talk to Police' Insights on the Lack of Cooperation in Police Investigations of Urban Violent Crimes Committed with a Gun." *Criminology and Public Policy* 18, no. 3: 623–48.

Bucerius, Sandra, Kendra Haggerty, and Luca Berardi. 2021. *The Oxford Handbook of Ethnographies of Crime and Criminal Justice*. Oxford: Oxford University Press.

Burns, Nick. 2022. "Elite Universities Are Out of Touch. Blame the Campus." *New York Times*, August 2, 2022. https://www.nytimes.com/2022/08/02/opinion/elite-universities-campus.html.

Burns, Robert. 2009. *The Death of the American Trial*. Chicago: University of Chicago Press.

Burton, Alexander, Matthew Logan, Justin Pickett, and Francis Cullen. 2021. "Gun Owners and Gun Control: Shared Status, Divergent Opinions." *Sociological Inquiry* 91, no. 2: 347–66.

Butts, Jeffrey, Caterina Roman, Lindsay Bostwick, and Jeremy Porter. 2015. "Cure Violence: A Public Health Model to Reduce Violent Crimes Committed with a Gun." *Annual Review of Public Health* 36: 39–53.

Calvey, David. 2018. "Covert Ethnography in Criminology: A Submerged Yet Creative Tradition." *Current Issues in Criminal Justice* 25, no. 1: 541–50.

Campeau, Holly, Ron Levi, and Todd Foglesong. 2021. "Policing, Recognition, and the Bind of Legal Cynicism." *Social Problems* 68, no. 3: 658–74.

Capers, Bennett. 2020. "Against Prosecutors." *Cornell Law Review* 105, no. 6: 1561–1610.

Carline, Anna, Clare Gunby, and Jamie Murray. 2020. *Rape and the Criminal Trial: Reconceptualising the Courtroom as an Affective Assemblage*. London: Springer Nature.

Carlson, Jennifer. 2015. "Mourning Mayberry: Guns, Masculinity, and Socioeconomic Decline." *Gender and Society* 29, no. 3: 386–409.

Carlson, Jennifer, and Rina James. 2021. "Conspicuously Concealed: Federal Funding, Knowledge Production, and the Criminalization of Gun Research." *Sociological Perspectives* 65, no. 1: 196–215.

Carroll, Jenny. 2014. "The Jury as Democracy." *Alabama Law Review* 66, no. 4: 825–70.

Carter, David, and Jeremy Carter. 2016. "Effective Police Homicide Investigations: Evidence from Seven Cities with High Clearance Rates." *Homicide Studies* 20, no. 2: 150–76.

CDC/Centers for Disease Control and Prevention, National Center for Health Statistics. 2021a. "Firearm Mortality by State, 2019." https://www.cdc.gov/nchs/pressroom/sosmap/firearm_mortality/firearm.htm.

———. 2021b. "WONDER Online Database, 1999–2019." http://wonder.cdc.gov/ucd-icd10.html.

Center for Justice Innovation. 2022. *Participatory Research: What Is It and How Can It Strengthen Your Reentry Evaluation?* April 2022. https://www.innovatingjustice.org/publications/examining-participatory-research-strengthening-reentry-programs.

Chakravarti, Sonali. 2020. *Radical Enfranchisement in the Jury Room and Public Life.* Chicago: University of Chicago Press.

Chambliss, William. 2018. *Power, Politics, and Crime.* London: Routledge.

Cloatre, Emilie. 2018. "Law and ANT (and Its Kin): Possibilities, Challenges, and Ways Forward." *Journal of Law and Society* 45, no. 4: 646–63.

Cobb, Charles. 2014. *This Nonviolent Stuff'll Get You Killed: How Guns Made the Civil Rights Movement Possible.* Durham, NC: Duke University Press.

Cobb, James. 2005. *Away Down South: A History of Southern Identity.* New York: Oxford University Press.

Cohen, Taya, and Lily Morse. 2014. "Moral Character: What It Is and What It Does." *Research in Organizational Behavior* 34: 43–61.

Colton, Emma. 2022. "Cornell Professor Warns Universities Are Eliminating the Meaning of 'Objective Truth' from Classrooms with CRT." *Fox News,* September 29, 2022. https://www.foxnews.com/us/cornell-professor-warns-universities-eliminating-meaning-objective-truth-classrooms-crt.

Combs, Thatcher. 2021. "Queers with Guns? Against the LGBT Grain." *Sociological Perspectives* 65, no. 1: 77–96.

Conley, John M., William O'Barr, and Robin Conley Riner. 2019. *Just Words: Law, Language, and Power.* 3rd ed. Chicago: University of Chicago Press.

Conley Riner, Robin. 2016. *Confronting the Death Penalty: How Language Influences Jurors in Capital Cases.* New York: Oxford University Press.

Conrad, Robert James, and Katy Lynn Clements. 2017. "The Vanishing Criminal Jury Trial: From Trial Judges to Sentencing Judges." *George Washington Law Review* 86, no. 1: 99–167.

Cook, Philip, Susan Parker, and Harold Pollack. 2015. "Sources of Guns to Dangerous People: What We Learn by Asking Them." *Preventative Medicine* 79: 28–36.

Cooper, Christopher, and H. Gibbs Knotts. 2017. *The Resilience of Southern Identity: Why the South Still Matters in the Minds of Its People.* Chapel Hill: University of North Carolina Press.

Copes, Heith, Tomislav Kovandzic, J. Mitchell Miller, and Luke Williamson. 2014. "The Lost Cause? Examining the Southern Culture of Honor through Defensive Gun Use." *Crime and Delinquency* 60, no. 3: 356–78.

Corsaro, Nicholas, and Robin Engel. 2015. "Most Challenging of Contexts: Assessing the Impact of Focused Deterrence on Serious Violence in New Orleans." *Criminology and Public Policy* 14, no. 3: 471–505.

Cowburn, Malcolm, and Azrini Wahidin. 2021. "Ethics and Criminology and Criminal Justice: From Conceptualizing to Conduct." In *The Encyclopedia of Research Methods in Criminology and Criminal Justice,* edited by J.C. Barnes and David Forde, 190–94. Oxford: Oxford University Press.

Coyne, Beth. 2018. *Courage of Our Convictions: Participatory Research in the Criminal Justice System.* London: Routledge.

Crewe, D.J. 2010. "Assemblage Theory and the Future for Criminology." In *New Directions for Criminology: Notes from Outside the Field,* edited by Ronnie Lippens and Patrick Van Calster, 39–57. Antwerp, Belgium: Maklu.

Crockett Thomas, Phil. 2020. "Crime as an Assemblage." *Journal of Theoretical and Philosophical Criminology* 12: 68–79.

Cullen, Francis. 2011. "Beyond Adolescence-Limited Criminology: Choosing Our Future." *Criminology* 49, no. 2: 287–330.

Dabney, Dean, and Fiona Brookman. 2018. "Fieldwork with Homicide Detectives: 60 Minutes of Reflections from a British and American Criminologist." In *Doing Ethnography in Criminology: Discovery through Fieldwork,* edited by Stephen Rice and Michael Maltz, 91–113. New York: Springer.

D'Antonio-Del Rio, Julia, Jessica Doucet, and Chantel Chauvin. 2010. "Violent and Vindictive Women: A Re-analysis of the Southern Subculture of Violence." *Sociological Spectrum* 30: 484–503.

Davis, Angela J. 2007. *Arbitrary Justice: The Power of the American Prosecutor.* New York: Oxford University Press.

Degenshein, Anya. 2022. "Ruptured Alliances: Prosecutorial Lobbying, Victims' Interests and Punishment Policy in Illinois." *Punishment and Society* 25, no. 2: 407–29.

DeKeseredy, Walter. 2014. "Mad Men in Bib Overalls: Media's Horrification and Pornification of Rural Culture." *Critical Criminology* 22: 179–97.

DeLanda, Manuel. 2006. *A New Philosophy of Society: Assemblage Theory and Social Complexity.* London: Continuum.

Delaney, David. 2010. *The Spatial, the Legal, and the Pragmatics of World-Making: Nomospheric Investigations.* London: Routledge.

———. 2016. "Legal Geography II: Discerning Injustice." *Progress in Human Geography* 40, no. 2: 267–74.

Deleuze, Gilles, and Félix Guattari. 1980. *A Thousand Plateaus: Capitalism and Schizophrenia.* London: Continuum.

Dewsbury, J.D. 2011. "The Deleuze-Guattarian Assemblage: Plastic Habits." *Area* 43, no. 2: 148–53.

Diamond, Shari Seidman, and Jessica Salerno. 2020. "Reasons for the Disappearing Jury Trial." *Louisiana Law Review* 81, no. 1: 120–63.

Didwania, Stephanie Holmes. 2018. *Gender-Based Favoritism among Criminal Prosecutors.* Columbia Law and Economics Workshop. https://law-

economic-studies.law.columbia.edu/sites/default/files/content/Didwania_
Gender%20Favoritism_Columbia%20(2020.11.09%20Law%20&%20
Econ%20Workshop).pdf.

Dimou, Eleni. 2021. "Decolonizing Southern Criminology: What Can the 'Decolonial Option' Tell Us about Challenging the Modern/Colonial Foundations of Criminology?" *Critical Criminology* 29, no. 3: 431–50.

Douglas, Mary. 1986. *How Institutions Think.* Syracuse, NY: Syracuse University Press.

Dowd-Arrow, Benjamin, Terrence Hill, and Amy Burdette. 2019. "Gun Ownership and Fear." *SSM-Population Health* 8: 100463.

———. 2021. "Introduction to the Special Issue on Guns and Society." *Sociological Inquiry* 91, no. 2: 249–52.

Eatley, Gordon, Harry Hueston, and Keith Price. 2016. "A Meta-analysis of the CSI Effect: The Impact of Popular Media on Jurors' Perception of Forensic Evidence." *Politics, Bureaucracy and Justice* 5, no. 2: 1–9

Ellison, Christopher. 1991. "An Eye for an Eye? A Note on the Southern Subculture of Violence Thesis." *Social Forces* 69: 1223–39.

Emerson, Robert, Rachel Fretz, and Linda Shaw. 2011. *Writing Ethnographic Fieldnotes.* Chicago: University of Chicago Press.

EveryStat. 2021. *Gun Violence in Alabama.* https://everystat.org/wp-content/uploads/2021/02/Gun-Violence-in-Alabama-2.9.2021.pdf.

Farr, Paddy. 2021. "Crashing Bodies: Towards an Intersectional Assemblage Theory of Domestic Violence." *Feminist Theory.* https://doi.org/10.1177/14647001211014764.

Farrell, Lauren, Bethany Young, and Janeen Buck Willison. 2021. *Participatory Research in Prisons.* Washington, DC: Urban Institute.

Fassin, Didier. 2013. *Enforcing Order: An Ethnography of Urban Policing.* Cambridge, UK: Polity Press.

Felson, Richard, and Paul-Philippe Pare. 2010a. "Firearms and Fisticuffs: Region, Race and Adversary Effects on Homicide and Assault." *Social Science Research* 39, no. 2: 272–84.

———. 2010b. "Gun Cultures or Honor Cultures? Explaining Regional and Race Differences in Weapon Carrying." *Social Forces* 88, no. 3: 1357–78.

Filindra, Alexandra, and Noah Kaplan. 2017. "Testing Theories of Gun Policy Preferences among Blacks, Latinos, and Whites in America." *Social Science Quarterly* 98, no. 2: 413–28.

Flango, Victor E., and Thomas M. Clarke. 2015. *Reimagining Courts: A Design for the Twenty-First Century.* Philadelphia: Temple University Press.

Garrett, Brandon, Alice Liu, Karen Kafader, and Chad Dodson. 2020. "Factoring the Role of Eyewitness Evidence in the Courtroom." *Journal of Empirical Legal Studies* 17, no. 3: 556–79.

Ghoddousi, Pooya, and Sam Page. 2020. "Using Ethnography and Assemblage Theory in Political Geography." *Geography Compass* 14, no. 10: 1–13.

Gilmore, Ruth Wilson. 2007. *Golden Gulag: Prisons, Surplus, Crisis and Opposition in Globalizing California*. Oakland: University of California Press.

Goldman, Barry, and Russell Cropanzano. 2015. "'Justice' and 'Fairness' Are Not the Same Thing." *Journal of Organizational Behavior* 36, no. 2: 313–18.

Gonzalez, Eric. 2019. "Using the Power of Prosecutors to Drive Reform." *Criminal Justice* 34, no. 3: 9–14.

Gonzalez Van Cleve, Nicole. 2016. *Crook County: Racism and Injustice in America's Largest Criminal Court*. Stanford, CA: Stanford University Press.

Goodman, Lisa, Kristie Thomas, Nkiru Nnawulezi, Carrie Lippy, Josephine Serrata, Susan Ghanbarpour, Cris Sullivan, and Megan Bair-Merritt. 2018. "Bringing Community Based Participatory Research to Domestic Violence Scholarship: An Online Toolkit." *Journal of Family Violence* 33: 103–7.

Goodman, Robert. 2001. "Community-Based Participatory Research: Questions and Challenges to an Essential Approach." *Journal of Public Health Management Practice* 7, no. 5: 5–7.

Goodwin, Amber, and T.J. Grayson. 2020. "Investing in the Frontlines: Why Trusting and Supporting Communities of Color Will Help Address Violent Crimes Committed with a Gun." *Journal of Law, Medicine and Ethics* 48, no. S4: 164–71.

Gordon, Sanford, and Gregory Huber. 2002. "Citizen Oversight and the Electoral Incentives of Criminal Prosecutors." *American Journal of Political Science* 46, no. 2: 334–51.

Granot, Yael, Emily Balcetis, Neal Feigenson, and Tom Tyler. 2018. "In the Eyes of the Law: Perception versus Reality in Appraisals of Video Evidence." *Psychology, Public Policy, and Law* 24, no. 1: 93–104.

Gray, Patricia. 2013. "Assemblages of Penal Governance, Social Justice and Youth Justice Partnerships." *Theoretical Criminology* 17, no. 4: 517–34.

Green, Bruce. 2018. "Prosecutorial Discretion: The Difficulty and Necessity of Public Inquiry." *Dickinson Law Review* 123: 589–628.

Green, Bruce, and Rebecca Roiphe. 2020a. "A Fiduciary Theory of Prosecution." *American University Law Review* 69: 101–58.

———. 2020b. "When Prosecutors Politick: Progressive Law Enforcers Then and Now." *Journal of Criminal Law and Criminology* 110, no. 4: 719–68.

Gregory, Derek, and Allan Pred, eds. 2007. *Violent Geographies: Fear, Terror, and Political Violence*. New York: Routledge.

Griffin, Brandon, Natalie Purcell, Kristine Burkman, Brett Litz, Craig Bryan, Martha Schmitz, Claudia Villierme, Jessica Walsh, and Shira Maguen. 2019. "Moral Injury: An Integrative Review." *Journal of Traumatic Stress* 32, no. 3: 350–62.

Grosjean, Pauline. 2014. "A History of Violence: The Culture of Honor and Homicide in the US South." *Journal of the European Economic Association* 12, no. 5: 1285–1316.

Grubb, Jonathan, and Chad Posick. 2021. *Crime TV: Streaming Criminology in Popular Culture*. New York: New York University Press.

Hagan, John, Bill McCarthy, and Daniel Herda. 2020. "What the Study of Legal Cynicism and Crime Can Tell Us about Reliability, Validity, and Versatility in Law and Social Science Research." *Annual Review of Law and Social Science* 16: 1–20.

Haight, Wendy, Erin Sugrue, and Molly Calhoun. 2017. "Moral Injury among Child Protection Professionals: Implications for the Ethical Treatment and Retention of Workers." *Children and Youth Services Review* 82: 27–41.

Hällgren, Markus, Ola Lindberg, and Oscar Rantatalo. 2021. "Sensemaking in Detective Work: The Social Nature of Crime Investigation." *International Journal of Police Science and Management* 23, no. 2: 119–32.

Haraway, Donna. 1988. "Situated Knowledges: The Science Question in Feminism and the Privilege of Partial Perspective." *Feminist Studies* 14, no. 3: 575–99.

Haverkate, Danielle, Travis Meyers, Cody Telep, and Kevin Wright. 2019. "On PAR with the Yard: Participatory Action Research to Advance Knowledge in Corrections." *Corrections: Policy, Practice and Research* 5, no. 1: 28–43.

Hawkins, Ian, and Kyle Scherr. 2017. "Engaging the CSI Effect: The Influences of Experience-Taking, Type of Evidence, and Viewing Frequency on Juror Decision-Making." *Journal of Criminal Justice* 49: 45–52.

Hayes, Rebecca, and Lora Levett. 2013. "Community Members' Perception of the CSI Effect." *American Journal of Criminal Justice* 38: 216–35.

Hayward, Keith. 2012. "Five Spaces of Cultural Criminology." *British Journal of Criminology* 52, no. 3: 441–62.

Hemenway, David, and Wilson Zhang. 2022. "Patterns of Household Gun Ownership and Firearm Suicide among Black Men Compared to White Men." *Preventative Medicine* 165, Part A: 107261–313.

Hill, Terrence, Benjamin Dowd-Arrow, Amy Burdette, and Tara D. Warner. 2020. "Gun Ownership and Life Satisfaction in the United States." *Social Science Quarterly* 101, no. 5: 2121–36.

Hill, Terrence, Benjamin Dowd-Arrow, Andrew Davis, and Amy Burdette. 2020. "Happiness Is a Warm Gun? Gun Ownership and Happiness in the United States (1973–2018)." *SSM Population Health* 10: 100536.

Hipple, Natalie, Kristina Thompson, and Beth Huebner. 2019. "Understanding Victim Cooperation in Cases of Nonfatal Gun Assaults." *Criminal Justice and Behavior* 46, no. 12: 1793–1811.

Hlavka, Heather, and Sameena Mulla. 2021. *Bodies in Evidence: Race, Gender, and Science in Sexual Assault Adjudication.* New York: New York University Press.

Hochstetler, Andy, Heith Copes, and Michael Cherbonneau. 2017. "It's a War Out There: Contextualized Narratives of Violent Acts." *Journal of Criminal Justice* 53: 74–82.

Hogan, Thomas. 2022. "De-prosecution and Death: A Synthetic Control Analysis of the Impact of De-prosecution on Homicides." *Criminology and Public Policy* 21: 489–534.

Holmes, Douglas, and George Marcus. 2008. "Collaboration Today and the Re-imagination of the Classic Scene of Fieldwork Encounter." *Collaborative Anthropologies* 1: 81–101.

Hough, Mike. 2014. "Confessions of a Recovering 'Administrative Criminologist': Jock Young, Quantitative Research and Policy Research." *Crime, Media, Culture* 10, no. 3: 215–16.

Hyndman, Jennifer, and Alison Mountz. 2007. "Refuge or Refusal." In *Violent Geographies: Fear, Terror, and Political Violence,* edited by Derek Gregory and Allan Pred, 77–92. London: Taylor & Francis.

Israel, Barbara, Amy Schulz, Edith Parker, Adam Becker, A. Allen, and John. Guzman. 2003. "Critical Issues in Developing and Following Community-Based Participatory Research Principles." In *Community Based Participatory Research for Health,* edited by Meredith Minkler and Nina Wallerstein, 53–76. San Francisco: Jossey-Bass.

Jackson, Bruce. 2009. *Pictures from a Drawer: Prison and the Art of Portraiture.* Philadelphia: Temple University Press.

Jacobsson, Katarina. 2008. "'We Can't Just Do It Any Which Way': Objectivity Work among Swedish Prosecutors." *Qualitative Sociology Review* 4, no. 1: 46–67.

Janoff-Bulman, Ronnie. 2009. "To Provide or Protect: Motivational Bases of Political Liberalism and Conservatism." *Psychological Inquiry* 20, no. 2/3: 120–28.

Jeffrey, Alex. 2019. "Legal Geography 1: Court Materiality." *Progress in Human Geography* 43, no. 3: 565–73.

Jinkerson, Jeremy. 2016. "Defining and Assessing Moral Injury: A Syndrome Perspective." *Traumatology* 22, no. 2: 122–30.

Jones, Helen, Fiona Brookman, Robin Williams, and Jim Fraser. 2021. "We Need to Talk about Dialogue: Accomplishing Collaborative Sensemaking in Homicide Investigations." *Police Journal: Theory, Practice and Principles* 94, no. 4: 572–89.

Kahn, Jeffrey. 2017. "Geographies of Discretion and the Jurisdictional Imagination." *PoLAR: Political and Legal Anthropology Review* 40, no. 1: 5–27.

Kaufman, Sarah Beth. 2020. *American Roulette: The Social Logic of Death Penalty Sentencing Trials.* Berkeley: University of California Press.

Kelley, Margaret. 2021. "Feminism and Firearms: Gun Ownership, Gun Carrying, and Women's Empowerment." *Sociological Perspectives* 65, no. 1: 77–96.

Kelley, Margaret, and Christopher Ellison. 2021. "Who Might Buy a Gun? Results from the Guns in American Life Survey." *Sociological Inquiry* 91, no. 2: 455–82.

Kindynis, Theo. 2014. "Ripping Up the Map: Criminology and Cartography Reconsidered." *British Journal of Criminology* 54: 222–43.

King Jr., Martin Luther. 1963. *Letter from Birmingham Jail.* August 1963. https://www.csuchico.edu/iege/_assets/documents/susi-letter-from-birmingham-jail.pdf.

Kirk, David. 2016. "Prisoner Reentry and the Reproduction of Legal Cynicism." *Social Problems* 63, no. 2: 222–43.

Kirk, David, and Mauri Matsuda. 2011. "Legal Cynicism, Collective Efficacy, and the Ecology of Arrest." *Criminology* 49, no. 2: 443–72.

Kitamura, Katie. 2021. *Intimacies.* New York: Riverhead Books.

Klein, Rebecca. 2021. "The Rightwing US Textbook That Teaches Slavery as 'Black Immigration.'" *Guardian*, August 12, 2021. https://www.theguardian.com/education/2021/aug/12/right-wing-textbooks-teach-slavery-black-immigration.

Koehler, Johann. 2015. "Development and Fracture of a Discipline: Legacies of the School of Criminology at Berkeley." *Criminology* 53, no. 4: 513–44.

Kohler-Hausmann, Issa. 2018. *Misdemeanorland: Criminal Courts and Social Control in an Age of Broken Windows Policing.* Princeton, NJ: Princeton University Press.

Kowalski, Gregory, and Don Duffield. 1990. "The Impact of Rural Population Component on Homicide Rates in the United States: A County-Level Analysis." *Rural Sociology* 55, no. 1: 76–90.

Kreag, Jason. 2019. "Disclosing Prosecutorial Misconduct." *Vanderbilt Law Review* 72, no. 1: 297–352.

Kruse, Corinna. 2016. *The Social Life of Forensic Evidence.* Berkeley: University of California Press.

Lantz, Brendan, and Marin Wenger. 2020. "Guns, Groups, and the Southern Culture of Honor: Considering the Role of Co-defendants in Southern Firearm Violence." *Psychology of Violence* 11, no. 4: 405–16.

Latour, Bruno. 2010. *The Making of Law: An Ethnography of the Conseil d'État.* Malden, MA: Polity Press.

Laurie, Emma, and Ian Shaw. 2018. "Violent Conditions: The Injustices of Being." *Political Geography* 65: 8–16.

Lee, Maggy, and Karen Laidler. 2013. "Doing Criminology from the Periphery: Crime and Punishment in Asia." *Theoretical Criminology* 17, no. 2: 141–57.

Lee, Matthew, and Graham Ousey. 2010. "Reconsidering the Culture and Violence Connection: Strategies of Action in the Rural South." *Journal of Interpersonal Violence* 26: 899–929.

Lee, Matthew, Shaun Thomas, and Graham Ousey. 2009. "Southern Culture and Homicide: Examining the Cracker Culture/Black Rednecks Thesis." *Deviant Behavior* 31, no. 1: 60–96.

Legg, Stephen. 2011. "Assemblage/Apparatus: Using Deleuze and Foucault." *Area* 43, no. 2: 128–33.

Levin, Leslie, and Lynn Mather. 2012. *Lawyers in Practice: Ethical Decision Making in Context.* Chicago: University of Chicago Press.

Levine, Kay, and Ronald Wright. 2013. "Prosecution in 3-D." *Journal of Criminal Law and Criminology* 102, no. 4: 1119–80.

MacNair, Rachel. 2015. "Causing Trauma as a Form of Trauma." *Peace and Conflict: Journal of Peace Psychology* 21, no. 3: 313–21.

Matthews, David. 2018. "If You Love Research, Academia May Not Be for You." *Times Higher Education*, November 18, 2018. https://www.timeshighereducation.com/blog/if-you-love-research-academia-may-not-be-you.

Matthews, Roger. 2014. "Rational Choice, Routine Activities and Situational Crime Prevention." In *Realist Criminology*, edited by Roger Matthews, 72–93. London: Palgrave Macmillan.

Mayhew, Pat. 2016. "In Defense of Administrative Criminology." *Crime Science* 5, no. 1: 1–10.

McGowran, Peter, and Amy Donovan. 2021. "Assemblage Theory and Disaster Risk Management." *Progress in Human Geography* 45, no. 6: 1601–24.

McMillan, Jordan, and Mary Bernstein. 2021. "Beyond Gun Control: Mapping Gun Prevention Logics." *Sociological Perspectives* 65, no. 1: 177–95.

Merelli, Annalisa, and Annabelle Timsit. 2018. "For Ten Years, Students in Texas Have Used a History Textbook That Says Not All Slaves Were Unhappy." *Quartz*, May 11, 2018. https://qz.com/1273998/for-10-years-students-from-texas-have-been-using-a-history-textbook-that-says-not-all-slaves-were-unhappy.

Metcalfe, Christi. 2016. "The Role of Courtroom Workgroups in Felony Case Dispositions: An Analysis of Workgroup Familiarity and Similarity." *Law and Society Review* 50, no. 3: 637–73.

Milam, Adam, Debra Furr-Holden, Philip Leaf, and Daniel Webster. 2018. "Managing Conflicts in Urban Communities: Youth Attitudes Regarding Violent Crimes Committed with a Gun." *Journal of Interpersonal Violence* 33, no. 24: 3815–28.

Miner-Romanoff, Karen. 2014. "Student Perceptions of Juvenile Offender Accounts in Criminal Justice Education." *American Journal of Criminal Justice* 39: 611–29.

Minton, Bennett. 2020. "The Lies Our Textbooks Told My Generation of Virginians about Slavery." *Washington Post*, July 31, 2020. https://www.washingtonpost.com/outlook/slavery-history-virginia-textbook/2020/07/31/d8571eda-d1f0-11ea-8c55-61e7fa5e82ab_story.html.

Moore, Dawn. 2011. "The Benevolent Watch: Therapeutic Surveillance in Drug Treatment Court." *Theoretical Criminology* 15, no. 3: 255–68.

Moore, Janet, Marla Sandys, and Raj Jayadev. 2015. "Make Them Hear You: Participatory Defense and the Struggle for Criminal Justice Reform." *Albany Law Review* 78: 1281–1316.

Moran, Dominique. 2012. "'Doing Time' in Carceral Space: Timespace and Carceral Geography." *Geografiska Annaler: Series B, Human Geography* 94, no. 4: 305–16.

Moran, Dominique, Jennifer Turner, and Anna Schliehe. 2017. "Conceptualizing the Carceral in Carceral Geography." *Progress in Human Geography* 42, no. 5: 666–86.

Moule, Richard, Bryanna Fox, and Megan Parry. 2019. "The Long Shadow of Ferguson: Legitimacy, Legal Cynicism, and Public Perceptions of Police Militarization." *Crime and Delinquency* 65, no. 2: 151–82.

Müller, Martin. 2015. "Assemblages and Actor-Networks: Rethinking Socio-material Power, Politics and Space." *Geography Compass* 9, no. 1: 27–41.

Müller, Martin, and Carolin Schurr. 2016. "Assemblage Thinking and Actor-Network Theory: Conjunctions, Disjunctions, Cross-Fertilisations." *Transactions of the Institute of British Geographers* 41, no. 3: 217–29.

Murley, Jean. 2019. "Aftermath: The True Crime Memoir Comes of Age." In *Crime, Deviance, and Popular Culture: International and Multidisciplinary Perspectives*, edited by Dimitris Akrivos and Alexandros Antoniou, 203–29. London: Palgrave.

Nader, Laura, ed. 1997. *Law in Culture and Society*. Berkeley: University of California Press.

Nail, Thomas. 2017. "What Is an Assemblage?" *SubStance* 46, no. 1: 21–37.

Nix, Justin, and Scott Wolfe. 2016. "Sensitivity to the Ferguson Effect: The Role of Managerial Organizational Justice." *Journal of Criminal Justice* 47: 12–20.

O'Donnell, Tayanah, Daniel Robinson, and Josephine Gillespie, eds. 2020. *Legal Geography: Perspectives and Methods*. London: Routledge.

Offit, Anna. 2021. "With Jurors in Mind: An Ethnographic Study of Prosecutors' Narratives." *Law, Culture, and the Humanities* 17, no. 3: 462–84.

———. 2022. *The Imagined Juror: How Hypothetical Juries Influence Federal Prosecutors*. New York: New York University Press.

Olsen, Robin, Leigh Courtney, Chloe Warnberg, and Julie Samuels. 2018. *Collecting and Using Data for Prosecutorial Decisionmaking*. Washington, DC: Urban Institute. https://www.urban.org/sites/default/files/publication/99044/collecting _and_using_data_for_prosecutorial_decisionmaking_0.pdf.

Oslender, Ulrich. 2008. "Another History of Violence: The Production of 'Geographies of Terror' in Colombia's Pacific Coast Region." *Latin American Perspectives* 35, no. 5: 77–102.

Papazoglou, Konstantinos, and Brian Chopko. 2017. "The Role of Moral Suffering (Moral Distress and Moral Injury) in Police Compassion Fatigue and PTSD: An Unexplored Topic." *Frontiers in Psychology* 8: 1–5.

Payne, Yasser Arafat, and Angela Bryant. 2018. "Street Participatory Action Research in Prison: A Methodology to Challenge Privilege and Power in Correctional Facilities." *Prison Journal* 98, no. 4: 449–69.

Petintseva, Olga, Rita Faria, and Yarin Eski. 2020. *Interviewing Elites, Experts and the Powerful in Criminology*. Cham, Switzerland: Palgrave MacMillan.

Pirie, Fernanda. 2013. *The Anthropology of Law*. Oxford: Oxford University Press.

Pizarro, Jesinia, Kristen Zgoba, and Wesley Jennings. 2011. "Assessing the Interaction between Defendant and Victim Criminal Lifestyles and Homicide Type." *Journal of Criminal Justice* 39, no. 5: 367–77.

Portillo, Shannon, Danielle Rudes, Jill Viglione, Matthew Nelson, and Faye Taxman. 2013. "Front-Stage Stars and Backstage Producers: The Role of Judges in Problem-Solving Courts." *Victims and Defendants* 8, no. 1: 1–22.

Ramchand, Rajeev, Enchante Franklin, Elizabeth Thornton, Sarah Deland, and Jeffrey Rouse. 2018. "Violence, Guns, and Suicide in New Orleans: Results from a Qualitative Study of Recent Suicide Decedents." *Journal of Forensic Sciences* 63, no. 5: 1444–49.

Reddit. 2021. "Fox News Moderator Suggesting 'Professor' Is a Lazy Job." https://www.reddit.com/r/Professors/comments/se3ewu/fox_news_moderator_suggesting_professor_is_a_lazy/.

Renkl, Margaret. 2021. *Graceland, at Last: Notes on Hope and Heartache from the American South*. Minneapolis, MN: Milkweed.

Rhineberger-Dunn, Gayle, Steven Briggs, and Nicole Rader. 2016. "The CSI Effect, DNA Discourse, and Popular Crime Dramas." *Social Science Quarterly* 98, no. 2: 532–47.

Richardson, Joseph, Christopher St. Vil, Tanya Sharpe, Michael Wagner, and Carnell Cooper. 2016. "Risk Factors for Recurrent Violent Injury among Black Men." *Journal of Surgical Research* 204, no. 1: 261–66.

Richland, Justin B. 2008. *Arguing with Tradition: The Language of Law in Hopi Tribal Court*. Chicago: University of Chicago Press.

Richman, Daniel. 2003. "Prosecutors and Their Agents, Agents and Their Prosecutors." *Columbia Law Review* 103, no. 4: 749–832.

Robinson, Carol. 2021. "More than 100 Guns Seized, 22 People Arrested in Tuscaloosa Gun Trafficking Probe." AL.com, November 8, 2021. https://www.al.com/news/2021/11/more-than-100-guns-seized-13-people-charged-in-tuscaloosa-gun-trafficking-probe.html.

Rockell, Barbara. 2009. "Challenging What They All Know: Integrating the Real/Reel World into Criminal Justice Pedagogy." *Journal of Criminal Justice Education* 20, no. 1: 76–92.

Roth, Jessica. 2020. "Prosecutorial Declination Statements." *Journal of Criminal Law and Criminology* 110, no. 3: 479–549.

Rudes, Danielle, and Shannon Portillo. 2012. "Roles and Power within Federal Problem Solving Courtroom Workgroups." *Law and Policy* 34, no. 4: 402–27.

Sandberg, Jorgen, and Haridimos Tsoukas. 2015. "Making Sense of the Sensemaking Perspective: Its Constituents, Limitations, and Opportunities for Further Development." *Journal of Organizational Behavior* 36, no. S1: S6–S32.

Sarat, Austin, and Conor Clarke. 2008. "Beyond Discretion: Prosecution, the Logic of Sovereignty, and the Limits of Law." *Law and Social Inquiry* 33, no. 2: 387–416.

Scarduzio, Jennifer, and Sarah Tracy. 2015. "Sensegiving and Sensebreaking via Emotion Cycles and Emotional Buffering: How Collective Communication Creates Order in the Courtroom." *Management Communication Quarterly* 29, no. 3: 331–57.

Schept, Judah. 2015. *Progressive Punishment: Job Loss, Jail Growth, and the Neoliberal Logic of Carceral Expansion*. New York: New York University Press.

Schlosser, Eric. 2015. "I'm a Liberal Professor and My Liberal Students Terrify Me." *Vox*, June 3, 2015. https://www.vox.com/2015/6/3/8706323/college-professor-afraid.

Schweitzer, Kimberly, and Narina Nunez. 2018. "What Evidence Matters to Jurors? The Prevalence and Importance of Different Homicide Trial Evidence to Mock Jurors." *Psychiatry, Psychology and Law* 25, no. 3: 437–51.

Semenza, Daniel, Richard Stansfield, Trent Steidley, and Ashley Mancik. 2021. "Firearm Availability, Homicide, and the Context of Structural Disadvantage." *Homicide Studies* 27, no. 5: 208–28.

Senger, Carolin, Richard Keijzer, Geni Smith, and Oliver Muensterer. 2011. "Pediatric Firearm Injuries: A 10-Year Single-Center Experience of 194 Patients." *Journal of Pediatric Surgery* 46, no. 5: 927–32.

Sepulveda, Carla, and Javier Wilenmann. 2022. "Structuring Prosecutorial Power." *Legal Studies* 42, no. 4: 680–95.

Shapira, Harel, Chen Liang, and Ken-Hou Lin. 2021. "How Attitudes about Guns Develop over Time." *Sociological Perspectives* 65, no. 1: 12–34.

Shaw, Ian. 2012. "Towards an Evental Geography." *Progress in Human Geography* 36, no. 5: 613–27.

Sherwin, Richard. 2002. *When Law Goes Pop: The Vanishing Line between Law and Popular Culture.* Chicago: University of Chicago Press.

Silbey, Jessica. 2012. "Images in/of Law." *New York School Law Review* 57: 171–83.

Sklansky, David. 2016. "The Changing Political Landscape for Elected Prosecutors." *Ohio State Journal of Criminal Law* 14, no. 2: 647–74.

———. 2018. "The Problems with Prosecutors." *Annual Review of Criminology* 1: 451–69.

Smith, Abbe. 2001. "Can You Be a Good Person and a Good Prosecutor?" *Georgetown Journal of Legal Ethics* 14: 355–400.

Soller, Brian, Aubrey Jackson, and Christopher Browning. 2014. "Legal Cynicism and Parental Appraisals of Adolescent Violence." *British Journal of Criminology* 54, no. 4: 568–91.

Sollie, Henk, Nicolien Kop, and Martin Euwema. 2017. "Mental Resilience of Crime Scene Investigators: How Police Officers Perceive and Cope with the Impact of Demanding Work Situations." *Criminal Justice and Behavior* 44, no. 12: 1580–1603.

Sommers, Ira, and Deborah Baskin. 2011. "The Influence of Forensic Evidence on the Case Outcomes of Rape Incidents." *Justice System Journal* 32, no. 3: 314–34.

Springer, Simon. 2011. "Violence Sits in Places? Cultural Practice, Neoliberal Rationalism, and Virulent Imaginative Geographies." *Political Geography* 30, no. 2: 90–98.

Stageman, Daniel, Nicole Napolitano, and Brian Buchner. 2018. "New Approaches to Data-Driven Civilian Oversight of Law Enforcement: An Introduction to the Second NACOLE/CJPR Special Issue." *Criminal Justice Policy Review* 29, no. 2: 111–27.

Steidley, Trent, and David Yamane. 2021. "Special Issue Editors' Introduction: A Sociology of Firearms for the Twenty-First Century." *Sociological Perspectives* 65, no. 1: 5–11.

Steinbauer, Robert, Nicholas Rhew, and Shawna Chen. 2015. "From Stories to Schemas: A Dual Systems Model of Leaders' Organizational Sensemaking." *Journal of Leadership and Organizational Studies* 22, no. 4: 404–12.

Survived and Punished. 2019. *Research across the Walls: A Guide to Participatory Research Projects and Partnerships to Free Criminalized Survivors.* January 2019. https://survivedandpunished.org/wp-content/uploads/2019/02/SP_ResearchAcrossWalls_FINAL-compressedfordigital.pdf.

Teubner, Gunther. 2017. "How the Law Thinks: Toward a Constructivist Epistemology of Law." In *Legal Theory and the Social Sciences*, edited by Maksymilian Del Mar and Michael Giudice, 205–35. London: Routledge.

Thomas, Shaun, Drew Medaris, and Cody Tuttle. 2018. "Southern Culture and Aggravated Assault: Exploring the Generality of the Southern Culture of Violence." *Sociological Spectrum* 38, no. 2: 103–16.

Thornton, Patricia, William Ocasio, and Michael Lounsbury. 2012. *The Institutional Logics Perspective: A New Approach to Culture, Structure, and Process.* Oxford: Oxford University Press.

Turner, Jennifer. 2016. *The Prison Boundary: Between Society and Carceral Space.* London: Palgrave MacMillan.

Ulmer, Jeffrey. 2019. "Criminal Courts as Inhabited Institutions: Making Sense of Difference and Similarity in Sentencing." *Crime and Justice* 48, no. 1: 483–522.

Umoja, Akinyele Omowale. 2013. *We Will Shoot Back: Armed Resistance in the Mississippi Freedom Movement.* New York: New York University Press.

Valasik, Matthew, Elizabeth Brault, and Stephen Martinez. 2019. "Forecasting Homicide in the Red Stick: Risk Terrain Modeling and the Spatial Influence of Urban Blight on Lethal Violence in Baton Rouge, Louisiana." *Social Science Research* 80: 186–201.

Vance, Stephen, Kerry Richmond, J. C. Oleson, and Shawn Bushway. 2019. "Weighing the Value of the Bargain: Prosecutorial Discretion after Sentencing Guidelines." *Criminal Justice Policy Review* 30, no. 7: 1086–1108.

Van Wezemael, Joris. 2008. "The Contribution of Assemblage Theory and Minor Politics for Democratic Network Governance." *Planning Theory* 7, no. 2: 165–85.

Vera Institute of Justice. 2022. *State Incarceration Trends: Alabama.* https://www.vera.org/downloads/pdfdownloads/state-incarceration-trends-alabama.pdf.

Waggoner, Catherine, and Laura Egley Taylor. 2018. *Realizing Our Place: Real Southern Women in a Mythologized Land.* Jackson: University Press of Mississippi.

Walenta, Jayme. 2019. "Courtroom Ethnography: Researching the Intersection of Law, Space, and Everyday Practices." *Professional Geographer* 72, no. 1: 1–8.

Wallerstein, Nina, and Bonnie Duran. 2003. "The Conceptual, Historical, and Practice Roots of Community Based Participatory Research and Related Participatory Traditions." In *Community Based Participatory Research for Health*, edited by Meredith Minkler and Nina Wallerstein, 27–52. San Francisco: Jossey-Bass.

Warner, Tara, and Shawn Ratcliff. 2021. "What Guns Mean: Who Sees Guns as Important, Essential, and Empowering (and Why?)" *Sociological Inquiry* 91, no. 2: 313–46.

Watts, Michael. 2008. "Violent Geographies: Speaking the Unspeakable and the Politics of Space." *City and Society* 13, no. 1: 85–117.

Webster, Daniel, Jennifer Whitehill, Jon Vernick, and Frank Curriero. 2013. "Effects of Baltimore's Safe Streets Program on Violent Crimes Committed with a Gun: A Replication of Chicago's CeaseFire Program." *Journal of Urban Health* 90, no. 1: 27–40.

Wehrman, Michael. 2010. "Race, Concentrated Disadvantage, and Recidivism: A Test of Interaction Effects." *Journal of Criminal Justice* 38, no. 4: 538–44.

Wesely, Jennifer. 2021. "Skimming the Surface or Digging Deeper: The Role of Emotion in Students' Reflective Journals during an Experiential Criminal Justice Course." *Journal of Experiential Education* 44, no. 2: 167–83.

Whitehill, Jennifer, Daniel Webster, Shannon Frattaroli, and Elizabeth Parker. 2014. "Interrupting Violence: How the CeaseFire Program Prevents Imminent Violent Crimes Committed with a Gun through Conflict Mediation." *Journal of Urban Health* 91, no. 1: 84–95.

Wilkinson, Blair, and Randy Lippert. 2012. "Moving Images through an Assemblage: Police, Visual Information, and Resistance." *Critical Criminology* 20, no. 3: 311–25.

Wright, Ronald, and Kay Levine. 2014. "The Cure for Young Prosecutors' Syndrome." *Arizona Law Review* 56: 1065–1128.

Xu, Jianhua, Karen Laidler, and Maggy Lee. 2013. "Doing Criminological Ethnography in China: Opportunities and Challenges." *Theoretical Criminology* 17, no. 2: 271–79.

Yamane, David. 2017. "The Sociology of U.S. Gun Culture." *Sociology Compass* 11, no. 7: 1–10.

Young, Richard. 2013. "Exploring the Boundaries of the Criminal Courtroom Workgroup." *Common Law World Review* 42, no. 3: 203–39.

Index

Founded in 1893,
UNIVERSITY OF CALIFORNIA PRESS
publishes bold, progressive books and journals
on topics in the arts, humanities, social sciences,
and natural sciences—with a focus on social
justice issues—that inspire thought and action
among readers worldwide.

The UC PRESS FOUNDATION
raises funds to uphold the press's vital role
as an independent, nonprofit publisher, and
receives philanthropic support from a wide
range of individuals and institutions—and from
committed readers like you. To learn more, visit
ucpress.edu/supportus.

www.ingramcontent.com/pod-product-compliance
Lightning Source LLC
Chambersburg PA
CBHW020855270326
41928CB00006B/715